Richard J. Jenks, PhD

Divorce, Annulments, and the Catholic Church
Healing or Hurtful?

D0143898

Pre-publication
REVIEW . . .

"While the Catholic hierarchy maintains that annulments are beneficial, one must ask for whom? Clearly petitioners want an annulment and thus say that annulment is the way for them to achieve `Catholic divorce.' But the majority of respondents with whom I have worked, and that number is over a thousand individuals, find what the individuals in Jenks' book have found—that the process is appalling at best, and devastating at worst.

Jenks' book highlights a key problem, not just with the annulment process, but with an aspect of the entire Catholic Church: the hierarchy's devastating mandate of silence on major issues of concern. The entire country has watched this conspiracy of silence in the sexual abuse revelations of our current time. This same attitude of mandated silence is key to keeping the annulment process in motion.

Jenks' research on the plight of respondents shows that many male respondents recognize the hypocrisy in the annulment process and choose to ignore Church policy; they simply do not participate in the process. But many Catholic women respondents do try to abide by tribunal annulment rules. These respondents do not realize that in the American Church they only have one chance in nine to defend their sacrament successfully. When these respondents, especially those with children, realize the sacramental grace of their marriage has been nullified and revoked, the resulting feeling most often is devastation."

Jan Leary, PhD, MEd, MDiv
Founder, "Save Our Sacrament:
Reform of Annulment
and Respondent Support"

Divorce, Annulments, and the Catholic Church
Healing or Hurtful?

THE HAWORTH PRESS
Divorce and Remarriage
Craig A. Everett, PhD
Editor

Divorce, Family Structure, and the Academic Success of Children by
William Jeynes

Divorce, Annulments, and the Catholic Church: Healing or Hurtful?
by Richard J. Jenks

Divorce, Annulments, and the Catholic Church
Healing or Hurtful?

Richard J. Jenks, PhD

The Haworth Press®
New York • London • Oxford

The Haworth Press, Inc., 10 Alice Street, Binghamton, NY 13904-1580.

PUBLISHER'S NOTE
Identities and circumstances of individuals discussed in this book have been changed to protect confidentiality.

Cover artwork by Sean Richard Jenks.

Cover design by Jennifer M. Gaska.

Library of Congress Cataloging-in-Publication Data

Jenks, Richard J.
    Divorce, annulments, and the Catholic Church : healing or hurtful? / Richard J. Jenks.
      p. cm.
    Includes bibliographical references and index.
    ISBN 0-7890-1563-3 (alk. paper)—ISBN 0-7890-1564-1 (pbk. : alk. paper)
    1. Divorce—Religious aspects—Catholic Church. 2. Remarriage—Religious aspects—Catholic Church. 3. Catholic Church—Doctrines. I. Title.

BX2254 .J46 2002
261.8'3589—dc21
                                        2001051590

To Sean, my son,
the joy of my life

ABOUT THE AUTHOR

Richard J. Jenks holds a PhD from the University of Missouri-Columbia, where he specialized in social psychology. He is currently Professor of Sociology at Indiana University Southeast, where he teaches courses on social problems, social psychology, and social movements. His research interests have included issues relating to social psychology, deviance, and the family. He has published articles in the areas of political sociology, smoking behavior, attitudes toward gays, co-marital sexuality, and divorce and annulments. In 1995, he was presented with the Outstanding Research and Creativity Award at Indiana University Southeast. Dr. Jenks is a member of the Society for the Scientific Study of Religion. He also acts as a group facilitator for New Beginnings, a group devoted to the concerns of the separated, divorced, and widowed, and is active in Big Brothers, Big Sisters.

CONTENTS

Foreword

It was the best of times; it was the worst of times
It was the age of wisdom; it was the age of foolishness
It was the epoch of belief; it was the epoch of incredulity
It was the season of Light; it was the season of Darkness. . . .

Charles Dickens

At the dawn of the French Revolution, Charles Dickens' well-known opening to *A Tale of Two Cities* gave voice and vision to nineteenth-century paradoxes. Today, these same words offer an eerie reminder that despite technological advances human beings remain as foolish as they have become smart. When we think we know what we believe—and too often what others should believe—we are confronted with the unbelievable. When we think our superior intellect and economic indicators will lead us into Light, we plunge into Darkness. While the events of September 11 shocked us into realizing that neither individual nor institution—regardless of history, wealth, power, or prestige—is immune from terror, many held to the misguided faith that the perpetrators of such "evil" had to have been oddballs raised on strange beliefs. Yet less than six months after the World Trade Center attacks, the Catholic Church is facing a crisis of epidemic proportions and the "evildoers" are not zealots, but ordained priests who preyed on vulnerable children entrusted to their care.

With the predictable anger at the crisis rising, some leaders are trying to remain calm and are urging followers to take a long-term perspective. They see the scandal as a catalyst for fundamental change. Some speak of a more open church with an involved laity and a church with married and women priests. Others hope for a time when the divorced might remarry without having to claim that their previous union was never valid. Of course, not everyone holds these views. Some traditionalists see the scandal as a result of America's "I can have what I want now" culture and a breakdown in church discipline and they see the salvation of their church in a return to its pre-Vatican II values. Yet increasingly as the scandal grows, more rank-and-file Catholics are becoming less interested in long-term solutions than in confronting unacceptable but inescapable truths: Crimes have been committed; children have been abused; there have been institutional cover-ups; trust has been shattered. And without trust even their beloved church will break down.

In keeping with Dickens' timeless paradoxes, Dr. Jenks' readable book, *Divorce, Annulments, and the Catholic Church: Healing or Hurtful?* enters a highly charged fray. Thankfully his work is written neither as an emotional roller coaster nor to convince readers of the moral righteousness of any point of view. Rather he begins his work with a calm, almost detached, cross-cultural history of divorce and then places that discussion in a much-needed standard sociological perspective. The author draws portions of his data from people divorced as little as six months, a model that not only enables him to observe participants in the immediate aftermath of their divorces but more importantly to establish baseline data so that sample members may be interviewed in their later years. Such scientific data has been sorely missing in most annulment analyses and should prove to be immeasurably useful in the future. Dr. Jenks is careful not to promise too much in his book and this humility may prove to be the work's greatest asset. He explains his methodologies carefully, painstakingly pointing out if and how he is relying on anecdotes, yet doing so in a way that is understandable to a reader not versed in statistical analysis. By taking this approach and respecting his readers, the author succeeds where others who have written on this topic have failed.

The reader trusts him and wants to keep his book for later reference. Such trust could not come at a more needed time. Without it, this book would be useless, but with it, Mr. Jenks' work might truly promote healing for those in the throes of annulment and for those who still love their church but at least temporarily are unable to trust it.

Sheila Rauch Kennedy
City planner and adjunct professor, Boston;
Author, *Shattered Faith: A Woman's Struggle to Stop
the Catholic Church from Annulling Her Marriage*

Acknowledgments

This book represents a number of years of work. I would like to thank my editor, Craig Everett, who spent untold hours giving comments and suggestions. I would also like to thank Linda Christiansen who came in virtually at the last minute and greatly contributed with astute comments and suggestions. In March 1999, I traveled to Boston to meet with Sheila Rauch Kennedy and Jan Leary. They took the greater part of a day to meet and discuss this project with me. I thank them from the bottom of my heart. I also thank Ms. Kennedy for the wonderful luncheon! Father Andrew Greeley and Father Ladislas Orsey of the Roman Catholic Church and Father John Matusiask of the Orthodox Church took time from their busy schedules and graciously consented to be interviewed. Father James Farrell kindly offered to help me contact individuals who had participated in the annulment process.

Above all, this book would not have been possible without the cooperation of over 400 individuals who consented to complete questionnaires, and the almost 100 individuals who also took their time to be interviewed over the phone. Finally, research grants from The Louisville Institute and Indiana University Southeast provided the necessary funds to complete this project.

On a personal note, I would like to thank Lavonne Sheets for her friendship and wise counsel. I am grateful for the writings of Reverend Harold Kushner. I was especially struck by a passage in his book, *When All You've Ever Wanted Isn't Enough.* The *Talmud,* he explains, suggests that a person do three things in life: plant a tree, write a book, and have a child. All of these show that we were here and that we made a difference. I must admit that I have not planted a tree. But at the right time and in the right place, that tree will be planted. This book has been a labor of love and, hopefully, it will make a difference in some people's lives. Finally, I would add the thought that having a child is only the start. We must care for and nurture that child to adulthood; to do this is the greatest pleasure and the greatest accomplishment of all.

Introduction

So they are no longer two, but one. Therefore, what God has joined together, let man not separate.

Matthew 19:6 (NIV)

Divorce is a stressful and devastating experience for many who go through the process. With nearly half of the marriages in the United States ending in dissolution, divorce is not an issue to be taken lightly. The spouses are not the only ones directly affected, but others close to them are too (e.g., their children, parents, and friends).

Society and its institutions also feel the impact of divorce. When a few marriages end, it is tragic but society remains unaffected. When thousands of marriages are dissolved, the very fabric of society is influenced and changed. One-parent families, with their increased economic and emotional hardships, become common. Political institutions become more involved by passing laws dealing with division of property, child custody, and child support. Religious institutions, which long have championed the idea of a marriage lasting "till death do you part," have to decide whether to keep their restrictive rules on staying married or give in to the reality of more frequent divorces. If the religion chooses the former it risks losing some of its members. If it chooses the latter, it risks being perceived as "caving in" for the sake of holding on to its members.

This is the dilemma the Catholic Church faces. Roman Catholics are the largest single religious denomination in the United States. They total close to 60 million (Gray, 1995) and make up approximately 27 percent of the population (Newport and Saad, 1997). Over the years the church has witnessed the assimilation of its members into mainstream American society. Although this has its advantages, it also has its drawbacks. Catholics have become more secularized, and the church has had less of an impact.

A consequence of this secularization is that Catholics are basically no different from non-Catholics in many areas, including divorce. Although more than 21 percent of Catholics have been divorced and another 23 percent are separated from their spouses (Kosmin and Lachman, 1993), the Church has not relented in its views on divorce. Catholics who are divorced face similar conflicts as they struggle to return to or retain an active role in their parish. As we shall see, the way out of this dilemma for both the divorced individual and the Roman Catholic Church is the religious annulment.

The annulment, or what is more aptly called a declaration of nullity, states that a real marriage did not exist. Although it may have appeared to be a valid union, something was missing from the onset. The Catholic Church maintains that an annulment differs from a divorce. The former declares there never was a valid marriage, and the latter recognizes that a marriage did, at one time, exist. This differentiation is used by those who argue that an annulment is not just a "Catholic divorce." Annulment proponents also quickly point out that the declaration of nullity is strictly religious; that is, it has no civil or legal repercussions. Therefore, although the marriage was declared not to have existed validly, any products of the union, such as property or, above all, children, are not affected. In other words, the children from the union are not declared illegitimate. Proponents also call attention to the fact that the remarriage of a Catholic without an annulment does not lead to being excommunicated from the Church. Indeed, this is the case. Although this penalty of excommunication was imposed in the United States, and the United States exclusively, it is no longer the case (Soule, 1997).

The sheer volume of annulment cases has increased tremendously. Prior to 1910, approximately 100 cases were heard worldwide. In 1994 alone, more than 54,000 marriages were nullified in the United States. This number represented almost 75 percent of all those granted worldwide. The figures indicated that the Catholic Church has spent over $20 million per year subsidizing marriage tribunals (Goodstein, 1997).

These figures also indicated that the vast majority of marriages were declared null and the reason for the nullification of the marriage was a "defect of consent." From this perspective, the consent of the couple when making the marriage vows is the crucial element. If this is missing, for whatever reason, then there is no valid marriage.

A majority of annulments today are granted for psychological reasons. It is here that the real controversy exists. Many feel that any marriage can be nullified under these kind of "ambiguous" circumstances. Although such disorders as schizophrenia and psychoses seem understandable, we might ask if other "lesser" offenses would qualify. For example, consider the following: a "sense of alienation or inadequacy, self-depreciation, hostility, sexual problems, impulsiveness or selfishness" can be serious enough to prohibit an individual from maintaining "the close, empathetic, cherishing relationship with a spouse which provides for mutual growth and the proper rearing of children" (Soule, 1997, p. 16).

Annulment awareness, even among Catholics, is somewhat limited and superficial. It is only when someone in the public eye seeks an annulment that most people hear anything about them.

I first became aware of annulments approximately eight years ago. As a sociologist I wondered, for example, if annulments are sought by all divorcing Catholics or if only certain "types" initiate an annulment. I searched the social scientific literature and found nothing on the topic. There was an occasional newspaper or magazine article; in addition, various articles and even books were written by scholars within the Catholic Church. It would not be until later that the case studies of Sheila Rauch Kennedy (1997) would appear in *Shattered Faith* followed by the largely archival approach of Ron Vasoli (1998) in *What God Has Joined Together.* However, there was nothing from a standard sociological perspective.

I decided that a social scientific study of annulments was needed. My purpose was to gain a better understanding of what annulments are, the extent to which they are being granted, on what grounds they are being granted, and the characteristics of those who seek annulments. Above all, however, was the attempt to bring a social scientific perspective to this area. I chose to use two standard sociological methods for gathering my information: the questionnaire and the interview.

With limited resources and no existing literature, I undertook my investigation. Given my experience and inquiries with the local tribunal, I concluded that I would not be able to get a list of petitioners and respondents from marriage tribunals. I therefore contacted Family Life groups from around the country and, informing them of my study, requested their cooperation. A number of group leaders responded affirmatively. I then proceeded to send questionnaires to these people, who then distributed them to both those who had gone through the annulment process and those who were divorced but had not had such an experience. In addition, a local priest was extremely helpful in locating respondents for me. I did not have a random sample of Catholics who were divorced, but I did have a sample with which to work.

I learned very quickly that the overwhelming majority of those who returned questionnaires and agreed to be interviewed were petitioners, and although they did have misgivings about annulments, they were generally favorably disposed to them. When I asked respondents to indicate their ex-spouses' addresses or phone numbers, virtually no one did.

I was aware that some people were opposed to annulments, but I did not know how to locate them. I did meet a few people who were opposed, but the number was very small.

My search for respondents took a positive turn when Sheila Rauch Kennedy (1997) published *Shattered Faith*. This book served notice that a group of people did exist who felt very hurt and betrayed by the Catholic Church. And then Jan Leary founded Save Our Sacrament (SOS), a group trying to reform the way in which the Catholic Church deals with divorce and remarriage. With the cooperation of both Ms. Kennedy and Dr. Leary, I was able to contact people who were not only respondents but were opposed to annulments. Many of these people agreed to complete the questionnaire as well as be interviewed over the phone. As a result, I arrived at a sample size of 126 petitioners and 35 respondents.

When I started thinking about the nature of my study I knew that I wanted to focus on those whose marriages had been annulled, but I also wanted to include two other groups: (1) those who were divorced but had not gone through the annulment process, and (2) those Catholics who were currently married and never divorced. Although I knew it would be important to describe the attitudes and characteristics of those whose marriages had been annulled, I would not know if their characteristics were any different from those who were divorced but whose marriages had not been annulled. Were the characteristics and beliefs of either of these two groups different from those who had never been divorced? It is for this reason that so-called comparison groups are often used by sociologists in their studies.

Finally, I wanted to explore in depth why some Catholics seek an annulment whereas others do not. To that end, I interviewed those individuals who favored annulments. Some of their stories are presented in this book. I also present the criticisms of annulments along with the stories of some who are opposed to them.

I hope this book will be a valuable source of information for both the person who is seeking or contemplating an annulment, and the divorced Catholic who is opposed to an annulment. It is my hope that therapists and priests who minister to divorced or separated Catholics will, after reading these stories, become more sensitized to the needs of their clients. This book will help tribunal personnel understand that although they must deal with Catholic Church law, they are also dealing with human beings who are typically going through a very traumatic time in their lives. Finally, this book will shed new insight into the annulment process, a process that is often shrouded in mystery and misunderstanding.

Chapter 1

Historical and Sociological Context of Divorce

I never considered divorcing but once it was clear that divorce was what I should do, the decision was instant (and final). After that decision, I had inner peace.

Alice, forty-three years old

IMPACT OF DIVORCE

Marriage is one of the most highly valued institutions in our culture. The vast majority of people not only *expect* to marry sometime in their life, but actually *do so*. The stigma attached to divorce has been great. Historically, it is far worse to divorce than to never marry. For the individuals, it was an indicator of failure and a sign of personal deviance. The individuals that made up the couple were typically viewed as immoral, mentally ill, or having some other individual problems (Feldberg and Kohen, 1980).

In 1950, the divorce rate in the United States was 2.5 for every 1,000 population (Kain, 1990); by 1980 the rate was at an all-time high—5.2 per 1,000 population (Zinn and Eitzen, 1999). In the 1990s, although divorces were occurring less frequently, they still remained very high. Figures currently indicate that approximately 43 percent of all first marriages in the United States end in divorce (Benokraitis, 1999).

Divorce became a social phenomena when its incidence increased. Today most people are more likely to interpret divorce as a personal misfortune rather than a sign of personal deviance or immorality. To some, the divorced are seen as innocent victims or "courageous survivors" (Levinger and Mokes, 1979).

With the soaring rates of divorce, thousands of men, women, and children have been affected. The consequences for divorced women often include lower standards of living; divorced men are more likely to experience a physical separation from their children.

The impact upon children in divorcing families can be even more devastating. Statistics indicate that about half of all couples who divorce have a child under age eighteen (Clarke, 1995). There have been two views about the impact of divorce on children. One holds that children suffer adverse psychological and behavioral consequences. The second argues that the situation for children of divorce would be much worse if they remained in a home in which there was constant tension and fighting (Shehan and Kammeyer, 1997).

A tremendous amount of research on the effects of divorce on children exists. Wallerstein has conducted some of the most recognized studies. She found, along with Kelly, such short-term effects of divorce as sadness, denial, and grief (Wallerstein and Kelly, 1980). It is also common for children to blame themselves and to fantasize about reuniting the parents. Wallerstein and Blakeslee (1989) also found long-term effects such as worry, underachievement, and self-deprecation among at least one-half of the children in their study.

Amato and Keith (1991a,b) reviewed existing studies on the consequences of divorce for children. They found that children of divorce do indeed suffer many negative consequences. Some of these are: low self-esteem, poor academic performance, difficulty in social relations, and lower life satisfaction. Other investigators have found higher levels of depression and withdrawal along with feeling less competent (Devall, Stoneman, and Brady, 1986; Peterson and Zill, 1986).

Not only do the children experience various psychological and behavioral changes, but it has been found that physical health is impacted. Guidubaldi and Cleminshaw (1985) found poorer physical health ratings among the children of divorce as compared to the children from intact families. A study by Mauldin (1990) found that the children of divorced parents averaged 13 percent more illnesses after the divorce than before. She argued that this was primarily due to increased levels of stress. Also, many single parents do not have the resources for getting their children medical care.

Another factor that has been studied in relation to divorce is *religion*. Historically, divorce has been either prohibited or, at least, discouraged by most religious organizations in the United States. Data that reveal individuals who are more actively involved in their religion have lower divorce rates. According to Glenn and Supancic (1984), there are differences among denominations, however. They found that Protestants had the highest rates of divorce and Jews the lowest; Catholics were in between. The percentage of Caucasian females who had been divorced or legally separated was 11.2 percent for Jews, 20.1 percent for Catholics, a range between 21.4 percent (Lutheran) and 32.9 percent (Episcopalian) for the different Protestant denominations, and 33.1 percent for those stating no religious preference. The findings for the males were in the same order as that for the females.

DIVORCE IN A HISTORICAL PERSPECTIVE

Many societies have attempted both to limit and to control the divorce experience. In some, divorce has been easy to obtain. In Islamic societies, for example, the husband does nothing more than say, "I divorce you" three times (Dyer, 1983). Among the Hopi Indians of the Southwest United States a woman could initiate a divorce. In order to obtain the divorce, she had only to place her husband's possessions outside their home (Queen, Habenstein, and Quadagno, 1985).

In other societies divorce has been, and still is, difficult to achieve. Until 1995 divorce was prohibited in Ireland. This prohibition was strongly backed by the Roman Catholic Church. The citizens in Ireland voted by a narrow margin (50.3 percent in favor) to allow divorce under certain circumstances. Specifically, if a couple has been separated for four of the last five years, a divorce is allowed (Barbash, 1995).

Divorce rates have typically increased in almost all societies around the world. Lester (1996), in a study of twenty-seven different nations between 1950 and 1985, found that the divorce rate had increased in all but two: Mexico and Yugoslavia. Table 1.1 presents the number of divorces that occur for every one hundred couples getting married for nineteen countries.

TABLE 1.1. Number of Divorces in Various Countries

Country	Divorces per 100 Couples
Russia	60
United States	51
Sweden	48
Estonia	46
Norway	44
United Kingdom	42
Denmark	41
Finland	41
Canada	38
Belarus	37
Lithuania	37
Ukraine	37
Switzerland	36
Austria	34
Moldova	34
Czech Republic	33
France	33
Belgium	31
Germany	30
Hungary	28
Netherlands	28

Source: Neft and Levine, 1997, p. 99.

English and American Law

English and U.S. cultures have witnessed similar histories in that divorce was extremely difficult to obtain. In England, up through the seventeenth century, the only option available to get out of a marriage was to obtain an annulment (Stone, 1990). Divorces could be granted on grounds such as: the husband and wife were too closely related biologically, physical cruelty, desertion, or adultery. A full divorce, however, was seldom granted even though it was necessary to allow a person to remarry. In contrast, a "bed and board" divorce, which the church did allow, dictated that the spouses could live apart but, legally, the obligations of marriage still existed between the parties (Stone, 1990).

Near the end of the seventeenth century the so-called "parliamentary divorce" was instituted. This type of divorce was the equivalent of a full divorce. The person who obtained this divorce was able to remarry. The dilemma was that not everyone could obtain this kind of divorce. In essence, the House of Lords had to pass an act granting it to the persons involved. Doing so was very expensive and, therefore, only available to the well-to-do. As a consequence, fewer than 100 full divorces were granted between 1697 and 1785. In every instance, it was the husband who was granted the divorce and the basis was always the wife's adultery (Cott, 1983).

Stone (1990) also reported that those of some means could engage in a "private separation" agreement. These were similar to today's accords in which the couple agreed to divide their accumulated resources. In addition, the husband typically was required to provide a form of alimony to the ex-wife. However, for the lower classes, the options for a divorce were more limited. Basically, the only possibility for these classes was desertion.

In 1857, the divorce laws in England were changed to allow women the right to file for divorce. Under the law, if the husband had abandoned the marriage for at least two years the wife was allowed to file. Cruelty was also permitted as grounds for divorce. Adultery, however, was allowed only as grounds for the husband (Stone, 1990).

Colonial America, even though consisting of a number of independent colonies having their own laws governing divorce, did have some consistencies. Though influenced by English law most states were more liberal than the "Mother Country." As a general rule, divorce was more common in New England than in the South, but even in New England divorce was not all that frequent during the seventeenth and eighteenth centuries (Gordon, 1978).

During the postrevolutionary period the trend in New England was for the courts to usurp the power of the legislature in divorce matters.

This did not occur in the South, however, until the 1800s. By the 1860s most states had abandoned the legislative divorce (Blake, 1962).

Some New England states had adopted very liberal laws. For example, Connecticut included as grounds for divorce not only cruelty and desertion but also alcoholism. A woman could also be granted a divorce in Connecticut if her husband was a "free thinker." In Massachusetts, grounds for divorce were adultery, bigamy, cruelty, and desertion. Starting with the latter part of the 1800s, women in this state not only were petitioning more for a divorce, but were being granted them (Gordon, 1978).

In the early nineteenth century, many states liberalized their divorce laws. Indiana, in 1824, included grounds of adultery, as well as cruelty, desertion, and what was termed an "omnibus clause." This clause stated that the court could grant a divorce for *any* reason it deemed fit. As a result, Indiana became somewhat of a haven for divorce. Not only was there the omnibus clause, but no residency requirements were needed (Gordon, 1978). Once the laws started to become more liberalized there seemed to be no turning back.

As the 1800s became the 1900s, religion started to play a role in divorce legislation. In 1902, twenty-five different Protestant denominations met at the Interfaith Conference on Marriage and Divorce. As a consequence of pressure placed upon then-President Theodore Roosevelt, he endorsed uniformity among the states in their divorce legislation.

Of particular concern during the early 1900s was migratory divorce. Spouses wishing to divorce but living in a state that had strict divorce laws would often go to states such as Indiana where, as previously mentioned, laws were more liberal or residency requirements were not established. Although this concern was great, only three states (New Jersey, Delaware, and Wisconsin) passed legislation preventing individuals from getting a divorce in a different state from the one in which they were permanent residents (Gordon, 1978).

A number of much-publicized cases in Nevada started the state on the road to being a "divorce capital." In addition to these cases, the legislature, in 1927, lowered the residency requirement for obtaining a divorce from six months to only three months. In 1931 it was lowered further to six weeks (Gordon, 1978).

Through the 1960s the grounds for divorce were fairly specific: desertion, cruelty, adultery, and nonsupport. Determining the grounds for divorce led to establishing wrongdoing (i.e., fault); in other words, someone had to be shown to be responsible for the breakdown of the marriage. Therefore, once wrongdoing was established it followed that the person had to be "punished." Typically this was done by way of a financial settlement (Guttman, 1993).

Most states expanded the grounds for divorce and, in 1969, California became the first state to adopt a "no-fault divorce" policy. This bill, signed into law by then-Governor Ronald Reagan (himself divorced), quickly became the norm for the rest of the country. The no-fault divorce was seen as a way of eliminating the negative consequences of divorce. A spouse no longer had to claim a specific reason for filing for a divorce, such as adultery; instead, one partner could seek a divorce on the grounds that the marriage was "irretrievably broken," claiming "irreconcilable differences." All that was now necessary was for one person to decide she or he did not want to be in the marriage and the courts supported it (Guttman, 1993).

In addition to no longer having to provide a specific reason for wanting a divorce, the no-fault law had three other effects:

1. eliminating the "adversarial confrontation," which existed before the new law;
2. dividing property in an equitable fashion; and
3. redefining the ex-spouses' responsibilities to the children.

The third effect has had an especially strong impact on the custody issue. During the colonial period, fathers were more likely to be granted custody of the children following a divorce. This was due to the mother being unable to support either herself or her children after a divorce. Mothers and children were seen as second-class citizens, nothing more than the property of the husband and father. In those cases in which the mother was awarded custody, the father was not required by the courts to pay child support. This pattern changed by the twentieth century with the coming of the Industrial Revolution. Now the father went outside the home to work while the mother stayed at home and cared for the children. This movement from an agrarian to an industrial society, along with the bourgeoning suffragette movement had, as a result, a growing respect for the role of mother. With the growing belief that the mother's role was crucial to the child's formative years, the courts began to grant custody to the mother. Consequently, by the middle of the twentieth century, a father was able to gain custody only by proving that his ex-wife was an unfit mother (Grief, 1985).

In the past two decades a shift has occurred in the granting of custody. No longer is custody of the child to be automatically awarded to the mother; rather, whatever is in the "best interest" of the child was to be the norm (Weitzman and Dixon, 1986). Still, fathers are awarded sole custody in only 9 percent of cases (Clarke, 1995). When fathers seek custody they are successful about one-half to two-thirds of the time (Hanson, 1988). Custody is most likely to be given to white fathers who are older and better educated (Donnelly and Finkelhor, 1992), and when the children are older and when the oldest child is male (Fox and Kelly, 1995).

The no-fault divorce has come under fire in the past decade. Using the argument that this "easy" divorce has lead to an increase in the divorce rate, many states have introduced legislation requiring a justifiable reason for divorce. There is debate as to the actual effect these laws have had. Nakonezny, Shull, and Rodgers (1995) found an increase in divorce rates from before no-fault laws were passed to after they were passed in forty-four of the fifty states. The actual average increase found was .80 divorces per 1,000 population. On the other hand, Glenn (1997), in his analysis of forty-three states, stated that the change in divorce laws had no impact. He found that in "states that adopted no-fault provisions at times other than during the divorce boom, the mean divorce rate was no higher in the 3 years after adoption [of the no-fault law] than in the 3 years before adoption" (p. 1022). Nakonezny, Shull, and Rodgers responded by saying that they never stated that "all" the increase in the divorce rate resulted from no-fault laws and that Glenn's analysis may be flawed in that he did not include three "crucial" states (Indiana, New Mexico, and Nevada) in his analysis. They argued that "when a no-fault divorce law was enacted in a typical state, divorce rates increased to a higher level than they would have reached otherwise" (Nakonezny, Shull, and Rodgers, 1995, p. 1026). Whether no-fault laws have led to an increase or not, many state legislatures have responded as if these laws have increased divorce rates (Glenn, 1997).

MODEL OF DIVORCE

Divorce, along with marriage, is a highly complex phenomenon. Although a number of perspectives help us to understand the divorce experience, I will focus on the one proposed by Bohannan (1971) along with Kaslow's (Schwartz and Kaslow, 1997) more recent "dialectic" model. The Kaslow model represents an expansion of Bohannan. Bohannan focused on what he called six "stations" or stages of divorce:

1. emotional,
2. legal,
3. economic,
4. coparental,
5. community,
6. religious (as added by Kaslow), and
7. psychic.

Kaslow added a seventh—the religious divorce.

The first station is the emotional divorce. This occurs when the couple is still married. One or both partners views the marriage as deteriorating and starts to question the desirability of remaining in the relationship. Although the marriage seems to be coming apart, a decision may be made to remain together, at least for the present (Bohannan, 1971). This stage includes such feelings as despair, anger, low self-esteem, and depression. Various behaviors such as avoiding issues, quarreling, and pretending that everything is fine are common. The couple may start seeing a therapist to deal with the problem issues (Schwartz and Kaslow, 1997). If the decision is made to divorce, the individuals move to the next step.

The second step is the legal divorce. During this stage an attorney is consulted. No-fault divorce laws may have eliminated demonstrating a cause for getting a divorce, but they have not eradicated the need for attorneys. Schwartz and Kaslow (1997) pointed to the fact that this stage encompasses self-pity and helplessness. Not only can behaviors such as bargaining, screaming, and threatening be found but even attempted suicide. Family, child, or individual therapy, along with mediation sessions, may be used in this phase.

The third stage Bohannan (1971) discussed was the economic divorce. This stage is crucial for it plays a significant role in both partners' financial future. Marriage may be about love and romance, but divorce typically comes down to money. Nobody really gains from divorce but the attorneys! It is argued that divorce is a major contributor to what is called the feminization of poverty. This refers to the high rates of poverty among families headed by single women. Originally it was an accepted fact that females experienced as much as a 73 percent reduction in their standard of living and males witnessed a 42 percent increase (Weitzman, 1985). More recent figures indicate that those percentages were too high. Peterson (1996) found that a woman's financial position decreased by 27 percent during the first year after separation and the man's increased by about 10 percent. In point of fact, however, the man's income may decline because of child support (which is not tax deductible), and/or alimony, mortgage payments for a home in which he no longer resides, rent on a new apartment, and so forth (Knox and Schacht, 1997).

Emotionally, the economic divorce may include confusion, sadness, feelings of loneliness, or relief. Typical behaviors during this stage are actual separation of the spouses, filing for divorce, and dealing with various legal issues (e.g., disposal of marital property and child custody) (Schwartz and Kaslow, 1997).

The fourth stage, the coparental divorce, represented the "most enduring pain of divorce" (Bohannan, 1971, p. 45). Although it is the parents who are divorced, the care and adjustment of the children needs to be recognized. Issues such as the daily care and financial obligations for the children along with visitation rights for the noncustodial parent need to be addressed. During this stage uncertainty, ambivalence, and concern for the children are exhibited. The parties may reveal the impending divorce to friends and family. A sense of grieving, but also a feeling of empowerment, may occur. If the wife was not in the workforce during her marriage, she may enter it now. Family therapy is an option (Schwartz and Kaslow, 1997).

Stage five, the community divorce, refers to the changes that come about in the divorced couple's social relations with friends and family. Divorced couples find that often they are dropped from the social gatherings of their married friends; some friends side with one ex-spouse or the other. In order to shore up these losses, the divorced individual may join new organizations not only for the companionship but for the support. It is very common, for example, for a newly divorced person to join a divorce support group. Kaslow pointed out that the community divorce can include indecisiveness, regret, and sadness, but also excitement and optimism. The divorce is now finalized and the former spouses start developing new activities and lives. One or both of the former partners may continue or seek individual counseling; the children may be placed in play or group therapy.

The sixth stage is the religious divorce. This stage was recently added by Schwartz and Kaslow (1997). The religious person seeks the approval of the church for the divorce and may fear God's disapproval. Behaviorally, individuals may seek a religious ceremony recognizing the divorce and may try in some way to make a "spiritual peace" with themselves. Unlike the previous stages in which individuals avail themselves of more secular therapy, ministerial counseling and advice is sought.

The final stage, the psychic divorce, comes after the divorce. When this occurs the person has successfully disassociated himself or herself from the previous spouse and has become a "new" person. Reaching this stage can take a considerable amount of time, especially if the individual had been married for a long time. This station may also take longer to reach when there are children involved, particularly if the children are young. What this means is that the parents must remain in contact with each other for an extended period of time to deal with issues concerning the kids. Feelings such as self-confidence, independence, and freedom come to the forefront. Working to help the children accept that the marriage is over, continuing a relationship with the children, and even parent-child therapy occur during this stage. Finally, the person may move on to a new relationship in the hopes of finding permanency (Bohannan, 1971; Schwartz and Kaslow, 1997).

The Bohannan model is a very popular one; it promotes an understanding of the difficulties that divorced persons experience. It also shows that the divorce experience, although unique to every individual, does have commonalties. Kaslow has added a significant dimension to the Bohannan model by incorporating the religious aspect. The religious institution is, after all, the dominant force in arguing against divorce. For the religious person, coming to terms with how her or his church sees divorce is important. For the Catholic, gaining the approval or at least the acknowledgment of the person's "existence," may be crucial. The way in which the Catholic can realize the Church's acceptance is the annulment.

FACTORS ASSOCIATED WITH DIVORCE

Studies indicate that many factors are associated with divorce. Research in the field can be grouped under three headings: cultural, demographic, and individual.

Cultural Factors

Industrialization

If asked why someone got a divorce, no one would blame industrialization. The change from an agricultural to an industrial society, with its attendant correlates, has produced change. These changes have been not only economic in nature but marital and familial as well.

In rural societies the strength of the extended family is apparent. These extended families include the parents and children as well as grandparents, aunts, uncles, and other relatives living together or in close proximity. In this system, no one is alone. Economic, social, and emotional support can be spread among many people. With the movement to an industrial society, however, the extended family has broken down. Industrialization has led to social and geographic mobility. The consequence is that the more isolated nuclear family (parents and children) has become the norm (Myers, 2000).

It is ironic that as many of the functions of the nuclear family have been given over to large corporations, schools, nursing homes, and hospitals, the one function that has become more important in family life is the affectional and companionship component. Because marriage offers the primary source of affection and companionship, it can put severe strain on the only other close person—the spouse. Among rural extended families, as I pointed out, the stresses and strains could be spread among several people. Now, when a spouse has problems, often only the other spouse is there to give support. Over a period of time the problems of one partner can create so much strain on the marriage that the relationship dissolves.

Gender Role Changes

Tremendous change has taken place in this country in regard to gender roles. Two of these concern economics and role expectations. Over half of all women are in the workforce and, although they still earn on the average only 72 percent of what the average man earns (Benokraitis, 1999), they now have greater financial independence than ever before. Thus, although many women may have stayed in a bad marriage in previous times due to an economic necessity, this is less often the case today. Data now indicate that when a divorce occurs the woman is more often the initiator. In fact, data from the National Center for Health Statistics in 1991 indicated that in 62 percent of all divorces, the female was the initiator and only in 32 percent of the cases was the husband the initiator. The remaining 6 percent jointly initiated the divorce.

In addition to economic changes, the women's movement has led to changing role expectations. No longer are women and wives expected to be meek, complacent supporters of their husbands. The wants and needs of the wife are now considered equally. The traditional marriage, where the husband was the breadwinner and the wife the child rearer and provider of emotional support, has gradually been replaced by more egalitarian marriages in which wives have equal rights. This sometimes has the effect of creating a marital battleground: the husband wants to hold on to his power and other privileges, and the wife believes she is entitled to more shared power and resources.

Values and Laws

Attitudes and laws change over time. American culture has always had an individualistic perspective but this seems to have become more prominent since the late 1960s. In previous decades, an individual contemplating divorce would usually consider others, asking: "What will my parents think?", "What will my friends think?", "What about the children?", "What will my church think?"

Although spouses undoubtedly still ask these questions, they now ask: "What is best for me?" Christopher Lasch (1978), in his book *The Culture of Narcissism,* discussed this emphasis upon the self. Lasch contends that in the period following the political and social upheavals of the 1960s, Americans turned inward and became preoccupied with the self and "psychic improvement" (p. 4). The rise of therapy became dominant and, according to the author, came to replace religion as one of the major components of American culture. The quest for self-improvement replaced a social consciousness. Lasch states: ". . . Americans have retreated to purely personal preoccupations . . . people have convinced themselves that what matters is psychic self-improvement: getting in touch with their feelings . . ." (p. 4). He contends that "This self-absorption defines the moral climate of contemporary society" (p. 25). During the 1980s, terms such as self-absorption, self-actualization, and self-improvement were more common. It is probably no accident that divorce rates were very high during this period. In 1979 and again in 1981 the rates were at an all-time high—over five divorces for every 1,000 population (Guttman, 1993).

In the late 1990s, the United States witnessed somewhat of a backlash to the individualism of a decade ago. Many people saw the influence of individualism and its consequent shift in laws as having had more negative than positive consequences. This shift has resulted in many state legislatures rethinking their liberal divorce laws. Louisiana, for example, passed a law in 1997 instituting two kinds of marriage—a "no-fault" and a "covenant" marriage. The latter would be much more difficult to obtain, requiring premarital counseling; specific grounds for a divorce such as adultery; the commission of a crime by the ex-spouse; abandonment for a period of one year; abuse; or living apart for at least two years. It finally requires the couple to seek counseling before a divorce is granted (Loconte, 1998).

In addition to Louisiana, covenant marriages exist in Arizona and bills relating to this type of marriage were introduced in seventeen other states during the 1998 legislative year. Statutes relating to mandatory counseling, either before marriage or divorce, have been introduced in some states, and others considered repealing their no-fault laws. Some states are mandating their schools to offer classes relating to marriage. Florida has passed such a bill (Otto, 1999).

In Michigan at least one judge has taken it upon himself to deal with the large number of couples getting a divorce. Starting in 1997, District Judge Sheridan borrowed the policy used by many church leaders of not marrying a couple unless they first complete a course in marital preparedness. Under his auspices, engaged couples are required to complete inventories that would identify their areas of agreement and disagreement. Also included is instruction on conflict resolution (Otto, 1999).

It should be noted that although many states are considering stricter laws, considerable opposition exists. Some states (e.g., Idaho and Georgia) have considered similar legislation but the proposals have not passed. Many academics and clinicians have voiced concern about the divorce laws becoming more restrictive. Craig Everett, editor of the *Journal of Divorce and Remarriage,* stated that many people believe that if a law is passed making it more difficult to get a divorce, it will lead to a decrease in the divorce rate. He says that this belief is probably false (Guttman, 1996).

Demographic Factors

Research over the years has found a number of demographic factors to be associated with divorce: education, income, age, race and ethnicity, and religion. The following is a brief look at each of these and their specific relationship with divorce.

Education

Generally, education is negatively associated with divorce. In other words, lower education increases the possibility of divorce (Kurdek, 1993). In a study by Glick (1984), for example, those with a high school education had a higher rate of divorce than those who held a bachelor's degree.

This educational factor seems to be stronger for men than for women. It has been found that women with very high levels of education (five years and more beyond high school) have high rates of divorce. The same relationship does not exist when looking at males who have a similar level of education (Glenn and Supancic, 1984). The reasons for the gender differences are not clear. Cooney and Uhlanberg (1989) discussed the possibility of a greater conflict for females between work and family responsibilities. Also, women who have higher educations will no doubt be more likely to have a higher level occupation with a correspondingly higher salary. The higher income will allow the woman to be more financially independent and, therefore, better equipped to leave an unhappy marriage.

Income

Income relates to the previous variable of education. Although the exception for well-educated women was noted, divorce rates generally are lower with higher incomes (Martin and Bumpass, 1989). Lester (1996) found a correlation between unemployment and a high divorce rate in nine of eleven countries studied

Age

The relationship between age at first marriage and divorce has been studied widely and the data indicate the same pattern—the younger the age at which marriage occurs, the greater the rate of divorce (Kurdek, 1993). In fact, evidence suggests that age is the strongest predictor of divorce, at least during the first five years of marriage (Martin and Bumpass, 1989). Other research indicates that the divorce rate for those who marry before the age of twenty was two to three times that of their counterparts who do not marry until their twenties (Norton and Moorman, 1987).

One obvious explanation for this relationship is the fact that young adults are typically not well-prepared for marriage. They are often still immature, just out of school, without jobs, and with no place to live. They are still convinced, at least when they are dating or engaged, that love conquers all. However, this belief can end very quickly. Evidence suggests that younger married couples are less happy than older spouses and, when compared to older spouses, they are more likely to complain about their spouse being moody, jealous, in trouble with the authorities, or using drugs and alcohol (Booth and Edwards, 1985).

Booth and Edwards (1985) also suggested that these young adults often marry without their parents' blessings. When trouble occurred within the marriage, the parents may not have discouraged a divorce; on the contrary a divorce may have been encouraged.

Race and Ethnicity

Research has consistently found that African Americans have higher rates of divorce than Caucasians. In fact, the rates have been twice that of Caucasians in the past two decades (Saluter, 1994). Differences still exist controlling for other variables such as occupation, income, and education (White, 1991). Recent figures indicate that 20 percent of all black females are expected to divorce within the first five years of marriage. The figure for white females is only 6 percent (Kposowa, 1998). The data also indicate that African Americans have a higher rate of separation (Glenn and Supancic, 1984).

Numerous explanations exist for this difference. Some researchers argue that there is a more tolerant view of divorce among African Americans than Caucasians (McKenry and Fine, 1993). Second, although differences still exist when controlling for socioeconomic variables, Jaynes and Williams (1989) reported that the differences in divorce rate is substantially reduced when education and income are taken into account. Third, African-American women have higher rates of teenage and premarital pregnancy (Garfinkel, McLanahan, and Robins, 1994). The age relationship, as mentioned earlier, has been clearly associated with divorce. Data also show higher rates of divorce when a premarital pregnancy or birth has occurred (Norton and Miller, 1992).

Religion

Different religions have various perspectives on marriage and divorce. Although most discourage divorce, some have attempted to prohibit it. Therefore, expect differences in the divorce rate among various religions but also when comparing the religious population with those who are not particularly religious. As Chapter 6 will detail, one of the duties of religion is to act as a socially cohesive force that provides support in times of trouble (Durkheim, 1951).

Research supports the belief that the religiously involved have lower divorce rates than those who are less religiously oriented. In fact, the less religious individuals have the highest divorce rates of all (Glenn and Supancic, 1984). Data also show that same-faith marriages have a lower divorce rate than interfaith marriages (Bahr, 1981; Lehrer and Chiswick, 1993). A common explanation for this is that same-faith marriages increase the shared values and traditions between the spouses (Wineberg, 1994).

Other Factors

Although the previous are some of the major demographic variables associated with divorce rates, they are by no means all variables. Other factors found by researchers to be associated with the divorce rate are: parental divorce, presence of children, and wives' employment. Specifically, research indicates that individuals whose parents divorced have more tolerant views toward divorce than those who grew up in intact families (Amato and Booth, 1991). Those in the former group also have higher divorce rates (Keith and Finlay, 1988). Data show that those who have no children have the highest divorce rates, and the lowest rates occur for those individuals who have a child under the age of three (Keith and Finlay, 1988).

Individual Factors

Despite my having discussed the general cultural and demographic factors relating to divorce, an individual's decision to divorce remains very personal. Therefore, more specific, or micro, factors are associated with divorce. These are most likely to be mentioned by people who have sought a divorce. In a survey by Geiss and O'Leary (1981), marriage and family therapists were asked to rate the most frequent and damaging problems of couples whom they counseled, along with those that were the most difficult to treat (see Table 1.2).

In their study of thirty-two divorced individuals, Rasmussen and Ferraro (1991) found extramarital sex, excessive drinking, and financial problems to be the most frequently mentioned factors causing divorce.

Colasanto and Shriver (1989) reported that personality incompatibility was the primary factor in 47 percent of cases. In second place, but far below that of personality incompatibility, was infidelity (17 per-

TABLE 1.2. Areas of Marital Conflict (Ranked from Most to Least) Seen by Therapists As Most Damaging and Most Difficult to Treat

Most Damaging	Most Difficult to Treat
1. Communication	1. Alcoholism
2. Unrealistic expectations for either the spouse or the marriage	2. Lack of affection
3. Power conflicts	3. Individual problems
4. Individual problems	4. Power conflicts
5. Role Conflicts	5. Addiction (other than alcoholism)
6. Loss of loving feelings	6. Value conflicts
7. Demonstrating affection	7. Physical abuse
8. Alcoholism	8. Unrealistic expectations
9. Extramarital affair	9. Extramarital affair
10. Sex	10. Incest

Source: Geiss and O'Leary, 1981, pp. 516-517.

cent). Other factors cited were alcohol/drug use (16 percent); disagreements about money, family, and children (10 percent); and physical abuse (5 percent). They reported that women were more likely to identify the role of alcohol or other drugs and less likely to cite the area of children and money.

Finally, Eels and O'Flaherty (1996) reported that the nature of the problems cited within the marriage have changed from what they term "individual behavioral problems" (e.g., alcoholism or abuse) to problems relating to communication. In their study of separated and divorced couples they found the top two areas of discord to be: (1) the ex-partner's inability to properly communicate his or her feelings, and (2) their partner's problem with listening to what he or she has to say.

SUMMARY

Divorce has become a major component of life in most societies throughout the world. One significant trend in the United States was the dramatic increases in the divorce rate during the 1970s and early 1980s. Although they have declined some, the rates still remain very high. A second major development was the enactment of no-fault divorce laws. There has been somewhat of a backlash, and many state legislatures are now considering rescinding their laws and making it tougher to be granted a divorce.

Many cultural, demographic, and individual factors are associated with and lead to divorce. One of these variables is religion. The figures indicate that those with no religion have the highest divorce rates when compared to those who have some religious identification.

Chapter 2

Religious Perspectives on Divorce

A murderer can be forgiven, reinstated. Drug addicts can wipe the slate clean of a past life and be heralded as heroes in part because of their past life. Many churches are proud to turn over pulpits to alcoholics, former prostitutes, released convicts. But let a person who has gone through the hell of a broken marriage seek the love and acceptance of the church, and for some the response will be rejection. And for others it will be conditional acceptance, conditional on the assumption that man or woman, father or mother, live alone the rest of his or her life.

(C. Wayne Zunkel, 1976, p. 155)

The following text discusses the views on divorce of four Protestant denominations: the United Methodist Church, the Presbyterian Church, the Southern Baptist Church, and the Mennonites. The first two bodies represent the more liberal Protestant denominations, and the latter two are more conservative in their approach to family issues. The views of those of the Jewish faith and Roman Catholicism are also included. Topics include how American Catholics view the Church's position, the growth of the Divorced Catholic Movement, and how the Church has responded to its divorced parishioners.

PROTESTANT DENOMINATIONS

United Methodist Church

The United Methodist Church is certainly not in favor of divorce, but it recognizes its inevitability in some cases. Remarriage is also acknowledged as not only unavoidable but acceptable. The church's

Book of Discipline states:

> We affirm the sanctity of the marriage covenant that is expressed in love, mutual support, personal commitment, and shared fidelity between a man and a woman. We believe that God's blessing rests upon such marriage, whether or not there are children of the union. . . .
>
> When a married couple is estranged beyond reconciliation, even after thoughtful consideration and counsel, divorce is a regrettable alternative in the midst of brokenness. It is recommended that methods of mediation be used to minimize the adversarial nature and fault-finding that are often part of our current judicial processes. . . .
>
> Divorce does not preclude a new marriage. We encourage an intentional commitment of the Church and society to minister compassionately to those in the process of divorce, as well as members of divorced and remarried families, in a community of faith where God's grace is shared by all. (*Book of Discipline of the United Methodist Church,* 1996, pp. 87-88)

Presbyterian Church (U.S.A.)

The Presbyterian Church takes the biblical view that marriage is sacred and should not be undone. At their June 1992 assembly, divorce was recognized as acceptable under certain conditions, i.e., on "biblical grounds" (e.g., "sexual immorality") (*Minutes of the General Assembly,* 1992, p. 60). When divorce occurs for any non-biblical reason the directive is either to reconcile or not to remarry. It is recommended that ministers and "ruling elders" provide counseling and direction for those who have engaged in sexual immorality and desertion. Finally, the General Assembly also adopted a resolution stating that remarriage is permissible when "an unbeliever separates from the marriage relationship with a believer" (p. 60).

Southern Baptist Church

The Southern Baptist Convention takes a very fundamentalist approach to all issues concerning the family, including marriage, divorce, and remarriage. They view divorce as totally unacceptable. However, they do make exceptions. Adultery is seen as a legitimate reason for a divorce. Resolutions were passed by the Convention in 1885 and again in 1904 that deplored divorce. In addition, ministers were discouraged from participating in the remarriage of two divorced persons. Apparently, some within the church were even dubious as to whether someone whose spouse had died was entitled to remarry (Leonard, 1996).

The Convention in 1975 pointed out that many people turn to divorce as a solution too soon when, in fact, the marriage could still be saved. Ministers were encouraged to provide necessary assistance to couples experiencing marital problems (Leonard, 1996).

Baptists have recognized the high divorce rate among their members, including pastors and other leaders. The issue of remarriage is still a difficult one for the church. For example, disagreement exists over the issue of allowing divorced and remarried Baptists to occupy positions of leadership (Leonard, 1996).

Recognizing the importance of providing information and assistance to married couples, the church started what are termed "Fall Festivals of Marriage." These conferences began approximately twenty-five years ago in Ridgecrest, North Carolina (Reyes, 2002). These are marital enrichment workshops for couples and are held in different locations around the United States. In 2001, approximately 9,000 people attended the conferences. In 2002, sixteen events will be held in nine different locations (Reyes, 2002). Topics covered at a 1994 conference included: intimacy, sexuality, parenting, marriage enrichment in your church, and two-career marriages. The church conducted these festivals in seventeen different states throughout 1994 ("Fall Festival of Marriage," 1994). Divorce recovery workshops for this segment of their population are now also offered by the church.

Mennonites

Historically, Mennonites were prohibited from divorcing except under the condition of adultery. As long as the ex-spouse was alive, remarriage was forbidden. Statistics indicated that divorce was rare among this group until the 1940s. However, by the 1970s, this religious group was facing the grim fact that, despite the frequency being less than most other denominations, more and more of its members were getting divorced (Kauffman, 1996).

In 1983, the Southeastern Mennonite Conference officially adopted a policy concerning marriage and divorce. Similar to other religions, they took the biblical position a person marries for life. The document states that the Old Testament allows divorce "as a concession." It was not "authorized by God." The New Testament grants two alternatives for the divorced person: to remain single and unmarried or to reconcile with his or her partner.

Remarriage was interpreted as adulterous, and seen as wrong and leading to solemn consequences. The 1983 policy based on the Bible, states: "Since the Scriptures teach that marriage is validated by God, whether contracted by believers or unbelievers, we believe the first marriage is still binding as long as both are living" (quoted in Statement of Position on Divorce and Remarriage, 1999, p. 2).

The Mennonite position is quite clear: divorce and remarriage are not to be tolerated. They are clearly in contradiction "to the original purpose of God and the true nature of marriage" (quoted in Statement of Position on Divorce and Remarriage, 1999, p. 2). The 1983 policy also states: "Scripturally, there is nothing which breaks the marriage bond except death. The act of adultery does not dissolve the marriage bond, although it decidedly affects the quality of a marriage relationship and leaves a permanent scar on the persons involved. A legal document called *divorce,* from God's point of view, does not break the marriage bond, else remarriage would not be adultery" (quoted in Statement of Position on Divorce and Remarriage, 1999, p. 1).

JUDAISM

Within the Jewish faith marriage has always been the ideal for the adult. At birth both the male and female are given a blessing asking that "they will mature into marriage" (Fishman, 1996, p. 100). Very few roles exist for an individual who does not marry and have children. Clergy are expected to marry, and congregations often avoid hiring either a rabbi or religious teacher who is single. Children who do not marry are often considered shameful by their parents. The fact that the vast majority (95 percent) of Jews wed can be understood given this cultural heritage (Fishman, 1996).

In the 1970s and 1980s, the divorce rate among Jews rose with the incidence being significantly greater among those who had a low level of "ritual observance" compared to those Jews who had a higher rate of religious observance (Brodbar-Nemzer, 1984). It is also estimated that approximately 10 percent of Jewish children currently are in single-parent homes, and another 20 percent live with a stepparent rather than a biological one (Fishman, 1996).

The Conservative and Orthodox communities are governed by traditional Jewish law (halacha). Under this law a civil divorce is not sufficient to end a Jewish marriage. In order for a marriage to legitimately end, a "get" must be obtained. A get states that a marriage never technically existed. This concept is equivalent to the Catholic annulment (Brozan, 1998).

Under traditional Jewish law only the husband is allowed to acquire the get. If he, for one reason or another, decides against acquiring the get, the wife is not free to remarry. However, in some limited instances (e.g., restriction of her freedom and lack of support), the wife can petition for the man to write the get (Kensky, 1996).

The husband typically appoints a scribe who writes the twelve-line document in Hebrew. Once written, witnesses testify to the fact that the husband has given his consent to have the get written out for him. This process takes no more than thirty to forty-five minutes. The next step consists of the husband presenting the get to his wife. Witnesses are also present at this stage of the process. Once the wife accepts the get, the divorce becomes final. The presence of the wife is not essential to this process. The procedure can even take place by way of proxy. Upon the wife's acceptance, the document is placed in the files of the participating rabbi. The document is also cut by the rabbi so that it can never be used again. The rabbi then prepares a certificate verifying that the process was properly conducted. There are no particular prayers or rituals and the entire process takes place in approximately one hour. There is a charge of approximately $400 if both parties are present. If the wife is not present, an additional meeting is required and another $100 is charged. If the parties are notable to provide the fee, subsidies are available. Once the process is complete they are divorced and the individuals are free to remarry (KAYAMA, 1997).

The get is required by traditional Jewish law, which is acknowledged by both Conservative and Orthodox faiths along with the state of Israel. The Reform Movement, however, does not require such a document. Many Reform rabbis do alert couples, however, to the fact that, without the get, they (along with their children) may encounter future problems arising from encounters with those within Judaism who do require the document.

Statistics indicate that anywhere from 20,000 to 30,000 Jewish couples divorce each year in the United States. As with their Catholic counterparts, very few (15 percent) actually obtain the get (KAYAMA, 1997). The consequences for not obtaining the get can be severe. If a woman has no get, remarries, and has children, those children are not considered legitimate. Those children would only be able to marry others in a similar position. They are also unable to marry in Israel (KAYAMA, 1997).

An organization by the name of KAYAMA was founded in 1985 by two attorneys, to increase the awareness of the restrictions that people face when they do not obtain the get. Their approach has been to try and reach as many people as possible to educate them to the obstacles they may face. Other services include making any necessary arrangement for acquiring the get and subsidizing the cost of the get, if necessary.

Again, this does not apply to Reform Jews. They view the fact that females are not allowed to initiate the process as wrong. Also, the idea that the children cannot have the same rights as those children whose parents acquired the get is also seen as unjust by the progressive (KAYAMA, 1997).

The get came under attack in 1987 when two Orthodox rabbis established their own court to assist women in obtaining a get. This was prompted by the fact that some husbands were not initiating the necessary proceedings to free the wife to remarry. Some withhold the get to reduce or eliminate child support payments; others want custody for themselves. Rabbi Rackman, one of the founders of the new court, stated that if the husband was refusing to initiate the get, the only alternative was to grant it to the wife. In this court, which consists of three judges, over 300 gets have been granted to wives (Brozan, 1998; Ragen, 2000).

ROMAN CATHOLICISM

In analyzing Catholic principles relating to divorce it can be stated that the doctrine, starting in the late Middle Ages, was very simple: marriage was dissoluble only with the death of a spouse. This included the principle that someone who was married could not marry someone else if the first spouse was alive (Phillips, 1988). There were two rather specific exceptions to this doctrine. The first permitted a Catholic to divorce and remarry if deserted by a spouse who was not a Christian. Second, if the marriage had not been sexually consummated and if either spouse wanted to join a religious order, then divorce was allowed. These two exceptions occurred only under rare circumstances (Rue and Shanahan, 1972; Phillips, 1988).

This doctrine started to erode in the sixteenth century. A debate incurred between those who favored legalizing divorce and those who were opposed to it under any circumstance. Among the former group were two camps. On one side were those who felt divorce was justifiable but only when infidelity was involved. In the other camp were those who argued that divorce should be allowed not only for adultery but for other grounds as well. One of the major advocates of the second position, that marriage is indissoluble, was the Catholic Church (Phillips, 1988).

Within Catholic doctrine, divorce was intertwined not only with marriage and remarriage but also with sexuality and celibacy. The preferred state was celibacy and virginity. If, however, an individual could not remain celibate and a virgin, marriage was accepted (Phillips, 1988).

Sex and marriage became inseparable. Doctrine dictated that God ordained marriage as the only means through which (1) children could be conceived, and (2) illicit sexual activity could be eliminated. Sex, however, was not to be pleasurable; it was to be restricted solely to procreation, the philosophy being that it had to be endured as a duty in order to have children born into the world (Phillips, 1988).

Phillips (1988) stated that, given the fact that marriage was second to celibacy, divorce might be interpreted as acceptable if it did not lead to remarriage or sexual relations. This was not the case. Church scholars, using various biblical passages, concluded that marriage was a lifelong pact between husband and wife; in short, marriage was indissoluble.

There were dissenters from this view. Saint Augustine, for example, believed infidelity was proper grounds for a separation. He also believed that, in such a case, neither spouse could remarry. In contrast, Pollentius believed that the church should allow the innocent party to remarry in the case of adultery. He also felt that if the couple was unable to have a proper sexual relationship because of an incurable disease, a separation should be allowed along with the possibility of the healthy partner remarrying (Phillips, 1988).

Despite various dissenting views the position of the church was "till death do you part." In order to uphold this position and "control" marriage, church law (canon law) was developed. Canon law was established to deal properly with marriage and divorce, bringing it into the hands of church law and courts. Marriage, which had been a private matter and outside court purview, became legally defined. In deciding whether a marriage was determined by consent or sexual relations, church law opted for the former. It decided that the marital partners had to give their mutual consent for the marriage to be valid. Until the sixteenth century this was all that was required. In other words, if two people agreed to the marriage then they were married even if there was no priest, witness, or formal ceremony (Phillips, 1988).

At the Council of Trent in 1563, the principle of indissolubility became part of canon law. Along with this precept came the addition of another crucial aspect of how the Church today views marriage—the principle that marriage is a sacrament. Although the sacramentality of marriage had been accepted much earlier, it became part of canon law only in the sixteenth century. Saint Augustine is often viewed as the first individual to treat marriage as a sacrament (Coleman, 1988).

Although the doctrine essentially remains intact, the twentieth century witnessed the declining influence of the Catholic Church and its teachings on marriage, divorce, and remarriage. In Latin America and Western Europe, where many countries are heavily Catholic in population, changes have also occurred. Divorce was permitted in Brazil in 1978 and Argentina in 1987. Brazil's original law allowed divorce after three years of a judicial separation and after five years of a de facto separation. A 1988 law reduced the necessary periods to one and two years, respectively. Argentina's 1987 law allowed divorce "by agreement" (Goode, 1993).

Western European countries have witnessed similar changes in their divorce laws. The situation in Italy prior to the ability to divorce was that individuals with the financial means would often go to another country long enough to be declared a citizen. He or she would then proceed with a divorce and return to Italy. For others of means, a church annulment was a possibility. This was costly and extremely difficult to obtain. The third alternative was to receive a legal separation. The difficulty here was that neither spouse was free to remarry. The situation changed in 1970 when the Italian parliament, despite the resistance of the Catholic Church, adopted a divorce law. The law was liberalized in 1975 when it dropped the provision for determining fault (Goode, 1993).

After Italy had gone through the process, Portugal and Spain followed suit. The law passed in Portugal in 1977 allowed three kinds of divorce. One form allowed a couple to divorce by mutual consent if they had been married for three years. Second, divorce could be obtained if "one of the spouses violated his or her marital duties in a repeated and serious manner, so as to make life in common impossible" (Phillips, 1988, p. 577). Also included here was the case in which there had been a separation or mental illness for at least six years, or desertion for at least four years. The third form of divorce was the possibility of converting a separation into a divorce after only two years (Phillips, 1988).

Spain legalized divorce in 1932, but under General Francisco Franco, who abided by the Catholic teachings, it was prohibited. In 1975 Franco died and, following the liberalization of many social policies, divorce was again made legal in 1981. Divorce could be obtained for a wide variety of reasons—infidelity, alcoholism or other drug addiction, desertion, or imprisonment for more than six years (Phillips, 1988).

Ireland was the last to legalize divorce. Prior to its legalization couples had few alternatives. Legal separation, though expensive, was available. Another possibility was having the marriage annulled, although very few were able to use this method. In fact, according to Dillon (1993), less than one-half of 1 percent of Irish Catholic marriages were recognized as invalid by the church. For example, only

828 annulments were granted between 1976 and 1984, an average of slightly more than 100 per year. Data also indicate, however, an increase in the number of annulments being granted. In a one-year period ending in 1990, over 1,000 applications were received, 250 decisions were made, and 234 were granted. Therefore, in a one-year period more than two and a half times the number of annulments were granted than was typical for each yearly period between 1976 and 1984.

In 1986, Prime Minister FitzGerald called for a referendum on divorce. If passed, divorce would become legal. Although one might guess that the Catholic Church played a major role in arguing for the defeat of the amendment, this was not the case. Officially, a position of nonintervention, reflecting a separation of church and state, was assumed. This did not keep priests and bishops from preaching from the pulpit the Church's position on divorce (Dillon, 1993).

Although polls indicated a majority in favor of the divorce proposal, support dwindled. After an active campaign by both pro- and antiforces the amendment was defeated by a two-to-one margin (Dillon, 1993). In 1995, however, a majority of the Irish voted in favor of a divorce bill (Barbash, 1995).

One might conclude that the Catholic Church is losing its battle to keep marriages intact until death. When such heavily Catholic countries such as Ireland and Spain legalize divorce, the Church finds itself at odds with the political and legal establishment. When the society is a highly religiously pluralistic one, such as the United States, the Church's doctrine carries little or no weight when states make their divorce policies.

Views on Divorce Among the Catholic Population

How does the American Catholic view the Church's stance on divorce and remarriage? Since 1987, *The National Catholic Reporter* has commissioned, at six-year intervals, the Gallup organization to conduct a survey of the American Catholic population. Questions relevant to divorce and remarriage, along with other church- and family-related issues, have been included in each of the three polls.

Respondents have been asked to indicate who they thought should have the "final say" when a divorced Catholic remarries without first obtaining an annulment: "church leaders," "individuals," or "both."

In 1987, 23 percent said "church leaders," 31 percent said "individuals," and 37 percent indicated "both." By 1993 the figure (23 percent) for the leaders had remained the same, but the percentage (38 percent) for the individual had increased. The 1999 data indicated lower support (20 percent) for the leaders and higher support (45 percent) for the individual ("American Catholics Still Seek Greater Role," 1999).

The 1993 results for the previous question were analyzed controlling for age, gender, and education. A higher percentage (27 percent) of males than females (20 percent) said "church leaders." Fewer individuals (20 percent) in the eighteen to thirty-four age category gave this response than those in the thirty-five to fifty-four age bracket (25 percent) or fifty-five and over category (26 percent). Finally, college graduates (20 percent) were the least likely to allow the pope and bishops to solely decide. Those with some college were next (21 percent), and 25 percent of those with a high school education or less believed the leaders should be the sole decision makers (Fox, 1993).

The 1999 survey included a breakdown of responses by church attendance and parish membership for the question regarding remarrying without an annulment. For those who attended Mass weekly, 32 percent said "church leaders" in contrast to the overall figure of 20 percent. Twenty-nine percent of weekly attenders said "individuals," compared to the overall figure of 45 percent. Parish members were also more likely to respond that the authority should rest only with the leaders—23 percent as opposed to 11 percent for the nonparishioners ("American Catholics Still Seek," 1999).

The survey also asked if a person could be a good Catholic "without obeying the Church hierarchy's teaching on divorce and remarriage." In the 1987 study, 57 percent said yes; in 1993 it was 62 percent; by 1999 the figure had increased to 65 percent.

Can a person be a good Catholic "without their marriage being approved by the Catholic Church?" According to the majority of American Catholics, the answer is "yes." The 1999 figure is 68 percent. In 1993 it was 61 percent, and in 1987 it was only 51 percent replying in the affirmative.

Results from the 1993 survey revealed that a majority (61 percent) felt that lay members should have the right to take part in making Church policy in the area of divorce and remarriage. In the 1987 poll the figure was only 50 percent. The 1993 survey also found a fairly large discrepancy based on gender. Women (67 percent) were more likely to favor lay participation than men (53 percent) (Fox, 1993). These results indicate a major shift from 1987 to 1999 favoring (1) more individual participation in the affairs and decisions of the church, and (2) the belief that a person could still be a good Catholic without obeying Church doctrine. Data also indicate that regular churchgoers and parish members are more likely to favor decision making by the leaders (Fox, 1993; "American Catholics Still Seek," 1999).

Rise of the Divorced Catholic Movement

In 1972, Rue and Shanahan published *The Divorced Catholic*. The book painted a picture of loneliness, frustration, and despair for the Catholic individual who had, or was contemplating, a divorce. The authors pointed to the fact that no mechanisms were in place within the Church to deal with the divorced Catholic. These divorced individuals often felt as though they did not belong, were not wanted, and that their spiritual needs were not being met. The need to deal with this ever-growing segment of divorced Catholics became increasingly important with the estimate that, as of 1988, a minimum of 6 million U.S. Catholics were divorced (Coleman, 1988). Studies show that in the United States the majority of spouses who divorce are not negative about marriage because they remarry, usually within three years of the divorce (Benokraitis, 1999). Catholics are no different. The problem from the Church's perspective is that about three-fourths of those Catholics who have remarried have done so without the "blessing" of the church (Coleman, 1988). No doubt many of these individuals are distraught over the fact that they divorced and remarried outside the Church.

Out of the need to deal with this large segment of the Catholic community, the Divorced Catholic Movement (DCM) arose in 1971 in Boston. Father James Young (1979) was instrumental in organizing this group. He noted that the divorced Catholic felt similar to an "outcast" from the Church. At that time divorce was highly stigmatized and even punished. The punishment was the inability to remarry. Many divorced Catholics also believed, although incorrectly, that they were not able to receive Holy Communion (Foster, 1999).

Although these divorced Catholics often felt discouraged, many did not want to leave the Church. On one hand they recognized the Church's position relating to marriage and its indissolubility. On the other, they recognized the reality of their own situation in a marriage that was causing them great stress and unhappiness. It was a time when their self-esteem was low and they experienced personal turmoil and often great anguish. It was also a time when they needed the Church. However, they felt that the Church was not there for them. The result for some was no doubt to leave the Church—a church that was seen as having failed them. Many did not choose this option; instead, they remained within the Church and attempted to find a constructive place. These Catholics ran counter to the stereotype of the "angry" divorced Catholic (Young, 1979).

Above all, the divorced Catholics who remained in the Church sought the ability to receive Holy Communion. Young (1979) notes that "Catholics are a deeply Eucharist people" (p. 9). A major aspect of the Mass is receiving the Eucharist and, if not allowed to participate in this ritual, most would feel a deep sense of loss.

Ripple (1990), who worked with Father Young, indicated that the Church needed to pay strict attention to all kinds of suffering, including that among the divorced. No one, she stated, should be "outside the family" (p. 5). The questions being asked prior to 1972 were, in her view, the incorrect ones. Instead of asking, "What is wrong with all these careless divorcing people?", the question should be, "How can we be present to and supportive of people who have experienced this human tragedy?" Instead of asking, "How can we prevent people from remarrying?", we should be asking, "What can we do to call people to faithfulness to life so that, if and when they do remarry, they have the possibility of that community of life and love they either did not have before or had and lost?" (pp. 5-6).

This led to the emergence of the Divorced Catholic Movement (DCG) and the subsequent development of over 500 Divorced Catholic Groups (DCG) throughout the United States and Canada. The original Boston support group provided the model for the other groups that followed. Young (1979) pointed to five characteristics that these groups shared.

1. *Self-help:* Young (1979) drew an analogy between the DCM and such groups as Alcoholics Anonymous and Weight Watchers. The challenge for these individuals was to take responsibility for their own actions and decisions. Young stated: "We begin with a theoretical assumption that divorced people are basically healthy, but might be exhibiting some transitory signs of distress while negotiating a difficult adjustment" (p. 5).

2. *Regular meetings:* Most groups met on a regular basis, typically once a month. At these meetings the group often heard a speaker or taped lecture. Sometimes a panel discussion was on the agenda. Two positive effects of these meetings were evidenced. One, the attendees were educated in a number of things that they needed to know, issues such as the law, taxes, single parenting, and church law. Second, the meetings brought together people who shared similar circumstances. These meetings, Young pointed out, often led to further meetings that month where members could sit and "rap." Usually these meetings were small, typically ranging from six to eight people, with a facilitator. The facilitator was either a long-standing member of the group or a professional.

3. *Availability of other resources:* Groups often developed working relationships with other helping resources. Individualized counseling, if recognized as being needed, was recommended. Groups also offered seminars for those individuals undergoing a separation.

4. *Members:* Young indicated that these groups were most effective with the newly separated or divorced. Very few people who had remarried attended group sessions. These people usually did not need the kind of support that was being provided.

5. *Religious identification:* A final aspect of these groups was a strong sense of religious identity. Although calling themselves the DCG, non-Catholics were not excluded. The point was, however, that they were Catholic and that by virtue of being Catholic, they had a "special set of problems and opportunities" (p. 6).

Brown (1979) analyzed the DCM during the 1970s and identified three major themes. (1) There was a sense of hope and a place for the divorced Catholic where they could receive care and concern. Early DCM leaders challenged the Church not to treat these people as persona non grata. (2) A sense of reconciliation was identified. The movement was instrumental in helping divorced Catholics contact tribunal staff members who might help them gain an annulment and priests who were sympathetic to their plight. If an annulment was not possible then a private reconciliation between the divorced individual and a caring priest might be attained. As the name implies, this process involves only the priest and the divorced individual; no other parties (such as the tribunal) are included. (3) The divorced themselves were the best equipped to minister to the newly divorced (as cited in Young, 1979).

The DCM took root and developed into the North American Conference of Separated and Divorced Catholics (NACSDC) (Ripple, 1990). NACSDC traces its roots to 1974 and the second meeting of a conference for the divorced and separated in the Boston area. The first Boston meeting was not only widely publicized throughout the Church but was featured in a 1973 *Time* magazine article. Other groups from around the country, unbeknown to one another, had also organized to help separated and divorced Catholics. In 1974, the Boston group invited representatives from those other organizations to attend their second conference. With Father Young as the director, delegates established a framework for NACSDC. A representative from each of the regions in the United States was elected to serve on the board of directors. One of their first decisions was to hold annual conferences to discuss issues concerning the divorced and separated. They chose Notre Dame as their meeting site because of its close association in individuals' minds with Catholicism (Comin, 1996).

One of the first things the board discovered was that in only two dioceses (Newark and Baltimore) were individuals appointed by a bishop to treat the concerns of the divorced and separated. Within the next few years, due mainly to NACSDC, things started to change. By 1981, 65 percent of dioceses reported they had some kind of ministry to the divorced and separated. The Canon Law Society, with its corresponding tribunals, has worked closely with NACSDC since the organization's inception. The early 1980s also saw support groups being founded in the majority of dioceses in the Unites States. In addition, groups were formed in Canada, Ireland, England, and New Zealand.

NACSDC acts as a "clearinghouse" for support groups, provides assistance in getting support groups started, holds annual conferences and workshops, and sells packets of materials and other resources (e.g., tapes). NACSDC also produces a quarterly newsletter, *Jacob's Well* (Comin, 1996).

The Church's Response to Divorce

One of the biggest concerns, and the ultimate form of punishment, for the practicing Catholic, was excommunication. During the 1800s American bishops were seriously concerned with the issue of divorce among their parishioners. As a consequence, divorce and remarriage without an annulment was penalized with excommunication. It should be noted that the remarriage, not the divorce, was to be penalized by excommunication. American bishops voted to drop this penalty in 1977. In other words, excommunication was no longer to be the case for Catholics who divorced and then remarried. Their decree, however, emphasized the fact that a remarriage could not be recognized as valid unless a determination could be made that the first marriage was null. This came in response to the estimated 75 percent of remarried Catholics who were in marriages considered by the Church to be invalid (Coleman, 1988).

In 1981, Pope John Paul II issued the *Familiaris Consortio* (Community of the family), which consisted of four major themes. The last three were directed specifically at those who remarry without the Church's blessing.

1. Those divorced Catholics who have not remarried maintain the full privileges of the Church, including receiving the Eucharist.
2. Those who have remarried are not excommunicated and "should consider themselves members of the whole community of the faithful" (Coleman, 1988, p. 10).
3. Those Catholics who have divorced and remarried outside the Church are not to participate in the Eucharistic right because their current marriage goes against the "real union," that is, the first marriage. Their current marriage is, then, invalid.
4. Those who have divorced may be prevented from separating for "serious pastoral reasons," for example, "care for children" (Coleman, 1988, p. 11).

It was the responsibility of the divorcing parties to approach the marriage tribunal for an annulment. If an annulment was not possible, the proper recourse was to continue to live together for the sake of the children.

SUMMARY

Although most religions oppose divorce, many Protestant denominations have softened their stance. No doubt this is at least partially due to the growing numbers of their members ending their marriages. Jews have also been divorcing in increasing numbers. In order to remain an Orthodox Jew "in good standing," divorcing spouses must obtain a get. While the Jewish ceremony unites a husband and wife in matrimony, the get is the religious ceremony that terminates the marital bond. The get is similar to the annulment found in the Roman Catholic Church.

The Council of Trent in 1563 formalized marriage with the Catholic faith and defined marriage as a sacrament. Although the Church's doctrine is "till death do us part," Catholics all over the world are divorcing. Even Ireland, a strongly Catholic nation, recently legalized divorce.

The growing assimilation and secularization of Catholics into American culture has led to increased divorce rates. Catholics in America are no different from other religious groups with respect to divorce. The DCM was an early attempt to recognize the plight of these "outcasts." Today, literally hundreds of divorced and separated groups exist within the various archdiocese to counsel and aid this growing segment of the Catholic population.

Chapter 3

Annulments and the Catholic Church

The faith community usually considers divorce an offense against the dignity of marriage, whether a Christian or a good and natural marriage, for it brings disorder into the family and society. It is especially injurious to a Christian marriage.

(Michael S. Foster, 1999, p. 27)

Within the Catholic Church there are two ways in which a marriage can be ruled invalid: (1) the internal and (2) external forum or solution. The former focuses upon the individual's conscience and whether she or he truly is convinced that no marriage ever existed. It is a process strictly between the priest and the individual. The external forum refers to the way in which the Church governs itself. Church law (canon law) is part of the external forum. It is within this context that the annulment occurs. Simply put, the internal is private and the external is public (Kelly, 1997).

THE INTERNAL FORUM

The internal forum solution involves an individual coming to terms with his or her conscience in the matter of his or her marriage and remarriage. The divorced Catholic is truly convinced that the first marriage did not exist in a true Christian sense. The individual may not be able to use the external forum for any number of reasons: there are no witnesses to the first marriage, a requirement of the external forum; there is an unwillingness to involve the former spouse for what is seen as some serious reason; undertaking the external route is believed to be morally impossible; or there is no marriage tribunal operating in the person's diocese (Davey, 1997).

For the internal forum solution to be applicable, a number of guidelines have been suggested:

1. reconciliation with the first spouse is not possible;
2. recognizing one's responsibility for the failure of the first marriage;
3. a second marriage exists and it would not be possible to separate because of certain obligations associated with the second marriage; and
4. by taking the Eucharist it in no way is interpreted as questioning the Church's teaching on the indissolubility of marriage. (Davey, 1997)

Coleman (1988) gave an example of a woman who approached the tribunal for an annulment on the grounds that her ex-husband never intended on having children. Although *she* knew that he never planned on having children, she could not prove it to the tribunal. After a period of time she remarried in a civil ceremony. However, she believed in her own conscience that her first marriage was invalid. Believing this, she continued attending Mass and participated in receiving the Eucharist in her new church. She still took communion believing in "good faith" that her prior marriage was not valid. She was also truly convinced, again in "good faith," that in her remarriage and participation in the sacrament of the Eucharist she was not committing a sin.

We have no statistics on the frequency with which this solution is used since it is a private affair between the individual and his or her priest. Even today it is probably the case that many individuals who are aware of the external solution (i.e., the annulment) are unaware of, or at least less well-versed in, the internal forum. This lack of knowledge even existed among many of the clergy. Archbishop Bernadin of Cincinnati wrote to Rome in 1974, inquiring about the matter of the internal solution (Davey, 1997).

It is possible that the internal forum is being used more frequently today as a result of a program started after the Second Vatican Council. This program is called the Rite of Christian Initiation of Adults (RCIA) and involves the gradual socializing of individuals into the

Catholic Church. Many individuals seeking to become Catholics are divorced and involved in second marriages but are not aware of the Church's position on divorce and remarriage. Many priests, in response to this dilemma, have taken an interest in the internal forum as a possible solution (Kelly, 1997).

A controversial letter, written by three highly respected bishops in Germany, appeared in 1993. This document addressed the need to bring the divorced Catholic back to the Church. The bishops advocated allowing the remarried individual to receive the Eucharist after a full and conscientious dialogue with a priest. Each case would be looked at individually on its own merits and the priest would not force his views on the matter. Instead, he would respect the decision the divorced Catholic reached. This would remain a private affair inasmuch as the official recognition by the Church would undermine the formal position regarding the indissolubility of marriage (Kelly, 1997).

Ladislas Orsy (1994), perhaps the leading authority on canon law, wrote that the bishops letter was to be commended not only for its clear presentation but its "theological depth" and the emphasis on conscience.

The letter quickly attracted the attention of Rome. The bishops were called to Rome to explain their intentions. The response by Rome was to send a letter to all the bishops of the world reiterating the Church's present doctrine. In other words, rather than the priest and the remarried parishioner coming to a determination privately that the remarried individual could receive the Eucharist, that determination still remained with the Church. This is accomplished by way of the external forum, that is, through the annulment process (Kelly, 1997).

Cardinal Joseph Ratzinger (1997) states that the internal forum has led to a number of abuses in some countries, and, therefore, is not a practical solution. He believes that the external forum is the only sound way to rule on the marriage.

Cardinal Ratzinger goes on to state that church law has broadened its rules for evidence and testimony within the external forum so that the internal solution does not need to be utilized. Although not directly stated, this might be interpreted to mean that the inclusion of psychological factors is to head off the possibility of using the internal forum. It is possible that there are priests who still use the internal forum. No statistics are available.

THE EXTERNAL FORUM: THE ANNULMENT

Pope John Paul II, in *Familiaris Consortio,* alluded to the possibility of annulment. He stated that the task for the divorced Catholic was to approach the tribunal concerning the obtainment of an annulment. If an annulment was not possible the couple was to live together as husband and wife for pastoral reasons (e.g., the good of the children) (Coleman, 1988).

If a Catholic wants to remarry and remain within the good graces of the Church, it becomes crucial that an annulment be obtained. Annulments have become fairly common in the United States and, because of their increasing frequency, somewhat controversial. Coleman (1988) reported that within a twenty-year period (1968 to 1988), grants for annulments in the United States rose from 368 annually to approximately 50,000, and that 80 percent of these petitions were granted. The data also indicated that the acceptance rate has been steadily increasing: in 1980, 62 percent; 1986, 85 percent; and 1992, 92 percent (Vasoli, 1998).

Between 1984 and 1994 over 638,000 annulments were granted, approximately 59,000 every year. This gives the United States the highest rate of annulment in the world. Although only about 6 percent of the world's Catholic population live in the United States, this country is responsible for 78 percent of the annulments that are granted worldwide (Vasoli, 1998).

What changes have led to the dramatic rise in granted annulments? Four factors must be considered:

1. the large number of divorced Catholics in the United States,
2. changes in the Church's definition of marriage,
3. institutional competition and
4. the belief that divorce means excommunication.

Divorced Catholic Population

As previously discussed, Catholics have been divorcing at about the same rate as other religious groups. In fact, the sheer size of the divorced Catholic population in the United States has exceeded that found in other countries. The United States has an estimated divorce rate of 3.8 per 1,000 Catholics. This figure is higher than most comparable nations. The closest is Canada; the rate is at 2.9 per 1,000 Catholics (Wilde, 1999).

Changes in the Definition of Marriage

Marriage within the Catholic Church was defined strictly as procreative until the middle of the twentieth century. Saint Augustine attempted to provide a middle ground between one extremist faction that defined all sex as bad and the other faction that defined all sex as good. He maintained that sexual relations within the context of the marital bond for the purpose of procreation was legitimate. For centuries this was the Church's position. This doctrine on marriage became official in 1917 with the passage of canon 1013. Now, according to canon law, marriage consisted of the procreation and education of the children (Wrenn, 1988).

Vatican II (1962-1965) called for a "new pastoralism" and a rethinking of the Church's position on marriage. The result of the council's work was to redefine marriage as a "covenant" between God and the spouses. Specifically, marriage was to include a procreative element and a "personalist" element (Wrenn, 1988; Foster, 1999). Individual responsibility was downplayed and replaced with the view that human behavior was due to environmental and genetic factors. Annulments were reflected in this new perspective also. The failure to grant an annulment was seen as "unpastoral, hard-hearted, and punitive" (Vasoli, 1998, p. 21).

There seemed to be a growing awareness that most Catholics who divorced and remarried did not do so because they wanted to break church law deliberately. Rather, they did so out of a desire that most people have for remarrying—to find a meaningful relationship with someone, companionship, or to have children.

In 1977, American bishops voted to end the excommunication of Catholics who had divorced and remarried without obtaining an annulment. Part of their statement read:

> We wish to help divorced and remarried Catholics without seeming to weaken the unbreakable bond of marriage covenant

entered into freely in Christ. . . . After study and reflection, the bishops of the United States have concluded that the removal of this particular excommunication . . . can foster healing and reconciliation for many Catholics remarried after divorce . . . it is a gesture of love and reconciliation from the other members of the church. (quoted in Coleman, 1988, p. 62)

The final major development was to incorporate into official church law the changes that Vatican II had rendered. In 1983, twenty years after the council was convened, marriage had officially been declared to be both procreative and "personalist." A crucial element in the changing definition of marriage was that it was now possible, under canon 1095, to examine a marriage from a psychological basis.

Until the Second Vatican Council and canon 1095, annulments were granted only on limited grounds (e.g., for reasons such as fraud, impotence, and homosexuality). Currently, the Church recognizes thirty criteria. These criteria can be placed under three general headings:

1. *Lack of canonical form* refers to going outside the laws of the Church, such as being married by a justice of the peace without first receiving permission from the bishop.
2. *Impediments to marriage* involves an ineligibility for marrying, such as the partner being underage, marrying a relative, or impotency.
3. *Defect of consent* (canon 1095) refers to the inability to engage in the marriage of one's own free will, such as being intoxicated at the time of the wedding; alcoholism; homosexuality; a forced marriage; a marriage entered into out of fear, fraud, or deceit; and, most important, *psychological* factors. (Coleman, 1988; Soule, 1997)

Father Orsy (1986), writing about canon 1095, stated:

Briefly, the overall meaning of the canon is that a person intending to marry must have the capacity to think rationally, to decide responsibly, and to carry out the decision by action. This capacity must be present *at the moment of the exchange of the promises.* If the validity of the promises is ever doubted, all that has happened before and all that has followed later can only serve as signs to determine the precise spirit of the person at the moment of the exchange of the promises. (p. 130)

"Lack of capacity" became a reason to grant an annulment. This specifically involves the presence of such significant psychological problems at the time of marriage that the individual is not able to "establish and maintain the close, emphatic, cherishing relationship with a spouse which provides for mutual growth and the proper rearing of children" (Soule, 1997, p. 16).

Defect of consent cases, especially for psychological reasons, represents the vast majority of nullity decrees (Lagges, 1991; Vasoli, 1998). The Church did recognize conditions such as psychoses and schizophrenia, but it is only since the inception of canon 1095 that such maladaptive reasons such as immaturity, lack of self-control, and the lack of sensitivity for the spouse have been included as possible reasons for an annulment. Tierney (1993) suggested that a person ask the following questions of himself or herself when considering his or her marriage:

- How sensitive were you to your spouse's needs?
- How sensitive was your marriage partner to your own needs?
- Did your marriage display a lack of thoughtfulness to the point that the lack of respect for the unique needs of the other led to gross insensitivity?
- Were you treated by your spouse as a person ought to be treated as a man or a woman?
- Did you treat your spouse as a man or a woman ought to be treated? (p. 20)

Tierney also states that if there is a lack of such sensitivity it is possible that the marriage has even "graver" problems and, if that is the case, "then your marriage was more than impoverished; it could even be null and void before God and the Church" (p. 20).

Although most individuals would no doubt recognize the acceptability of declaring a marriage null and void when a person was deceived in some way or was forced into marriage, there is considerable room for debate when considering certain psychological reasons. Many see this as nothing more than a loophole that allows the Catholic Church to acknowledge divorce. Church scholars are quick to point out, however, that this is not the case; annulments are not a "Catholic divorce" (Foster, 1999, p. 175).

Institutional Competition

Wilde (1999) points to a crucial factor for the rise of annulments being granted in the United States—institutional competition. This refers to the fact that, in religiously pluralistic societies, religions have to market their "product" to attract and keep members. Wilde maintains that an annulment is such a marketing device.

In her research, Wilde has calculated the annulment rates of the United States and other countries. She found that these rates have also risen in other countries, such as Canada, Great Britain, and Australia. All of these countries are designated as "competitive" societies. Still, the United States has a substantially higher rate than the other competitive societies. For example, Wilde found that the rate of annulment in the United States was 23 percent, and the rate for Canada was only 10 percent (Wilde, 1999).

Equating Divorce with Excommunication

The United States has a higher rate of annulments than other "competitive" societies. What makes the United States distinct from these other countries? Wilde (1999) points to the fact that an American Catholic, in contrast to his or her counterparts in other nations, could be excommunicated for remarrying after obtaining a civil divorce. This declaration, she stated, has been widely misinterpreted and was applied to *anyone* who obtained a divorce. Therefore, the divorce became associated with a "grievous" sin. The effect was to create a highly alienated group of divorced Catholics. As they became more mobilized the Church took notice. One way to bring these estranged people "back into the fold" was to rescind the excommunication decree and grant more annulments.

We can conclude, then, that the annulment rate in the United States is higher because of the sheer size of the divorced Catholic population, the changing definition of marriage brought about by canon 1095, the Church's competition for members, and the mistaken belief that divorce meant excommunication.

THE ANNULMENT PROCESS

For simplicity, this process has been broken down into eight steps starting with a presentation of these steps in abbreviated form and then discussing each in more detail (see also Table 3.1). I should point out that two or more of these steps may be combined and considered at the same time.

Step 1: Civil Divorce

The Catholic Church will not consider a petition for annulment unless the person has already received a civil divorce (or annulment).

Step 2: Discussion with the Parish Priest

The person considering the annulment talks with a priest concerning the petition and where the petition will be filed. This preliminary discussion is followed by a more formal interview with the parish priest.

The diocesan court hearing the case can be:

1. "where the parties were married,
2. where the respondent lives,
3. where the petitioner lives, or
4. where most of the testimonies will be collected" (Foster, 1999, pp. 115-116).

No one diocesan court takes precedence.

TABLE 3.1. Steps in the Annulment Process

Step 1: Obtaining a civil divorce
Step 2: Discussion with a parish priest
Step 3: Collection of information
Step 4: Collection of testimonies
Step 5: Hearing the case
Step 6: Decision by Court of First Instance
Step 7: Review by Court of Second Instance
Step 8: Appeal to Rome

Step 3: Collection of Information

One of the spouses formally initiates the process. This person is referred to as the petitioner. The grounds for the annulment are determined along with a determination of exactly which tribunal will hear the case. Once a petition is filed the ex-spouse (referred to as the respondent) is notified. The respondent has three options: (1) oppose the petition, (2) favor the petition, or (3) indicate an indifference to the petition. If the third option is chosen, there is no further contact with the respondent relevant to information gathering (Foster, 1999).

The petitioner provides certain kinds of preliminary information. This includes a copy of the marriage license and the civil divorce decree. If the parties were born and raised Catholic, such documents as the baptismal and confirmation records are obtained. In addition, signed releases for any relevant materials the tribunal may want to consider (e.g., relevant medical or counseling records) are requested by the tribunal. Questionnaires (often very extensive in nature) are completed relating to his or her childhood (e.g., What was it like to grow up in your family? Were there any specific problems at home that had an effect on your later life? What was your parents' marriage like?); his or her dating history (e.g., At what age did you begin dating? How did you meet your spouse? Were there any problems when dating him or her?); and married life (e.g., Were there any problems on the wedding day? Was your sexual relationship ever a problem? Were either of you impulsive, selfish, or ungrateful on a regular basis?). See Appendix A for a sample questionnaire.

Step 4: Collection of Testimonies

The petitioner (and respondent) may provide the names of witnesses who the tribunal may contact. These witnesses should be familiar with the party or parties before the marriage. Counselors or medical doctors may provide relevant information. This stage may require anywhere from two to six months.

Step 5: Hearing the Case

Once the evidence has been gathered the case is considered. Typically (but not always) three judges are expected to hear the case: the petitioner's advocate, a defender of the bond, and a third judge.

The defender of the bond is a person who has the duty of arguing for the validity of the marriage. This represents the Court of First Instance.

Step 6: Decision by Court of First Instance

Once all the evidence has been heard the judge(s) renders a verdict. The decision consists of four parts:

1. The judge and tribunal are identified along with names and addresses of both the petitioner and respondent and any court officials who served on the case.
2. The facts of the case are cited along with the grounds for the annulment appeal.
3. This consists of the "dispositive" and "expositive" sections. While the former entails the decision, the latter consists of the "facts of the case in light of Church law" (Foster, 1999, p. 142).
4. The case is ended with the date and place and the signatures of the judge(s) and a Church notary.

Ideally, the Court of First Instance should have concluded its business within one year (Foster, 1999).

Step 7: Review by the Court of Second Instance

The fact that the Court of First Instance may have ruled for the nullity of the marriage does not mean that the marriage is null, even if none of the parties (petitioner, respondent, or defender of the bond) objects. The decision goes automatically to the Court of Second Instance. This review process may take one to two months. However, it is the right of an individual to bypass this step and proceed directly to *Step 8.*

There are twenty-nine courts of Second Instance in the United States (Vasoli, 1998). This court reads the decision by the Court of First Instance; evidence collected by the expert, if one is used; along with the defender of the bond's statement. The panel of judges then gives a voice vote with a two-to-one majority being necessary.

Although this court may overturn the Court of First Instance, this seldom occurs. Data indicate that when the tribunal of First Instance rules that the marriage is null, in less than 1 percent of cases does the Second Instance go against this ruling. In one diocese, for example, 2,652 cases were submitted to the Second Instance tribunal and only two were reversed (Vasoli, 1998). If a respondent wants the decision for nullity overturned, the chances are not great. Most cases end here.

Step 8: Appeal in Rome

An option for the party who disagrees with the ruling of the "lower" court(s) is to appeal the case to the Rota in Rome. And, as stated in *Step 7,* the person may request that the Rota in Rome be the Court of Second Instance. The odds are much greater for the marriage to be declared valid by the Rota. In fact, the rate of reversal is 92 percent in contrast to the .004 percent rate among American Second Instance tribunals. The problem as far as the respondent is concerned is that, oftentimes, this option is not made known to him or her. When the respondent takes advantage of this option, the burden for incurring the expenses involved often falls upon his or her shoulders. Foster (1999) states that the party appealing the case is responsible for the expenses. Vasoli (1998) states that the National Council of Catholic Bishops and Rota "reportedly agreed to facilitate Rotal appeals by petitioners and respondents of limited means. For a fixed fee of $800 or thereabouts, waived for those who qualify, First Instance sentences can be appealed directly to the Rota" (Vasoli, 1998, p. 198).

THE MARRIAGE TRIBUNAL

What exactly is a marriage tribunal? Basically it is a type of legal system headed by three judges. They are typically, but not always, priests. In 1983 the system changed so that nonpriests can be named to the panel if they are deemed qualified. The judges, along with the defender of the bond, are to be highly conversant with canon law and expected to hold a doctorate or license. Appointments to these positions are by the bishop. The tribunal hears the case for nullity (Tierney, 1993).

The evidence indicates, however, that a large percentage do not have the necessary credentials. In a study of twenty-five tribunals it was found that less than half had the necessary credentials as specified in the revised code of 1983. In some cases, the same individual acts as both judge and defender (Vasoli, 1998).

The data also indicated that U.S. tribunals are able to handle far more cases than their foreign counterparts. The tribunal responsible for Rome, Italy, and its surrounding area processed 147 cases at the First Instance level in 1985. In the same year Chicago processed 1,360 cases at the same level. In addition, the Rome staff, which complained of not having enough time to devote to the cases, was twenty-five, and Chicago, in contrast, only had fourteen (Vasoli, 1998).

Dioceses and their tribunals have often become very adept at getting the word out to possible petitioners. Some dioceses publish brochures that provide basic information about annulments and how to proceed. Others, such as the Philadelphia diocese, have made information available on the Internet. When one logs onto their Web site, information on the following questions can be found: What is an annulment? Can I petition for an annulment? What tribunal is competent to hear my case? What is the annulment process? How can I start an annulment? What is the court fee? In reference to this last question it is pointed out that both MasterCard and Visa are accepted to cover the cost.

According to Orsy (1990) the tribunal was established, ideally, to "uphold certain values precious to the community" (p. 141). Some of these values included

1. upholding the sanctity of marriage,
2. reinforcing the indissolubility of marriage,
3. administrating justice in an impartial manner,
4. protecting the rights of everyone involved,
5. determining the truth, and
6. providing a healing experience for the parties involved.

On the other hand, as Orsy (1990) points out, tribunals may not serve some of these values. In addition, there are other important values. These include the following:

1. The "rules for the tribunals are not conceived from a pastoral point of view; the primary focus is not on the healing process" (p. 143).

2. Rather than supporting the integrity of the marriage doctrine the granting of large numbers of annulments actually undermines church doctrine.
3. Only in developed societies such as the United States are well-organized, functioning tribunal systems possible. Less developed societies do not have the appropriate funding or personnel.
4. The time delay in deciding a case can prevent the person from getting remarried in a reasonable amount of time.
5. Going through this process can be far from a healing experience. For some it is intrusive and can bring back painful memories.
6. "The law has overreached its own capacity. . . . When in specifically psychological cases (as most cases are), the judges are required to determine (often in the testimony of third parties) with utter precision the internal state of the petitioners as it was at the moment of the exchange of marital vows, perhaps many years ago, one cannot speak of precise justice in the ordinary sense of the term" (p. 143).

The question becomes: Can it be possible at all to determine with "utter precision" what the intent was on the part of the spouses at the time they exchanged their wedding vows?

One final point needs to be made. Although the annulment process is a Catholic one, it is often assumed that the only ones affected are Catholics. This is not the case. A non-Catholic can also apply for an annulment or be the respondent in an annulment case. For example, consider a case in which a Protestant couple has divorced. One of them wants to marry a Catholic. In order for the marriage to take place in the Catholic Church, the Church has to nullify the previous Protestant marriage.

OBJECTIONS TO ANNULMENTS

Although the number of annulments being granted in the 1970s was low and the attention paid to them was slight, there were still objections. First, in a book, *Divorce and Remarriage for Catholics?,* then in an article for *Commonweal,* Monsignor Stephen Kelleher

(1973, 1977) referred to annulments as "dehumanizing." At various places in his article he stated:

> I find it difficult to conceive that a therapist can say in retrospect that he is sure either or both were simply and unequivocally unable to succeed in their marriage when they exchanged their marital vows. (1977, p. 10)

> It is a paradox that today's Church, the self-proclaimed champion of personal responsibility and freedom, in an effort to help more and more divorced persons be free to remarry, is downgrading the responsibility and freedom of more and more persons in their decision to marry. (p. 11)

He argued that the tribunal process is simply bad.

Kelleher believed that a person should have the right to divorce. In fact, he believed that the Church should even encourage it in certain situations:

> When a marriage is dead, that is when it has become irreparably intolerable for one or both parties, divorce is the only answer and a person has the right to remarry. The Church should often encourage such a person to divorce and remarry. (1973, p. 179)

In sharp contrast to Cardinal Ratzinger, Monsignor Kelleher (1973) felt that the internal forum solution is preferable to the tribunal route.

With the growing number of annulments being granted, many objections are being raised. At times, the criticism is scathing. Especially noteworthy are the objections related to an annulment being a healing process for all parties and the fact that almost all annulments in the United States are being granted on a psychological basis.

Two more recent criticisms of the annulment process have come in the form of books. The first, *Shattered Faith* (Kennedy, 1997), was written from a very personal point of view, and the second, *What God Has Joined Together* (Vasoli, 1998), is a more analytical approach.

The Kennedy (1997) work is a condemnation of the annulment process. The impetus for this book came from the fact that Kennedy's husband of thirteen years, Representative Joe Kennedy, sought an annulment after they were legally divorced. Ms. Kennedy does not deny the fact that there were problems and that a divorce was the only way out. She argues against the ruling by the Boston tribunal that the marriage never did exist—that is, either or both parties was not really capable of entering into a valid marriage.

She sees the Church as being very hypocritical in this matter. Her perspective can probably best be summarized as to how the church (in her view) skirts various issues (such as denying the marriage but saying the children are legitimate) by the title of the first chapter of her book, "Gobbledygook."

She and her ex-husband knew each other a total of twenty-two years, nine before marriage and thirteen in marriage. They had two children. One of the ironies is that, although the children were raised Catholic, she is not Catholic. Born and raised Episcopalian, the Catholic Church told her that her marriage was not valid.

After receiving notification that her ex-husband was seeking an annulment she, unlike most others, decided to fight back. She was enraged at the idea that she could be told what her marriage was like or not like. She wrote that her personality started to change. One change was that now, contrary to the past, she was able to stand up to her ex-husband. She stated:

> For me a marriage, even one that was over, remained a sacred bond. Though divorced, I remained loyal to it. Now by denying the sanctity of our marriage, Joe had broken that bond. He had in essence drawn a line in the sand and by opposing him, I had crossed it. Neither of us would ever be able to go back. I could not back down and face myself or my children. (Kennedy, 1997, pp. 26-27)

Elsewhere she stated:

> How could he possibly believe that the marriage that produced our children had never been valid? We had known each other for nine years before our wedding and we had been married close to thirteen. I could not go along with him on this. (p. 7)

On October 23, 1996, she was informed by the tribunal that the marriage had been annulled. The reason given was her ex-husband's "lack of due discretion" (the inability to freely contract marriage due, usually, to some "psychic" cause). She exercised her right to bypass the Court of Second Instance and appealed directly to Rome. Her case is now under review and, at this writing, no decision has been reached. Until the Rota in Rome upholds the ruling of the Court of First Instance, her ex-spouse does not have the annulment.

Vasoli (1998) also takes the annulment process to task. Whereas Kennedy offered her own situation, along with other case studies, Vasoli (1998), a former professor of sociology at Notre Dame University, attacked annulments from a more analytical perspective. His method involved using canon law, statistics compiled by church agencies, and conversations with people involved with tribunals.

Vasoli stated that he was married more than fifteen years before he and his wife divorced. His wife filed for an annulment; the filing was completed in a tribunal 600 miles from his place of residence. In his particular case he received two forms: one seeking permission to appoint a "procurator-advocate," and the other, a questionnaire.

A priest, though not a canon lawyer, was appointed to his case. The questionnaire asked several questions concerning his preference to be interviewed in person at the tribunal office or over the phone, his position on annulments, and so forth. He was also asked to write about his marriage, childhood, and dating behavior.

Expressing displeasure with the whole process, he sought assistance. He discovered that there were few canon lawyers available and the ones that were relatively close geographically were "annulment friendly." Finally, he was directed to a monsignor who had some experience with annulments. After familiarizing himself with Vasoli's marriage the monsignor agreed to lend his assistance.

Vasoli discovered he knew practically nothing about church law, despite his background and occupation. He was born and raised Catholic and attended Catholic schools, including at the graduate level. As a professor of sociology he taught courses on marriage and the family and the sociology of law. In addition, he "kept abreast of key Church pronouncements on marriage found in the documents of Vatican II" (Vasoli, 1998, p. xi).

Despite his opposition, his marriage was annulled by the court of First Instance. The reason was psychological, again the most frequent reason given for annulment in the United States. This decision was affirmed by the Court of Second Instance. However, he decided to appeal the case to Rome. Five years and over $8,000 in expenses later, two Rota panels of judges overturned the annulment decision.

Vasoli brings up two important arguments: (1) how tribunals have changed in their perspective toward marriage and divorce, and (2) the tribunals' greater use of psychology to help grant annulments.

Vasoli points to the works of Lawrence Wrenn (1973, 1988, 1995) as providing the guidelines for modern-day U.S. Catholic writers who are seeking to broaden the concept of marriage. The purpose of changing the concept of marriage is to enable more annulments to be granted. Wrenn emphasizes the "personalist" nature of marriage, arguing that marriage is not only for procreation but involves a relationship which is based on sharing, a "joining of souls" (quoted in Vasoli, 1998, p. 39).

The word "covenant" replaces contract. This had the effect of changing the idea of what constitutes marriage. Covenant implies "a higher marital ideal; out of reach for a large percentage of couples who merely 'contract' marriage" (p. 36).

In short, Vasoli maintains that tribunals are focusing on the "rarely idealized ideal—intimacy, effective communication, shared fulfillment, enrichment, self-esteem, and harmony" (p. 44). When tribunals get involved in this kind of view of marriage they are opening a whole new area by which annulments can be granted. In Vasoli's view, it has allowed tribunals to "invalidate hundreds of thousands of marriages" (p. 73) using nebulous phrases such as "lack of due discretion."

Within the Catholic jurisprudence system there is an appellate court, known commonly as the Rota. The Rota is responsible for hearing all kinds of cases including those relating to marriage. It also can review cases in reference to whether the lower courts followed proper procedures or applied the law correctly. Within the United States civil court system, it is analogous to the Supreme Court.

One of Vasoli's points is that the lower courts have granted annulments too easily using the new definition of marriage. When the Rota hears the case, however, the typical ruling is to overthrow the lower court's decision of nullity. What if the Rota heard all of the approximately 433,000 annulment cases that were granted on the grounds of defective consent between 1984 and 1994 instead of the 200 per year that it currently handles? Vasoli's review of the literature found that the Rota overturns nearly 92 percent of the cases. If that is applied to the total annulments (again, 433,000), nearly 390,000 of those granted would be overturned.

One can conclude from reading Vasoli that American tribunals have become "loose cannons," annulling marriages on the grounds that either or both parties were not fully understanding of or capable of entering a marriage. But, given the extremely idealistic view of marriage that the tribunal holds, no couple is capable of this. As a result, in the words of one anonymous tribunal member: "There is no valid marriage which, given a little time for investigation, we cannot declare invalid" (quoted in Vasoli, 1998, p. 7).

Vasoli also attacks the new perspective that draws from counseling and psychology in making the case for nullity. He argued that canonists' "use of the massive body of psychological theory and research has been generally superficial and tendentious" (p. 70).

He stated that today's tribunals are relying heavily upon self-theory. Self-theory (which stresses such tenets as self-actualization, self-enhancement, self-esteem, and so forth) has not been highly regarded within the field of psychology for several decades. The so-called recovery movement stresses the importance of getting in touch with one's feelings, positive self-esteem, being nonjudgmental of the person, and, certainly, not feeling guilty. This is in stark contrast to the idea of "toxic shame" that is characterized by such traits as low self-esteem. Vasoli discusses an article by Garrity (1991), who argues that defective consent is causally linked with toxic shame and comes from a dysfunctional family (Vasoli, 1998).

The concept of the "dysfunctional family" has become one of the key phrases in modern-day mental health counseling, as well as the self-help and pop psychology literature. The problem with this concept is that it includes so many variables that almost everyone can argue that they come from such a dysfunctional family of origin.

This fact is used by the proannulment advocate since it allows the tribunal to rule that toxic shame and dysfunctionalism within one's family of origin have affected the ability for informed consent.

Although Vasoli does not say that the psychological aspect should be eliminated altogether, he believes it has been misused. He wrote:

A history of unhappy marriage followed by divorce impels the presumption that something psychological had to be amiss when the parties consented to marriage. A finding of lack of due discretion or incapacity is virtually assured. Such reasoning is more decisive in annulment proceedings than in civil trials because there are fewer legal and psychological checks and balances. (1998, p. 87)

Elsewhere he stated:

A lot of psychological chaff is mixed in with the juridically relevant wheat. Some of the material could possibly be linked to defective consent, but much of it is extraneous, far more germane to marriage counseling than to a Church tribunal investigating marital consent. Taken as a whole, the instructions are a psychological exploration, on a grand scale, for personality and behavior traits that may be employed to initiate and justify a trial. There are tens of millions of validly married spouses who at one time or another are insensitive to the needs of others, quick tempered, moody, jealous, selfish, and ungrateful. (p. 130)

Other criticisms are discussed by Vasoli. For example, he stated that engaged Catholics are required to go through premarital counseling, where such issues as children and fidelity are covered.* This counseling should enable the priest to determine if there is some valid reason why the couple should not be married. The question then becomes: How did the priest miss this when counseling the couple before marriage but the tribunal is able to ascertain this five, ten, fifteen, or even twenty years after the marriage?

To date, although there has been criticism of the annulment process and the large number being granted, Kennedy and Vasoli have been the most vocal in their criticism of annulments. A group has recently formed, partially due to the Kennedy book, seeking to change the Church's view on marriage, divorce, and annulment. The group,

---

*It should be pointed out that not all engaged Catholic couples go through the same process of direct one-on-one contact with a priest. As we shall see in Chapter 4, there are at least three options. For example, the couple can go through a Pre-Cana course where they, along with other couples, spend a day or more with a priest and married couples.

formed by Dr. Jan Leary, is known as Save Our Sacrament (SOS). This group, along with its views, will be discussed in Chapter 9.

SUMMARY

As the number of divorced Catholics has grown, annulments (i.e., the external forum) have become more numerous and more scrutinized. The annulment provides that if there were problems in existence before the marriage then these preexisting difficulties can lead to a declaration of nullity.

The four major reasons for the growth of the granting of annulments were discussed, and the annulment process was broken down into a series of eight steps with special attention given to the marriage tribunal. The tribunal is the Church court. Within the Catholic Church three levels exist. The first level is at the diocesan level; the second consists of a number of dioceses; the third, at the Vatican, represents the highest court of appeal. Once a decision on the annulment petition is made it automatically goes to the second level. Although many are not aware of it, an appeal can be made to the Vatican in Rome.

Chapter 4

Demographic and Marital Issues

The marriage contract is intended to be binding until death.

I Corinthians 7:39

The remainder of this book focuses on a study the author conducted between 1994 and 1998. The study is based on questionnaires and interviews gathered from a sample of annulled, divorced, and married individuals. In this chapter two major topics are considered: (1) the scope of the study and the sample, and (2) the participants' views on marriage and divorce and the differences, if any, among three groups (divorced, annulled, and married) in how they view these issues.

NATURE OF THE STUDY

Overview

The purpose of this study was to fill a gap in the social scientific literature on religious annulments. Using standard questionnaire items, I assessed the attitudes and characteristics of the three different Catholic samples: (1) the divorced and annulled, (2) the divorced and not annulled, and (3) the married. My goals were twofold: (1) to determine if there were any differences among the three groups on any social or psychological measures, and (2) to look at the issue of Catholic annulments as they currently exist.

Methodology and Procedure

This study utilized questionnaires and interviews. Although the statistics relating to the incidence of annulments and the percent granted is useful, as is the history of divorce and annulments within the Catholic Church, such information does not provide a perspective about how people who are divorced and annulled view their lives, their former marriages, and the annulment process.

I began this study in 1995 by contacting Family Life groups representing the different dioceses in the United States (and one in Canada). I informed each group of the nature of the study and asked if they would be willing to cooperate. Ninety groups were contacted, and twenty-seven offered their help by encouraging their participants to complete my questionnaire.

In addition to these respondents, I contacted a local parish priest who had an interest in canon law and annulments. With his cooperation, notices were placed in local parish bulletins throughout the southeastern Indiana area. As a result, I identified and wrote to these fifty-four divorced Catholics and asked if they would participate in the study. All consented.

These two sources, the Family Life groups and the local priest, produced a total sample of 235 divorced and annulled persons. Respondents came from eighteen states. Approximately 70 percent of the sample resided in: California, Florida, Indiana, Kentucky, and Louisiana. Of these 235, 136 individuals had had their marriages annulled, and the remaining 99 had not. Seventy-three also indicated that they would be willing to be interviewed.

Out of the seventy-three who indicated a willingness to be interviewed, a random sample of fifty was drawn. These individuals were contacted by phone and asked again if they were willing to be interviewed. All agreed. The interviews lasted from twenty to forty-five minutes depending on the individual. Each interview consisted of twenty-six open-ended and twenty-two closed-ended questions.

My research design also included a sample of currently married Catholics who had never been divorced. I contacted the same Family Life groups that had cooperated in my obtaining the divorced samples and asked if they could assist in obtaining a sample of married individuals. This process resulted in a sample of 163 individuals. These respondents received the same questionnaire as my divorced samples with the exception that the questions relevant to divorce and annulment were eliminated. My purpose in including a married group was to determine if any differences existed among those individuals who were annulled, divorced, and married.

Table 4.1 includes the breakdown of the number of respondents from the different states for both those completing a questionnaire and those being interviewed. Appendix B contains the questionnaire and Appendix C contains the interview outline.

Demographic Characteristics of the Sample

I asked the respondents some standard questions in order to determine the exact demographic profile of the three samples. This information is presented in Table 4.2.

Education

Nationally, almost 85 percent of Catholics are high school graduates, and about 24 percent are college graduates (Kosmin and Lachman, 1993). As Table 4.2 illustrates, my sample was highly educated. Over 98 percent of the sample were high school graduates and over 29 percent have at least some college education. Over 45 percent of the annulled sample have at least sixteen years of education. Both the divorced and married groups have higher percentages of sixteen or more years of education than the annulled sample. The median (the point where half the respondents are above the figure and half are below) years of education for the two divorced samples, however, is approximately equal—fifteen years. For the married sample the median year of education is slightly higher—15.6 years. Statistically* there are no differences among the groups in terms of the education variable.

Gender

Overall, females comprised over 65 percent of the sample. Although they accounted for approximately 75 percent of the annulled and divorced samples, females represent only a little over 50 percent of the married sample.

---

*Stating that something is statistically significant means that the chances that there are true differences between the two groups are 95 out of 100.

TABLE 4.1. Number of Participants and Percent of Total from Each State, by Marital Status

State	Annulled No.	%	Divorced No.	%	Married No.	%
California	6	4.4	13	13.1	0	0
Florida	26	19.1	25	25.3	28	17.2
Indiana	22	16.2	22	22.2	37	22.7
Iowa	1	.7	0	0	0	0
Kansas	1	.7	1	1.0	0	0
Kentucky	15	11.0	14	14.1	18	11.0
Louisiana	15	11.0	5	5.1	10	6.1
Maryland	1	.7	0	0	0	0
Massachusetts	3	2.2	1	1.0	0	0
Michigan	8	5.9	1	1.0	16	9.8
Minnesota	1	.7	0	0	5	3.1
Missouri	4	2.9	0	0	0	0
Montana	1	.7	0	0	0	0
New Hampshire	5	3.7	3	3.0	0	0
New Jersey	0	0	1	1.0	0	0
New York	3	2.2	3	3.0	9	5.5
North Carolina	0	0	1	1.0	0	0
North Dakota	6	4.4	0	0	0	0
Tennessee	2	1.5	0	0	0	0
Texas	6	4.4	4	4.0	11	6.7
Virginia	2	1.5	0	0	0	0
Wisconsin	5	3.7	3	3.0	29	17.8
Canada	3	2.2	2	2.0	0	0
Total	**136**		**99**		**163**	

TABLE 4.2. Demographic Characteristics: Percentages of Total Sample and by Marital Status

Characteristic	Annulled (N = 136)	Divorced (N = 99)	Married (N = 163)	Total Sample (N = 368)
Education				
0-11 years	1.6	1.6	1.2	1.5
12	18.7	16.5	19.4	18.0
13-15	34.2	31.6	23.7	29.2
16+	45.5	50.3	55.7	51.2
Median (in years)	15.0	15.2	15.6	16.0
Gender				
Male	25.0	20.8	49.7	34.3
Female	75.0	79.2	50.3	65.6
Age				
Under 40 years	10.5	15.5	28.2	20.0
41-50	27.1	33.0	27.0	28.5
51-65	57.1	45.4	36.2	44.8
66+	5.3	6.2	8.6	6.7
Median (in years)	53.0	51.0	49.0	51.0
Race/ethnicity				
African American	0.8	1.8	1.2	1.0
Hispanic American	5.3	1.8	6.8	5.0
White	92.5	93.6	85.8	90.2
Other	1.4	2.8	6.2	3.8
Family income				
$0-$24,999	29.0	33.3	5.7	20.6
$25,000-$54,999	43.5	43.0	27.6	37.0
$55,000-$84,999	17.6	16.1	40.3	26.5
$85,000+	9.9	7.6	26.4	15.9
Political ideology				
Conservative	40.3	30.2	39.9	38.0
Moderate	41.8	51.0	44.8	44.5
Liberal	17.9	18.8	15.3	17.5

Age

Only 10.5 percent of the annulled group and 15.5 percent of the divorced group were under the age of forty. In contrast, approximately 28 percent of the married individuals were younger than forty years of age. The majority of participants in all three groups were between forty-one and sixty-five; less than 7 percent of the total sample were age sixty-six or older. The median age for those married was forty-nine; the divorced group, fifty-one; and the annulled group, fifty-three.

Race/Ethnicity

The vast majority of all three samples was white. Hispanic Americans make up the next largest category. Approximately 1 percent of all three sample groups was African American.

Family Income

Significant differences existed among the different groups according to family income. Almost 30 percent of the annulled and over 33 percent of the divorced had incomes less than $25,000 a year. Thus, the annulled and divorced have very similar incomes. This similarity is expected given that most respondents (70.3 percent) in these two groups are single. In contrast, the married respondents often have two wage earners and, as a consequence, 94 percent of this group make more than $25,000 a year.

Political Ideology

Gallup and Castelli (1987) reported that 33 percent of Catholics are liberal in political ideology, 12 percent are moderate, and 55 percent are conservative. Kosmin and Lachman (1993) reported a lower percentage (38 percent) as conservatives.

The respondents were also asked to identify their current political ideology. When I looked at the total sample, the plurality identified themselves as moderates. Almost 38 percent identified as conservative, almost exactly what Kosmin and Lachman reported; less than 17 percent say they are liberals. Among the annulled, over 40 percent labeled themselves as either conservative or very conservative, the highest of the three groups giving this designation. Statistically, however, there was no difference in terms of this variable.

Summary of Demographic Characteristics

The annulled, divorced, and married do differ in some important ways. The marrieds, as compared to the annulled and divorced, are represented by a higher percentage of males. This group also has a higher average income. Otherwise, the samples are similar demographically. The annulled sample, which is the main focus, is above average in education; predominantly female; concentrated in the fifty-one to sixty-five-year-old age range, with more than 84 percent between the ages of forty-one and sixty-five; are white; politically moderate to conservative; and the plurality earn between $25,000 and $55,000 a year.

MARRIAGE AND DIVORCE

This section offers first a review of some demographic information concerning the makeup of the three samples: age at first marriage, length of marriage, and whether they have children. I then consider whether the couple has had any premarital counseling and, if so, with whom, their expectations concerning their respective marriage, and how they perceived their marriage compared with other couples. Finally, the samples' attitudes concerning issues of their divorce are reviewed, such as whether divorce is justified and, if it is justifiable, what reasons make it so.

Demographics

Age at Marriage

Although the annulled sample had a lower average age (22.8 years) at marriage, it was not significantly different from the divorced sample (23.2 years). The married sample had the highest average age (24.1 years) at marriage.

Length of Marriage

On average, the married respondents have been together twenty-three years. The annulled group was married an average of almost sixteen years and the divorced group was married almost seventeen years. Certainly one cannot argue that the partners did not try to make their marriages work. The length of marriage might also be used by some to argue against an annulment. After all, if a marriage lasted that long (and some lasted as long as thirty to thirty-five years), how could one contend that there was no marriage or that it was doomed from the start?

Children

As I have discussed, divorce can produce difficult adjustment issues for children. Nearly 60 percent of all divorcing couples have a child (Zinn and Eitzen, 1999). This represents over half a million children each year who are in single-parent homes (Knox and Schacht, 1997). Approximately 60 percent of divorcing couples have children. In the sample, approximately 80 percent of the divorced and annulled had children. For the married sample the figure was even higher—90 percent. The figure is somewhat higher than what Gallup and Castelli (1987) report nationally for Catholics—68 percent. Opponents of annulments might also point to the issue of children. An often stated criticism is, "What about the legitimacy of the children?" Eighty percent of the marriages in my two divorced samples produced children, with some couples having as many as five children.

Counseling

Within the Catholic Church premarital counseling is a firm expectation. Couples who are preparing for marriage often have a number of options. The first is a weekend retreat typically headed by two to three married couples and a priest. During the course of this retreat presentations are given about marriage. Practical matters such as finances and effective marital communication along with religious issues are considered. In addition, the individuals are asked directed reflective questions. They are instructed to think about these questions, first on their own, and then together.

The second option, which also consists of a retreat, is less structured and relies more on reflection and individual initiative. The third option involves Pre-Cana counseling. Here, a group of engaged couples meet with a team of married couples and a priest. This usually involves eight hours of contact time. Also, a premarital inventory is involved. The inventory measures the compatibility between the two engaged individuals.

The priest with whom I discussed premarital counseling indicated that, at least in his twenty-five years of experience, the latter option has been the most used. In addition, he noted that within his parish some marriage preparation is a requirement and that over the course of his years of counseling for marriage, the percentage of couples going through these programs has increased.

The respondents were asked if they had undergone any counseling prior to their wedding.* The majority of all three groups said that they had experienced some form of premarital counseling. For the annulled group, 56 percent had some counseling. For the divorced sample it was higher, a little over 59 percent; for the married sample it was even higher, almost 73 percent. Table 4.3 shows with whom the respondents had their counseling.

Statistically, differences did occur. A higher percentage (58.9 percent) of the married sample sought the advice/counseling of a priest whereas both the divorced and annulled samples (38.8 percent and 42.5 percent, respectively) were more likely to have had no counseling prior to their marriage. More than 27 percent of the married sample had no counseling before marriage. Still, the married respondents were more likely to seek some kind of counseling when compared with the two divorced groups. It is interesting to note that the respondents made little use of professional counselors and therapists. One could hypothesize that the advice and counseling of a priest would lead those contemplating marriage to recognize potential serious problems. As a result the couple may decide that the marriage should not take place.

---

*Although I did not ask the question it would be interesting to learn how many Catholics sought counseling from a priest *after* the divorce. One might hypothesize that the person who did not initiate the divorce would be more likely to do so. For these individuals, to hear a priest say that "it was not their fault" could provide some needed comfort.

TABLE 4.3. Percentage Having Counseling Prior to Marriage and with Whom

Counselor	Annulled	Divorced	Married
Priest	35.1	37.8	58.9
Minister/preacher	1.5	7.1	1.3
Counselor/therapist	3.7	3.1	0.0
Other	15.7	11.2	12.7
None	44.0	40.8	27.2

Marital Expectations

Marital expectations in the United States are very high. No doubt many of our expectations about marriage, and the socialization process into marriage, comes from the mass media, especially the movies and television. In many films, and in particular the older romances, couples fall in love and live happily ever after. A man from the upper-upper class falls in love with, and marries, a woman from the lower class. A strictly raised Jew marries a strictly raised Catholic. Someone who has a great deal of education marries someone who has dropped out of high school. The idea conveyed is that love conquers all, and social class, religious, and educational differences are all minor when in love.

There are other reasons for marriage—economic, legitimizing sex and children, companionship, and security. Yet in the United States, romantic love rates very high as the reason for marriage.

I asked two questions relating to marital expectations: (1) "Compared with your expectations of marriage *before* you were married, how did (or has for the married) your marriage turn(ed) out?", and (2) "Compared with other couples you have known, how would you rate the degree of satisfaction that you *felt* with your marriage?" Respondents were asked to choose one of six options. See Tables 4.4 and 4.5 for a list of the options and the response numbers.

The annulled and divorced groups are weighted toward the negative responses. The majority of the married responded in the positive direction. If we combine the two categories identified as "much worse" and "somewhat worse," the two divorced groups are almost identical (82 percent). In contrast, a majority (55.2 percent) of the married sample fall into the "somewhat better" and "much better" categories. More than 30 percent of the married respondents believed it is about as expected; in contrast, a small percentage of the other two groups reported this expectation/experience. For these two groups, annulled and divorced, the marriage fell far short of expectations.

Statistically, there were significant differences among the three groups. The difference, however, was a result of the married sample. When the annulled and divorced groups were compared, no statistical difference was found. In contrast, the married sample differed significantly from both the annulled and divorced groups.

TABLE 4.4. Premarital Expectations Compared to Postmarital Perceptions of Marriage

Perception	Percent of Group		
	Annulled	Divorced	Married
Much worse	64.7	52.5	0.6
Somewhat worse	17.3	29.3	11.7
About the same	12.8	8.1	30.1
Somewhat better	3.0	7.1	17.8
Much better	3.3	3.0	37.4
Don't know	0.0	0.0	1.9

TABLE 4.5. Perception of Respondents' Marriages versus Other Couples' Marriages

Perception	Percent of Group		
	Annulled	Divorced	Married
Much less satisfied	44.4	28.6	0.6
Somewhat less satisfied	20.7	23.5	5.6
About the same	17.8	24.5	13.0
Somewhat more satisfied	12.6	17.3	24.1
Much more satisfied	4.4	6.1	54.9
Don't know	0.0	0.0	1.9

The second question concerned the perception of respondents' own marriages versus the marriages of other couples they knew. These results are presented in Table 4.5. As with the previous question, the vast majority have an opinion and, also similar to the last question, the results would be as expected. Both the annulled and the divorced perceived their marriages as less satisfying than that of other couples they know. For the annulled group approximately 65 percent fall into the two less-satisfied categories while a slight majority (52.1 percent) of the divorced group fall into the same two categories. In contrast, 79 percent of the married respondents perceived their marriages, as compared to other couples' unions, as either somewhat more satisfying or much more satisfying. For all three groups, however, only a minority saw their marriage, in comparison to that of others, as about the same. The percentage of the divorced (24.5 percent) giving this response is higher than either of the other groups. Finally, even among the two divorced groups, 17 percent of the annulleds and over 23 percent of the divorced perceived their marriages as better than other couples they knew.

There are significant statistical differences between the married sample and both the annulled and the divorced groups. The married respondents were, as expected, more likely to perceive their marriages as more satisfying than the two divorced groups. Although a higher percentage of the annulled perceived their marriages as less satisfying than the divorced, the difference was not large enough for a statistical difference to exist.

Is Divorce Justified?

The United States has the world's highest divorce rate (Goode, 1993). Nearly 50 percent of all marriages in the United States end in divorce. By contrast, approximately 40 percent of all marriages in Britain, Sweden, and Denmark result in divorce. The rate is much lower (about 10 percent) in France (Norton and Miller, 1992).

I asked all three samples to what extent they agreed with the view that there are valid reasons for a divorce. Among the annulled sample 86.5 percent respond in the affirmative, and 84.5 percent of the divorced gave this response. The lowest affirmative response was from the married group—75.5 percent. However, this was still a large majority. Statistically there are no differences among any of the groups.

I then provided a list of ten possible reasons for divorce. Respondents were asked to check all those items that they believed were justifiable grounds for pursuing a divorce. The annulled checked, on the average, 4.5 reasons justifying divorce and the divorced checked 4.1. These two figures were significantly higher than the 2.4 listed by the married group.

The specific reasons, along with the percentage checking each response, are outlined in Table 4.6. The responses are arranged from highest to lowest, using the annulled group as the base.

The four highest-rated categories in each group were (1) physical abuse, (2) infidelity, (3) alcoholism or substance abuse, and (4) neglect of children.

Being in a physically abusive relationship was clearly viewed by all the groups as the number one justification for divorce. Less than 8 percentage points separated the divorced (76.6 percent) from the annulled (84.4 percent). Infidelity was reported by 71.1 percent of the annulled as a justification while 61.7 percent of the divorced gave this reason. Only 39.9 percent of the married reported this as a sufficient motive for divorce. The married sample was significantly less likely than the other two groups to report this as an allowable reason for divorce.

TABLE 4.6. Possible Reasons for Divorce

Reason	Percent of Group		
	Annulled	**Divorced**	**Married**
Physical abuse	84.4	76.6	82.2
Infidelity	71.1	61.7	39.9*
Drugs/alcohol	69.6	69.1	49.1*
Child neglect	49.6	48.9	25.8*
Emotional problems	48.9	40.4	12.3*
Immaturity	45.2	23.4	9.8*
No longer in love	31.9	40.4	10.4*
Sexual problems	26.7	24.5	2.5*
Financial problems	10.4	17.0	1.2*
Problems with in-laws	8.1	7.4	2.5

*Indicates that the married group had significantly lower percentages than either the annulled or divorced.

Alcohol or some other kind of drug abuse was named by 69.6 percent of the annulled and an almost identical 69.1 percent of the divorced. The married group (49.1 percent) placed this reason second but were significantly less likely to give this as a reason than either of the two other groups. Child neglect was reported by almost half the annulled (49.6 percent) and divorced (48.9 percent), and one-fourth the married (25.8 percent).

Since our culture recognizes "falling in love" as the major reason to marry, then "falling out of love" might logically be expected to be a significant factor justifying divorce. However, no longer being in love was ranked only seventh by the annulled (31.9 percent) and sixth by the married (10.4 percent). Among the divorced (40.4 percent) it tied for fifth place along with emotional problems.

There was a clear trend with this data for a lower percentage of the married, with the exception of physical abuse, to name any particular reason as sufficient justification for obtaining a divorce. In fact, the married sample had a significantly lower percentage than either the annulled or divorced on eight of the ten possible reasons. The only exceptions were physical abuse and problems with the in-laws.

It is reasonable to assume that those who are divorced would see divorce as more justifiable, whereas those who have never been divorced would be less likely to do so. One respondent commented: "I think it is interesting that I only checked the boxes that were the reasons for my divorce—feeling all other situations could be worked out with help. . . ." This individual had great insight. No doubt many respondents gave as justifications those things that led to their divorce.

It is possible that many married individuals had experienced some of these problems in their marriages and resolved them. Perhaps these issues made their resolve about marriage stronger. The result can be that this group saw issues such as infidelity as less valid grounds for divorce.

When the divorced and annulled groups were compared, only one statistically significant difference existed: immaturity. Although 45.2 percent of the annulled reported immaturity as a suitable justification for divorce only 23.4 percent of the divorced did so. This difference is not without explanation. Although immaturity is rarely listed by the general population as a factor leading to divorce, it is seen as a crucial variable by the Catholic Church when a possible annulment is being considered.

The most common reason now cited for annulling a marriage is based on psychological dimensions. One of the considerations under this heading is immaturity. Those looking for reasons that the marriage was null and void typically point to the "fact" that the partner was never really capable of entering into a full-fledged marriage. Thus the spouse lacked maturity. It should be of no surprise, therefore, that immaturity would be listed by the annulled because they have been made aware of this criteria by their priest or tribunal. In other words, they have been "primed" to give this response.

Respondents were asked the reason(s) for their own divorce. Of those responding the most often cited reason (44 percent) was an affair. Alcoholism was listed second (18 percent). In some instances it was the partner's; in other cases it was the respondent's own drinking problems. One respondent said that they both were alcoholics. Physical abuse, personality disorders, and incompatibility were also mentioned. Some gave unique responses. One respondent wrote: "Her worldly values versus my spiritual values." A second person wrote: "I liked her but did not love her. She loved me but did not like me." A third responded: "She quit being a wife."

Finally, I asked four additional questions regarding variables that may be viewed as affecting the legitimacy of divorce: (1) if there are no children involved, (2) divorce and remarriage if there are children, (3) divorce with no remarriage, and (4) marriage to a divorced person who has never been married in the Catholic Church. These questions, along with the responses, are presented in Table 4.7.

Over 77 percent of the annulled sample approved of divorce when no children are involved. This group showed more approval than the married sample (approximately 38 percent) but less so than the divorced sample. For the latter group, the approval rate was over 82 percent. It is interesting to note that the married sample showed a high rate of uncertainty with almost 25 percent of the sample declaring their indecision. Statistically, there were significant differences among these three groups.

When we compare the responses for divorce with no children and divorce when children are involved in a marriage, the data indicate a significant reduction in the justification of divorce. For the annulled group there was almost an 11 percent decline (all in the "strongly agree" category). For the divorced group there was a similar decline of about 13.3 percent (again, in the "strongly agree" grouping)

TABLE 4.7. Issues That May Be Used to Justify Divorce

		Percent Response				
Question	Group	Strongly Agree	Agree	Don't Know	Disagree	Strongly Disagree
Divorce and remarriage when no children are involved	Annulled	26.7	50.4	7.6	7.6	7.6*
	Divorced	31.3	51.0	7.3	7.3	3.1
	Married	4.4	33.1	23.1	23.1	16.3
	Total Sample	18.6	43.6	13.8	14.0	9.9
Divorce and remarriage when children are involved	Annulled	16.0	50.4	13.7	9.9	9.9
	Divorced	16.5	52.5	15.5	12.4	3.1
	Married	2.5	29.4	22.5	21.3	24.4
	Total Sample	10.7	41.2	7.8	15.0	14.2
Divorce with no remarriage	Annulled	6.1	36.6	14.5	22.1	20.6*
	Divorced	13.4	25.8	15.5	19.6	25.8
	Married	4.3	33.2	26.5	21.0	13.0
	Total Sample	7.2	32.4	19.1	20.8	18.3
Marriage to a divorced person who has never been married in the Catholic Church	Annulled	16.7	56.8	16.7	7.6	2.3*
	Divorced	23.7	50.5	18.6	5.2	2.1
	Married	5.0	55.3	24.5	10.7	4.4
	Total Sample	13.4	53.0	19.8	8.2	3.0

*Indicates there is a statistically significant difference among the groups on this question.

and for the married group there was a 5.6 percentage decline. However, the order of support remains the same as for the previous question. The divorced (69 percent either agreeing or strongly agreeing) have the highest approval, followed by the annulled (66.4 percent), and then the married sample (31.9 percent). The married sample had a significantly lower percentage agreeing that divorce is justified when there are children involved than either the annulled or the divorced groups.

Less than a majority of all three groups "agreed" or "strongly agreed" with divorce with no remarriage (ranging from 39.2 percent to 42.7 percent). The married group (37.5 percent) was least likely to respond in either of the agree categories, and the annulled group (42.7 percent) was most likely to either agree or strongly agree. The married group also had a high percentage (26.5 percent) who were in the "don't know" category.

Finally, when asked if a person were to marry a non-Catholic who had been divorced, the annulled (73.5 percent) and divorced (74.2 percent) samples were very similar in the percentages saying either "agree" or "strongly agree." The married sample (60.3 percent) was less likely to agree and, as compared to the two divorced groups, had higher rates of both indecision and disagreement.

ANALYSIS OF FINDINGS BY GENDER

Did men and women differ in terms of any of the questions asked? Only two differences stood out as statistically significant (see Table 4.8). They occurred on the divorce and remarriage questions. Seventy percent of females either "agree" or "strongly agree" with the acceptability of divorce when no children are involved. In contrast, only 45.7 percent of males were in these two categories. Females (57.3 percent) were also more likely than the males (37.8 percent) to accept divorce when children are involved.

SUMMARY

This study, based on mailed questionnaires, consisted of 136 annulled, 99 divorced, and 163 married individuals who were contacted through local parish bulletins and national Family Life groups. The majority of these respondents were *white females* with *some college*

TABLE 4.8. Significant Differences by Gender

		Percent Response				
Question	Gender	Strongly Agree	Agree	Don't Know	Disagree	Strongly Disagree
Divorce and remarriage when no children are involved	Male	10.7	35.0	17.1	20.7	16.4
	Female	23.9	45.7	13.2	10.0	7.1
Divorce and remarriage when children are involved	Male	7.1	30.7	18.6	20.7	22.9
	Female	12.5	44.8	18.9	12.8	11.0

education with the majority earning *less than $55,000 a year in income.* The sampled individuals were also *middle-aged* and identified themselves as *moderate in political ideology.* In most respects, this sample was not that different from the general Catholic population.

One important finding with reference to the annulled and their former marriages is that the *average length of the marriage* was almost sixteen years. Furthermore, 80 percent of the marriages resulted in *children,* with some producing as many as five children. It should be noted that the Church stresses neither the length of the marriage nor the presence of children as having a bearing on whether the marriage was valid.

Although the majority of the sample had some form of *counseling,* a substantial percentage did not. Today, the Church stresses the role of premarital counseling, either personally with a priest or more typically through the Pre-Cana program.

A large majority of the annulled respondents *perceived their marriages* to have turned out worse than they originally thought upon entering into the marriage. Also, when asked to *judge their marriage against those of other couples,* the annulled individuals perceived their marriages as less satisfying. It is interesting to note that their perceptions in both of these areas was the most negative of any of the three groups. One could ask: Were their marriages really that bad, or did they justify their divorces and annulments by perceiving their marriages in that manner?

Did the annulled respondents see divorce as justified? The answer is an emphatic *yes.* Physical abuse, infidelity, and drug and alcohol abuse headed the list, and child neglect, emotional problems, and no longer being in love were also rated highly as justifiable reasons for divorce. The married sample had a lower percentage reporting the reason was a justifiable one for divorce in nine of the ten instances. Furthermore, the percentage for the married group was significantly lower than the other two groups in all but the physical abuse and problems with in-laws reasons. The only significant difference between the annulled and the divorced samples was immaturity. Again, this is no fluke; priests and others who currently counsel the divorced Catholic lead the individual down this path.

Finally, almost everyone in the study who was divorced indicated they found it extremely difficult, if not painful, to proceed with the marital dissolution. Yet they did get the divorce; they found divorce *justifiable;* and they accepted it under many conditions. This was so despite the Church's official view that marriage is a lifelong proposition.

When all the measures in this chapter were reanalyzed employing the variable of gender, only two significant differences were found. Both differences occurred on the divorce and remarriage questions. Since females have been found to be more likely to initiate a divorce (London, 1991), it could be argued that they would also be less likely to disapprove of divorce.

Chapter 5

Religion and Marriage:
Psychological Factors

There is a lot of anger and rage against my first wife and against
God because I felt that this was the person that He wanted me to
marry. Emotionally I went through eighteen months of grieving.
I went through three different support groups, two for divorce. I
moved to an apartment with a chair and a cot. I basically started
over.

> Jack, a divorced father,
> married ten years
> and divorced for two years

After a divorce, the life changes are enormous. One major adjustment has to do with the legal ramifications of the end of the marriage
that define such issues as division of property and child custody. In
addition to the legal issues, however, are the emotional aspects of the
dissolution. It is not unusual for the divorced individual to deal with
very strong emotions concerning their ex-spouse, such as anger and
bitterness, as well as adjustment issues that may include lowered self-
esteem, depression, or anxiety.

Dealing with divorce is similar to riding a roller coaster. One minute the individual feels disbelief. The individual asks, "How could
this be happening to me?" The next minute anger is experienced.
"How could she or he have done this to me, to leave without a word,
without a gesture of kindness?" The next minute a deep depression
descends. "If only a train would come by and hit me and end it all." To
go on without him or her does not seem to be an option. The next minute the individual wants to ask that person he or she has always had
his or her eye on out on a date. After all, the "ex" is probably dating

also and is living it up. Disbelief, anger, depression, relief—all these emotions, plus countless more, can be experienced with divorce. A survey of postdivorced individuals by Buehler and Langenbrunner (1987) found that 87 percent reported they felt anger toward their ex-spouse, 86 percent reported that they felt insecure, and 86 percent reported that they felt depressed.

Almost all the divorced respondents experienced these kinds of feelings. Depression was by far the dominant emotion. One woman indicated such a depression that she lost between thirty-five and forty pounds. Another respondent, a female who is now in her forties, said she practically stopped functioning for a year. Such tasks as going to work, grocery shopping, running errands, etc., became overwhelming at times. A woman who had been married almost thirty years attempted suicide and, although the marriage ended almost ten years ago, says that she is still depressed. Although these were more extreme cases the same kinds of things were heard over and over: divorce was psychologically damaging and it took at least several months to "get back on track."

MARRIAGE AND WELL-BEING

Research shows that marital status is positively associated with numerous measures of well-being. In other words, higher levels of well-being are reported among those who are married as compared to those who are not. One very common measure of well-being is happiness. Glenn and Weaver (1988) found that the separated and divorced were less likely to say they were "very happy" with their lives when compared to the married. The National Opinion Research Center (NORC) reported that, throughout the 1970s and 1980s, 39 percent of married adults indicated that they were "very happy." Only 24 percent of the "never married" reported being "very happy" (Lee, Seccombe, and Shehan, 1991). It should be noted that in the 1980s there was a slight decline in the reported happiness for married females (Glenn and Weaver, 1988).

Distress as a variable has also been found to be related to marital status. As with happiness, those who are not married have been found to report higher levels of stress and mental health problems. It has been found that this relationship still exists when controlling for other factors such as income and emotional support. In other words, when one compares levels of depression for individuals who are of the same income level and have the same amount of emotional support, those who are married still have lower rates of depression than those who are not married (Ross, Mirowsky, and Goldsteen, 1990). Kurdek (1991), using a sample of 6,000 individuals, found higher rates of depression and suicidal tendencies along with lower rates of happiness among the divorced.

Research has also found that, among psychiatric populations, the married were underrepresented, and the divorced and separated were overrepresented. Bloom (1975) found that divorced or separated males were nine times more likely to be admitted to some kind of mental health facility than their nondivorced counterparts. Divorced or separated females were three times more likely to be admitted than their counterparts.

Studies have shown a positive relationship between various physical measures and one's marital status. Rogers (1995) studied over 36,000 individuals and reported that unmarried males had higher rates of all kinds of illnesses (e.g., diabetes and cirrhosis of the liver) and higher death rates (e.g., from accidents and suicide). In addition, research shows that the married are less likely to say they are sick, to visit a physician, or to be hospitalized. Married individuals also have lower mortality rates in relation to comparable unmarried persons (Kaprio, Koskenvuo, and Rita, 1987; Litwack and Messeir, 1989).

Risk-taking behaviors are also found to be higher among those not married, especially the divorced. A study of automobile accidents, for example, showed that the fatality rates were higher for the divorced than other marital groups. The difference existed for both males and females, whites and nonwhites (National Center for Health Statistics, 1970). McMurray (1970) studied the accident rate for those individuals both six months prior to and six months after their divorce. He found that the accident rate during this one year period doubled.

Various explanations exist for the relationship between marital status and well-being. The two primary hypotheses suggest social selection issues and the social causation hypothesis. The former states that those individuals who are the most psychologically adjusted and physically healthy are those most likely to be desirable partners and actually marry. In other words, psychological health leads to marriage. For those individuals whose marriages fail, it can be hypothesized that they had poor mental and/or physical health before their marriage (Booth and Johnson, 1994; Marks, 1996).

The social causation explanation argues that marriage is directly linked to better emotional and physical health (Marks, 1996). In contrast to the previous explanation that argues that the mental state precedes the marriage, this model holds that marriage leads to the mental state. Having a mate to rely upon provides a form of stability, a blanket of security that may lower anxiety and depression. In addition, marriage leads to less-risky behaviors (e.g., less or no smoking and drinking) that can affect not only health but life expectancy (Benokraitis, 1999). To be sure, arguments can be made for both of these explanations. However, the research supports the latter hypothesis—that is, the idea that marriage leads to better emotional and physical well-being (Marks, 1996).

RELIGION AND WELL-BEING

The relationship between religion and well-being, similar to that of marriage, is strong. Studies have focused on three areas: (1) mental health measures, including depression and anxiety; (2) physical state of health and perceived state; and (3) life satisfaction.

Numerous studies have documented the effects of various kinds of religious behaviors (for example, an active prayer life) on mental health (Crawford, Handal, and Wiener, 1989; Poloma and Pendleton, 1990). Research also has shown that highly religious individuals manifest less distress and better psychological adjustment than individuals rated either as medium or low in their religious activities. This has been found to be especially true for females (Crawford, Hendal, and Wiener, 1989). Another report (Gartner, Larson, and Allen, 1991) has shown that "religiosity is associated with lower levels of depression" (p. 11).

A similar relationship also exists when we look at different measures of both subjective and actual physical health. In a review of the literature, Levin and Vanderpool (1987) found a relationship between church attendance and subjective health ratings in the twenty-eight studies that they assessed.

In regard to actual physical health, Dwyer, Clarke, and Miller (1990) conducted a study utilizing over 3,000 counties in the United States and found lower rates of cancer in those counties where there were a large number of church members. Levin (1994) reported a negative relationship between religion and illnesses such as heart disease, stroke, and various forms of cancer. Comstock and Partridge (1972) found lower mortality rates for heart disease, emphysema, cirrhosis of the liver, cancer of the rectum, and suicide for those individuals who attended religious services at least once a week as compared to those who did not attend. Finally, Koenig and George (1998) focused on those individuals over the age of sixty-five. They reported that those persons who had high rates of religious participation (e.g., attended services weekly or regularly studied the Bible) were 40 percent less likely to experience hypertension.

Jarvis and Northcott (1987) suggested that religion has an effect on physical well-being in two related ways: (1) First, religious doctrine can prohibit, or at least discourage, behavior that is harmful to one's health. (2) Second, religion can encourage behavior that can prevent or eliminate illness.

The Mormons, for example, prohibit the use of substances such as tobacco and alcohol, and even caffeine. Southern Baptists, Seventh-Day Adventists, and other similar fundamentalist religions also discourage such behaviors as drinking alcoholic beverages. Among their practitioners, then, we would expect to witness fewer cases of diseases (e.g., cirrhosis of the liver and lung cancer) symptomatic of the use of such drugs as alcohol and tobacco.

We should also note the role of positive thinking in preventing illness and disease. It has been found that maintaining a positive outlook in dealing with disease and religion are related (Paloutzian, 1996). One's religious beliefs might also help an individual cope more effectively with negative effects (such as illness) by interpreting the sickness as part of God's plan. In other words, religion may provide individuals with a framework or belief system that allows them to deal effectively with different kinds of adversity (Spilka, Hood, and Gorsuch, 1985).

In addition to the finding of better physical and mental health among the religious, research has documented higher levels of satisfaction among the devout. Furthermore, this relationship has been found not only in the United States but in other countries. Inglehart (1990), in a survey of fourteen European countries, found a higher rate of life satisfaction among those individuals who attended services at least once a week compared to those who did not.

Pollner (1989) conducted a study utilizing three different measures of well-being: general well-being (e.g., general happiness, marital happiness, and life excitement); stress (e.g., unemployment, divorce, and death of a relative); and social interaction (e.g., spending time with relatives or friends). He found these factors to be highly correlated with various indicators of a relationship with a "divine other." Those indicating such a relationship scored better on the measures of general well-being, manifested lower levels of stress, and spent more time with others.

This study suggests that the role of religion (along with marriage) seems to be critical in distinguishing those who express higher feelings of life satisfaction and well-being. As mentioned earlier, one particular explanation for the higher reports of physical well-being involve religion's role in encouraging (or dictating) a lifestyle that might include healthy diet, exercise, and avoiding alcohol and tobacco. This can also be applied to marriage.

FINDINGS ON WELL-BEING

In this study I was interested in ascertaining if differences on different measures of well-being existed among the married sample and the two divorced samples. Based on the past research, I would expect to find that the married sample will exhibit greater levels of well-being and lower levels of psychological distress.

I examined four statements to determine current feelings of well-being in this sample population:

1. I feel like a failure.
2. I am satisfied with my life as a whole.

3. Overall, I am satisfied with my physical health.
4. Overall, I am satisfied with my emotional and mental health.

Table 5.1 presents the percentage in each of the three groups that either agreed or strongly agreed with the question.

Results indicated that only 5.8 percent of the annulled and 1.8 percent of the married either agreed or strongly agreed that they felt like a failure. On the other hand, 18.8 percent of the divorced reported this feeling. Comparing the groups, the divorced were more than three times more likely than the annulled, and ten times more likely than the married sample either to agree or strongly agree that they felt like a failure.

When the three groups were compared on the life satisfaction question 84.5 percent of the annulled, 68.3 percent of the divorced, and 92 percent of the married responded in either of the agree categories. Satisfaction with health resulted in similar figures, although a smaller percentage of both the annulled and married were in the two agree categories. Finally, of the three satisfaction questions, the highest rated for all three samples was on the following: "Overall, I am satisfied with my emotional and mental health." A total of 87.7 percent of the annulled, 75.2 percent of the divorced, and 94.5 percent of the married either agreed or strongly agreed with this question.

The responses to these four questions on well-being clearly indicate that the divorced group are the lowest in satisfaction and highest in feelings of failure while the married group is highest in satisfaction and lowest in feelings of failure. The annulled fall in between the married and divorced but are closer to the figures for the married sample than the divorced sample.

In comparing the married with the divorced sample, it was found that the two groups were significantly different on all four measures of well-being. Similarly, significant differences occurred on all four measures when the divorced and annulled were compared. Finally, the annulled and married groups were different only on one question: "I feel like a failure."

The three groups were also compared on other measures relating to physical and psychological distress (see Table 5.2).

One of the questions I asked was: "Have you felt so sad, discouraged, hopeless, or had so many problems (during the past month) that

TABLE 5.1. Well-Being by Marital Status

Question	Group	Percent Response					
		Strongly Agree	Agree	Don't Know	Disagree	Strongly Disagree
Failure	Annulled	0.6	5.2	5.8	39.6	48.7
	Divorced	5.9	12.9	10.9	35.6	33.7
	Married	0.0	1.8	1.2	38.7	58.3
Satisfied life	Annulled	24.5	60.0	5.2	9.0	1.3
	Divorced	12.9	55.4	5.9	23.8	2.0
	Married	33.7	58.3	2.5	3.7	1.8
Satisfied physical health	Annulled	21.7	59.2	0.6	15.3	3.2
	Divorced	7.9	61.4	2.0	19.8	8.9
	Married	19.9	62.1	1.9	15.5	0.6
Satisfied emotional and mental health	Annulled	26.0	61.7	3.2	8.4	0.6
	Divorced	16.8	58.4	5.0	17.8	2.0
	Married	30.9	63.6	1.9	3.1	0.6

TABLE 5.2. Physical and Psychological Distress by Marital Status

Question	Response	Percent of Group		
		Annulled	Divorced	Married
Felt sad	Extremely/very much	12.0	18.4	1.2
	Quite a bit/some	13.3	28.1	10.5
	Little/not at all	74.7	53.4	88.3
Happy with personal life	Very/fairly happy	66.5	48.5	71.6
	Satisfied	14.8	16.5	13.0
	Somewhat/very dissatisfied	18.7	34.9	15.5
Illness in past month	All/most of time	7.0	11.6	5.0
	Good bit/some	21.0	25.2	25.6
	Little/none	72.0	63.1	70.2
Needed help	Yes, sought help	26.9	34.0	14.2
	Yes, did not seek help	3.8	7.8	3.1
	Few/no problems	69.3	58.2	83.7

you wondered if anything was worthwhile?" Respondents were able to give one of six responses ranging from "extremely" to "not at all." Among the annulled, 12.0 percent responded either "extremely" or "very much"; for the divorced it was 18.4 percent; for the married it was only 1.2 percent. At the other end of the scale ("a little," "not at all"), the figures were 74.7 percent for the annulled, 53.4 percent for the divorced, and 88.3 percent for the married sample. Thus, the married were least likely to feel this way, followed by the annulled, and then the divorced. Significant differences in their responses were found between the married and annulled, the married and the divorced, and the annulled and the divorced.

A second question asked if they had been happy with their personal lives in the last month. Over 66 percent of the annulled and 71 percent of the married reported being either "very happy" or "fairly happy." In contrast, less than 49 percent of the divorced gave this response. And, 34.9 percent of the divorced, compared with only 18.7 percent of the annulled and 15.5 percent of the married, responded either "somewhat dissatisfied" or "very dissatisfied." We see, then, that the order for satisfaction was the same as for the previous question—the married, the annulled, and then the divorced. However, even though significant differences appeared between the married and divorced groups, along with the annulled and divorced, no statistical difference occurred between the annulled and the married.

The third question stated: "Have you been bothered by any illness, bodily disorder, pains, or fears about your health during the past month?" The divorced population reported the lowest in physical well-being. Although 11.6 percent of the divorced gave either the "all the time" or "most of the time" responses, only 7 percent of the annulled and 5 percent of the married were in these two categories. On the other hand, 72 percent of the annulled, 70.2 percent of the married, and 63.1 percent of the divorced responded either "a little of the time" or "none of the time." Although the divorced reported a higher percentage indicating some kind of illness, they were not significantly higher than either of the other two groups.

Finally, I included a question relevant to the past year: "Have you had severe enough personal, emotional, behavioral, or mental problems during the past year that you felt you needed help?" Although only 14.2 percent of the married respondents said that they had problems and sought help, 26.9 percent of the annulled and 34 percent of the divorced gave an affirmative response. The married (83.7 percent) were also most likely to report few or no problems. The annulled (69.3 percent) were next, followed by the divorced (58.2 percent). Statistical tests revealed differences between the married and both the annulled and the divorced. The difference between the annulled and divorced was not large enough to be statistically significant.

Since the divorced and the annulled scored lower on most of the measures of well-being, I assumed that this would manifest itself in higher rates of seeing a counselor than among the married. This was indeed the case. When I asked if they had seen some kind of counselor almost 82 percent of the divorced, 75 percent of the annulled, and only 32 percent of the married responded "yes." The statistical analysis indicated no significant difference between the annulled and divorced. The married sample had visited a counselor significantly less often than either of the divorced groups.

Virtually all of the results strongly support the previous research which has shown that the married experience not only higher feelings of well-being but fewer signs of distress. Differences among the groups existed not only currently, but within the past month and the past year. That the divorced experience emotional and psychological effects should come as no surprise. The extreme pain that many divorced individuals suffer as a result of detaching themselves from a significant other often takes a toll through higher rates of illness, levels of depression, and even suicidal ideation.

What particular role does a spouse play when considering psychological and physical factors? Ross, Mirowsky, and Goldsteen (1990) indicated that a spouse can improve one's health in a number of ways: through "emotional health, by reducing risky behavior, by aiding early detection and treatment, and by helping recovery" (p. 1063). Even the opportunity to talk to someone else about personal problems can reduce stress and the incidence of health problems (Clark, 1993). As previously stated, it is possible that people who are better adjusted are more likely to get married. It may be more likely that receiving social and emotional support from a marital partner actually promotes well-being and better health. Marriage can reduce risky forms of behavior. Married individuals are more likely to give up behaviors such as drinking, speeding, fighting, smoking (Benokraitis, 1999).

In addition, there is a correlation between income and health. A higher income can provide the means to sustain a healthy lifestyle. Rogers (1996) found that a higher income improves health behavior and access to quality health care. Since most marriages involve two wage earners the likelihood of a higher income exists for the married than for the divorced.

However, it should be noted that some studies do not support the observation that the married experienced better health. There is evidence, often in families with low incomes and young children, that married women are not as healthy as married men (Anson, 1989). Ross, Mirowsky, and Goldsteen (1990) have argued that the sheer fact of marriage does not always lead to better health; the important variable is being happy in the marriage. With these qualifications marriage does seem to be a crucial factor leading to higher levels of happiness along with lower levels of anxiety, depression, and illness.

ANNULLED VERSUS DIVORCED

One aspect of this study focused solely on the divorce experience. The literature reports a broad range of evidence that psychological turmoil occurs both during and after the divorce process. In fact, divorce ranks in the top ten in terms of major life stressors (Holmes and Rahe, 1967; Hobson et al. 1998). Therefore, it is not surprising to find high levels of depression, feelings of failure, insomnia, and other emotional problems among these people.

Respondents were asked if they had experienced certain behaviors or feelings just after their divorce. Twenty questions were examined. Statistically significant differences occurred on seven of the twenty measures. In addition, there were fairly large differences on three other items. The differences were not quite large enough, however, to reach statistical significance. Table 5.3 summarizes the variables for which either statistical differences appeared or the differences almost reached significance between the annulled and divorced.

Six questions were worded such that agreeing with the statement indicated a poorer adjustment. These are presented first in the table. Although 22.6 percent of the annulled reported having a poor appetite "all the time," 34.2 percent reported experiencing this problem

TABLE 5.3. Behaviors or Feelings the Annulled and Divorced Expressed Just After Divorce

Behavior/feeling	Group	Percent Response		
		None of the Time	Some/Occasionally	All the Time
Indicating negative adjustment				
Poor appetite	Annulled	34.2	43.2	22.6*
	Divorced	23.7	56.4	10.9
Could not shake off blues	Annulled	27.2	44.4	28.5*
	Divorced	15.0	62.0	23.0
Could not keep mind on things	Annulled	17.8	63.8	18.4*
	Divorced	6.9	69.3	23.8
Felt depressed	Annulled	17.2	51.6	31.2*
	Divorced	6.9	66.3	26.7
Felt sad	Annulled	14.2	55.5	30.3*
	Divorced	4.0	65.7	30.3
Could not get "going"	Annulled	28.1	62.1	9.8
	Divorced	17.8	65.3	16.8
Indicating positive adjustment				
Was as good as others	Annulled	16.9	41.6	41.6*
	Divorced	10.9	60.4	28.7
Was happy	Annulled	19.6	58.2	22.2*
	Divorced	18.0	72.0	10.0
Hopeful about future	Annulled	18.5	46.5	35.0
	Divorced	14.4	60.8	24.7
Enjoyed life	Annulled	13.8	56.6	29.6
	Divorced	17.2	65.7	17.2

*Indicates differences between the groups were statistically significant.

99

"none of the time." Only 10.9 percent of the divorced reported this "all the time," but 23.7 percent reported feeling this way "none of the time." The same trend occurred with the questions concerning being able to shake off the blues and feeling depressed. A higher percentage of the annulled than the divorced were in the "all the time" category, but also a higher percentage of the former group than the latter was in the "none of the time" category.

The annulled had a lower percentage responding "all the time" to not being able to keep their mind on things and not being able to get "going," and a higher percentage responding "none of the time." Both the annulled and divorced had the same percentage (30.3 percent) responding "all the time" on feeling sad. However, a higher percentage of annulled (14.2 percent) than divorced (4.0 percent) responded "none of the time."

The remaining four questions were worded such that agreeing with the statement indicated positive adjustment. On all four of the questions the annulled had a higher percentage responding "all the time." However, they also had a larger percentage responding "none of the time" on the following questions:

1. I felt that I was just as good as other people.
2. I was happy.
3. I felt hopeful about the future.

In attempting to answer the question of which group, the annulled or divorced, is better adjusted, the data favor the annulled. A way of determining an overall adjustment score is to construct a new figure based on the two *extreme* categories. For example, to determine the score on the poor appetite question:

1. Take the 22.6 percent for annulled on the "all the time" response and subtract the 10.9 percent figure for the divorced. This resulted in a difference of 11.7 percent. In other words, 11.7 percent more of the annulled scored in the "poorer" adjustment direction.
2. Then do the same with the "none of the time" category. Here, 10.5 percent fewer (34.2 percent to 23.7 percent) of the annulled gave this response than the divorced.

3. Then arrive at an overall score by subtracting 10.5 percent from 11.7 percent. In this instance 1.2 percent more of the annulled fell into the "poorer adjustment" category.

After going through the same process for each question, I found that the annulled scored higher on adjustment on all but the poor appetite question. The range was from 5.8 percent on the depressed question to 18.9 percent on the feeling good about oneself question.

Finally, it should be noted that the annulled had higher percentages scoring in the two extreme categories. This would seem to indicate that there were two separate annulled groups. Indeed, this was the case. Some of the annulled individuals in this study initiated the annulment process (i.e., were petitioners), and others did not (i.e., the respondents).

Findings on Recently Divorced Individuals

I also wanted to examine the divorced groups' *current* feelings on various psychological measures. The literature often finds support for the idea that "time heals all wounds." In other words, as time passes people usually get over whatever emotional trauma they have experienced, become less depressed, and start looking forward to the future again. If you asked recently divorced persons if they felt sad they would no doubt be more likely to respond affirmatively than those individuals who were divorced five or ten years ago. The latter individuals would have had time to heal their wounds and move on. What I did, therefore, was to take only those individuals who had recently been divorced and compared the annulled and divorced on various psychological measures—feelings of hopelessness, meaninglessness, life satisfaction, and so forth. I used both one and two years as the cutoff point for defining recently divorced. The results are summarized in Table 5.4.

The annulled scored in the better adjusted direction on sixteen of the nineteen questions for those who had been divorced one year or less. Significant differences existed on three of these questions. The differences were more pronounced when we use two years as the cutoff point for time since the divorce. Here, the annulled scored in the better adjusted direction on eighteen of the issues; ten of the differences were statistically significant.

TABLE 5.4. Psychological Measures for the Divorced

Question	Divorced One Year or Less		Divorced Two Years or Less	
	Annulled (N = 15)	Divorced (N = 29)	Annulled (N = 30)	Divorced (N = 44)
Little control over things	3.9	4.0	4.0	3.9
Cannot solve problems	1.8	1.7	4.1	3.4*
Can do anything I set my mind to	1.6	2.1	1.7	2.1
Future depends on me	2.1	1.7	1.9	1.8
Now is dreariest time of my life	3.5	2.9	3.8	3.1*
Just as happy now as when I was younger	3.2	3.6	2.8	3.8*
Most things I do are boring	3.9	3.5	4.2	3.4*
Things I do now are just as interesting as ever	2.5	2.9	2.1	2.9*
As I look back on life, I am satisfied	2.6	3.1	2.2	3.0*
Things are getting worse	3.7	3.4	4.0	3.5*
I feel like a failure	4.2	3.4*	4.4	3.4*
I like myself	1.6	1.9	1.5	2.0*
My life is on the right track	1.8	2.4*	1.6	2.4*
My future looks good	2.1	2.3	1.8	2.5*
I wish I could change my life	2.0	2.0	2.2	2.0
I am satisfied with my life	2.1	2.7*	1.9	2.6*
No control over life	4.2	3.7	4.1	3.8
Satisfied with physical health	2.0	2.5	1.9	2.6*
Satisfied with emotional and mental health	2.0	2.4	1.9	2.6*

Note: Responses were given from a low of 1 (strongly agree) to a high of 5 (strongly disagree).

*Indicates that there was a significant difference between the groups.

Throughout this chapter we have seen that the annulled, as compared to the divorced, scored in the more positive direction on almost all of the measures. When we considered four different measures of well-being, the annulled scored higher. When we considered different measures of physical and psychological distress the annulled were less likely to have those problems. We also found that the annulled scored higher on adjustment after the divorce. Finally, when I controlled time since the divorce, the annulled had scores indicating higher levels of adjustment.

These differences might lead one to believe that having obtained an annulment produced a different frame of mind for this population, as compared to those who have not had an annulment. It is possible, for example, that more of the annulled joined some kind of support group that provided such things as lowered feelings of sadness, higher levels of life satisfaction, and being hopeful about the future.

Another possibility is that the annulment "theology" led to higher levels of well-being for the annulled. This theology states that a marriage was doomed from the start. In essence, there was nothing the person could have done to make the marriage work. This belief can possibly relieve a tremendous amount of guilt from the divorced individual. Believing this to be true, the annulled person (at least the petitioner) can proceed with the healing process more quickly than the person who has not acquired an annulment. For the divorced person (along with the respondent to an annulment petition) who may not have this mind-set, the healing process can take much longer.

Finally, I noted earlier that the married were less likely to see a counselor than the divorced or annulled. I also noted no statistical difference between the divorced samples although a slightly higher percentage of the divorced had seen a therapist. I found the same kind of difference in how many times they had seen a therapist (annulled, 5.2 times on average; divorced, 6.2). Thus, although the divorced had seen a counselor more often, the difference was not statistically significant.

Does Gender Matter?

Gender is a significant variable considered in the analysis of variables such as happiness, well-being, depression, and life satisfaction. Although gender may not be crucial in studying some topics (e.g., happiness), studies have found that females display more symptoms of depression (Seiden, 1976; Cleary, 1987) along with other kinds of emotional disorders such as phobias and anxiety attacks (Cocker-ham, 1989; Kessler et al., 1994). I did an analysis to see if there were any gender differences on any of the questions included in my study.

In comparing the total sample of males with females, I found only five significant differences (see Table 5.5). Two related to emotional problems and the need for counseling. The first appeared in the area of reporting severe enough problems within the *past year* that they felt they needed help. A total of 32.5 percent of females responded that they needed help, and 21 percent of the males responded in this manner. The second difference occurred in the area of having *ever* seen a therapist. Females (67 percent), in comparison to the males (42.1 percent), were more likely to have reported having seen a thera-pist. This finding is not unusual. This difference is typically attributed to females being more likely to recognize their feelings and to seek out help when they do experience any kind of personal or emotional problem. However, socialization has taught men to be "tough," and often to refrain from recognizing the emotional. As a consequence, they are less likely to seek treatment (Doyle and Paludi, 1995).

TABLE 5.5. Significant Differences by Gender

Question	Response	Male (%)	Female (%)
Needed help	Yes, sought help	15.4	28.3
	Yes, did not seek help	5.6	4.2
	Few/no problems	79.0	67.5
Seen a counselor	Yes	42.1	67.0
Felt fearful	None of the time	38.6	16.6
	Some/occasionally	49.1	60.6
	All the time	12.3	22.8
Enjoyed life	None of the time	12.3	16.0
	Some/occasionally	47.4	64.9
	All the time	40.4	19.1
Had crying spells	None of the time	32.8	15.4
	Some/occasionally	51.7	59.5
	All the time	15.5	25.1

Finally, females were much more likely to have felt fearful and to have crying spells after the divorce and much less likely to report enjoying life after the marital breakup.

These differences may be attributed to the different gender roles that have been assigned to males and females. I have already mentioned the greater likelihood of females recognizing their emotions and seeking therapy. It is also possible that the *males* reported a brighter future and all that goes with it for two reasons: (1) because they were romantically involved with someone else. Although this is just speculation I did find a number of women during the course of the interviews who said that their husbands left them for another woman. This was especially true for the males who were seeking an annulment. (2) Males enjoy a higher standard of living after a divorce (Weitzman, 1985; Hoffman and Duncan, 1988; Peterson, 1996).

Again, these differences were for the entire sample of males compared to the entire sample of females. In other words, I did not compare males and females by marital status. When I did proceed with this kind of analysis I found that there were a total of six significant gender differences: four for the annulled, one for the divorced, and one for the married. The differences for the three samples are presented in Table 5.6.

The results indicated that the annulled males were (1) more hopeful about the future and (2) enjoyed life more. Conversely, males were less likely to (1) feel like a failure in life and (2) be fearful. Divorced males, similar to their annulled counterparts, were less likely than the females to be fearful. The only difference for the married sample was with the counseling variable. Although 24.1 percent of males reported having visited a counselor, 40.7 percent of females had done so.

SUMMARY

Both marriage and religion are very strong forces in many people's lives. Marriage comes with obligations. These obligations require that one take care not only of oneself but others. The result is often a better lifestyle, which, in turn, leads to a change in physical health. This change is typically for the better.

TABLE 5.6. Significant Gender Differences by Marital Status

Question	Gender	Percent Response		
		None of time	Some	All the time
Annulled				
Hopeful about future	Male	13.9	22.2	63.9
	Female	19.5	54.2	26.3
Enjoyed life	Male	11.4	37.1	51.4
	Female	14.9	63.2	21.9
Failure in life	Male	50.0	30.5	19.4
	Female	24.3	53.0	22.6
Felt fearful	Male	40.0	48.6	11.4
	Female	20.2	59.6	20.2
Divorced				
Felt fearful	Male	38.1	52.4	9.5
	Female	12.2	60.8	27.0
Married				
Have seen a counselor (yes)	Male	24.1		
	Female	40.7		

These results support the research of others: marital status and religion have an impact on all kinds of psychological, emotional, and physical indicators. The divorced have the lowest levels of both general and physical well-being. In addition, most of the differences are statistically significant. Again, this indicates that there is a real difference among the three groups on the different measures.

On many of the measures, the annulled (when compared to the divorced) scored better on adjustment. In many instances the annulled, although scoring lower on adjustment than those who are married, were sometimes not significantly lower. In other words, they were closer to the married sample than the divorced one.

Chapter 6

Social Integration

It was a choice [being Catholic]. When I was young, it was how I was raised. Maybe it's a feeling of being part of a community, being a part of a group of people that have values that I share.

Sarah, a lifelong Catholic age forty-three,
divorced and annulled

In Chapter 5, I noted the positive relationship between both marriage and religion and physical and emotional well-being. I suggested that, according to the research, both of these play a role in promoting a healthy lifestyle. However, research also shows that the role of social integration is crucial in understanding emotional well-being. Social integration refers to the extent to which an individual is tied into the community and its various institutions. Individuals who have religious, familial, friendship, and community associations are said to be high in social integration. In contrast, those who are isolated, who lack communal ties, are low in social integration. Social integration, as a variable, has been used to explain a wide range of occurrences, including substance abuse (Umberson, 1987), illness (Berkman and Breslow, 1983), and mortality (Blazer, 1982).

One of the first authors to write on the importance of social integration was Durkheim (1951). He argued that when strong social ties exist among individuals they are less likely to engage in nonnormative or deviant behaviors. Durkheim is noted for conducting the very first social scientific study, a study of suicide. He hypothesized that social integration led to different suicide rates. Specifically, individuals with few ties would have higher suicide rates than those with numerous social ties. He found that this was the case. The unmarried, for example, had higher suicide rates than the married. Those who are single do not have the obligations and attachments to others that married individuals do. He also found that Protestants had higher rates of suicide than either Jews or Catholics. He argued that Protestantism is more of an "individualistic" religion whereas Judaism and Catholicism have a set of rituals that foster cohesiveness and a bond among its participants.

Some of the married respondents indicated this sense of integration. One individual felt that if it were not for his marriage he would have been "adrift at sea." Another, married to the same person for over thirty years, wrote that she could not imagine having another spouse. Her husband, along with her children, gave meaning to her life. A third respondent, having experienced some bouts with depression, said he may have committed suicide if he had not had his marriage, his children, and his faith.

Others, especially the divorced and not annulled, feel isolated and alone. An older woman felt the extreme sting of isolation from her church. After her divorce she saw herself as a "nonperson all of sudden." She states that "You do not exist and that is a very hard thing. You have to find your own way somehow. And I am sure a lot of people do not make it." Her last comment no doubt rings true for many. Some of the divorced respondents felt neglected and abandoned at a time when they needed a church to support them. Many dealt with this "ostracism" by leaving the Catholic Church and becoming members of other religious organizations that they felt were more accepting of a divorced person. Several became active in these churches and developed friendships and the acceptance they had sought in their Catholic parish.

The argument that social integration is tied to both religion and marriage is highly important and has been documented. A large percentage of individuals who are divorced and annulled have friends or relatives who proceeded them in divorce. In the words of one of the respondents: "Why not, it's the norm among my friends and family." On the other hand, married respondents were much less likely to have friends or relatives who are divorced. Many indicated that, in their family and among their friends, divorce is frowned upon. Among these individuals divorce is a sign of failure.

Religious integration is important and married respondents are much more likely to have married other Catholics; the divorced and annulled are much more likely to have married outside their faith and, as a consequence, to have attended Mass less frequently when married. I also found that the annulled are a unique group. Although they are similar to other divorced individuals, in many instances they are closer to the married sample on some measures.

MARRIAGE AND SOCIAL INTEGRATION

A very significant variable relating to divorce is social integration. The idea that forming bonds with others may have a dampening effect on divorce has been noted by Booth, Edwards, and Johnson (1991). They examined these variables in a longitudinal national sample of married persons on three different occasions over an eight-year period. In their study of different forms of integration they found that some kinds of integration related to divorce and others did not. When they looked at the number of friends reported and the number of community organizations to which the individual belonged (referred to as communicative integration), they found the relationship to be a weak one. Booth, Edwards, and Johnson did find a tendency toward divorce among those individuals with fewer friends and a lack of organizational ties, but it was not a very strong relationship.

The researchers also looked at the relationship between divorce and the rate of divorce for their friends or siblings, referring to this as normative integration. Norms are rules or guidelines for behavior. When we see others who are close to us breaking the norms, then it may weaken our own attachment to the norm. They found this form of social integration to be highly related to the divorce rate among their respondents. That is, having a divorced friend or a sibling was related to the respondent's also experiencing a divorce.

I employed communicative and normative measures of social integration in this study. Given the findings of Booth, Edwards, and Johnson (1991), I expected to find more support for the normative measures of integration than the communicative. If a person had a friend(s) or sibling(s) who had divorced (normative integration), the greater would be the probability that this person would be divorced. When I did the analysis, this was the case. I found little support for the communicative integration measures.

RELIGION AND SOCIAL INTEGRATION

Studies show religion is critical in leading to higher levels of integration in communities. However, all religions may not offer the same degree of integration. Some may be very loosely organized and promote individuality, and others may be highly integrated and focus on engaging in common rituals and activities along with conforming to its norms and principles. Within religious communities there are many variations in their levels of social support, adherence to the church doctrine, and emphasis on conformity. Jarvis and Northcott (1987) have argued that there are differences among the structural elements of religions. Those religions that are more structured involve the person more in the group and, as a consequence, have a greater impact on the person's life, including physical and emotional well-being and life satisfaction. Catholicism is highly structured and stresses the individual's participation within the Church and his or her religion.

Catholicism and Integration

Durkheim's (1951) early study found that Catholics had lower suicide rates than Protestants. He argued that this was due to the Catholics requiring a social network. In a more recent study of Catholics, Burr, McCall, and Powell-Griner (1994) reported that membership in the Church may provide "stronger networks and more social support, thereby insulating individuals from suicidal impulses" (p. 314).

In the United States from the 1930s through the 1950s, Catholics and Catholicism were generally perceived negatively. Protestantism and its values were dominant. This resulted in an emphasis on Catholics sticking together, and the Church itself placed a premium on conformity. It seemed to produce a sense of identity for these individuals. As Catholics, they shared a characteristic that separated them from the dominant Protestant culture. Participating in common rituals tends to bring people closer together and can make the group more cohesive.

Today there is greater acceptance of Catholics and their faith. There is also a greater diversity shown among Catholics themselves (Davidson et al., 1997). Still, many writers view Catholicism as quite unique. Andrew Greeley (1990), in his book *The Catholic Myth,* argued this distinctiveness. He stated that Catholics were different from others in that they possess a more "sacramental" imagination:

> By that I mean that Catholics are more likely to imagine God as present in the world and the world as revelatory instead of bleak. Much that is thought to be distinctively Catholic results from this distinctive style of imagining—the importance of community, institution, and hierarchy; the emphasis on ritual and ceremonial; the interest in the fine and lively arts; devotion to saints, angels, holy souls, and especially the Mother of Jesus; reverence for statues and images; the use of blessings, medals, and prayer beads. (p. 4)

Because of the importance of social integration as a sociological variable I included a number of related variables in the study. I compared the three groups of annulled, divorced, and married on these measures.

Communicative and Normative Integration

Communicative integration concerns the extent to which the individual is engaged in a social network of ties (Booth, Edwards, and Johnson, 1991). I asked the respondents two questions relating to communicative integration: (1) "I belong to a network of friends," and (2) "I get a lot of satisfaction from the groups I participate in." The annulled had the highest percentage responding either "often" or "very often"—78.5 percent. The figure for the divorced was 76.6 percent, and for the married respondents it was 72.7 percent. The majority of all three groups answered in the affirmative. Statistically, however, there were no differences among the groups. The majority of all three groups also gained satisfaction from group participation. The annulled (88.9 percent) were most likely to give this response, and the married (78.9 percent) were next. The divorced had the lowest percentage giving this response—70.8 percent. There were significant differences between the annulled and both the divorced and the married. No differences occurred between the divorced and the married. The annulled were more likely to be satisfied with their group experiences, and the divorced were not.

It should be pointed out that these questions are not the best measures of communicative integration in that they asked only about the current situation. It is very possible that the divorced and annulled were more isolated from groups prior to their divorce and became involved with groups (such as divorce encounter) only after the divorce. It is interesting to note the gap between the two divorced groups with respect to their level of satisfaction. Although I did not ask what specific groups they were members of, the difference may be in the type of group to which they belonged. It is possible that the annulled may be more likely to belong to a religious group that is attempting to integrate the individual back into the Church, and the divorced may belong to a more secular group.

Normative integration involves conforming to the existing standards or norms (Booth, Edwards, and Johnson, 1991). I asked three questions in order to measure this form of integration: (1) "How many of your close friends are divorced?" (2) "Were your parents ever divorced?" (3) "Were your ex-spouse's (just spouse for the married sample) parents divorced?" (4) "Were any brothers or sisters divorced before your divorce?" (for the married sample: "Are any of your brothers or sisters divorced?").

While 28.6 percent of the annulled and 19.4 percent of the divorced samples responded "most" or "all" when asked about close friends being divorced, only 6.2 percent of the married individuals gave either of these responses. In contrast, 25.9 percent of the married sample, 13.9 percent of the divorced, and 9.3 percent of annulled gave "none" as their response. The married and annulled samples were very similar in their responses when asked about their parents: 9.9 percent of the former and 9.1 percent of the latter said their parents were divorced. Higher percentages of the two divorced groups indicated that their former spouse's parents were divorced: 26.1 percent for the divorced and 22.4 percent for the annulled sample. About 12.5 percent of the married group said their spouse's parents are divorced. When I asked them about any sisters or brothers being divorced, 51.8 percent of the divorced, 49.1 percent of the married, and 36.8 percent of the annulled responded affirmatively.

These results were not clear-cut as far as the annulled and the divorced. Although these two divorced groups did have more friends and spouse's parents who were divorced, the married group was the most likely to have divorced siblings. If we consider the divorced a definite pattern emerges: they are most likely to have divorced parents (both their own and that of their former spouse), friends, and siblings. Booth, Edwards, and Johnson (1991) argued that having some-one close who has obtained a divorce exposes the individual to significant others who have gone against the norms. My findings certainly confirm that for the divorced group.

Attitudinal Integration

I have suggested that one's ties with the Church are partially dependent upon one's marital status. Within the Catholic Church, marriage is seen as insoluble. Therefore, one who is married and never divorced has an indisputable place within the Church along with total access to its sacraments. Divorce, on the other hand, can place the person in a more precarious place within the Church. The person who has experienced a divorce within a church that has such a strong stance on that behavior may experience feelings of abandonment, or at least the feeling that they are not "full" members of the Church.

The way in which a person may choose to deal with a divorce in the Catholic Church is by getting an annulment. The effect of the annulment is to restore the person's role within the Church. Still, as can be argued, that place may not be as secure as for the married individual. I tested this idea in another study (Jenks and Woolever, 1999), which hypothesized that the divorced would have the lowest scores on various attitudinal measures of Catholicism, the married would have the highest integration scores, and the annulled would fall in between these two groups.

In that study, six attitudinal questions that measured the person's integration into the Catholic Church were asked. These integrative questions go beyond the measures used in many other studies. Rather than just asking if they belong to the Church, the extent to which they actually identify, and take pride in, their church is being asked. These measures, then, represent more of a social psychological integration. Table 6.1 presents this information.

A large majority of all three groups indicated a sense of pride in being Catholic. However, the married sample reported the greatest sense of pride and the divorced the least. A minority of all three groups indicated they put the Church's goals ahead of their own. Again, the married individuals were most likely to give this response, and the divorced were the least likely to do so. When I analyzed the question of

TABLE 6.1. Percent Agreeing with Questions Measuring Integration into the Church

Question	Annulled	Divorced	Married
I feel a sense of pride in being a member of the Catholic Church.	90.9	79.4	93.9
I put the Church's goals ahead of my own personal interests.	42.6	26.3	47.5
I am committed to the Church's goals.	70.8	51.0	84.6
To be perfectly honest, I do not care what the Catholic Church does or says.	5.7	11.5	2.5
It is important to maintain the values of the Church.	87.0	64.9	96.9
I am to the point where I do not know if I belong to the Church.	10.0	27.4	1.2

commitment to the Church's goals I found a very large difference of almost 20 percent between the divorced group and the annulled and over 33 percent between the divorced and the married. Although a small minority indicated that they did not care what the Church said, the divorced were more likely to agree. The question regarding maintaining the values of the Church displayed another large difference. Sixty-five percent of the divorced agreed compared to 87 percent of the annulled and almost 97 percent of the married. Finally, the divorced were more likely to question whether they belong to the Church. Among the married sample, barely 1 percent questioned this.

The results for all six questions were clear: the married individuals were the most integrated into the Church, the divorced the least. For some of the questions these differences were quite significant. When I did the usual statistical tests I found significant differences on all the questions. Furthermore, I found that the divorced sample's percentages differed significantly from that of the annulled sample on four of the six questions: "committed to the Church's goals," "do not care what the Catholic Church does or says," "maintain the values of the Church," and "do not know if I belong to the Church." In addition, the other two (feeling a sense of pride in being a Catholic and placing the Church's goals ahead of one's own interests) were very close to achieving statistical significance. Results also indicated that the divorced scores differed from the married on all six questions. Finally, the annulled and married differed on the commitment to the Church, maintaining the values, and do not really care what the Church thinks questions.

Behavioral Integration

Behavioral indicators such as (1) frequency of church attendance, (2) intensity and length of exposure to church doctrine, and (3) involvement in church groups and organizations can also be used to measure commitment and integration into the Church and organizations.

Church Attendance

Prior to the Second Vatican Council it was reported that between 75 and 80 percent of Catholics attended church weekly. Other reports indicate that figure has dropped to 59 percent: 51 percent attending once a week and 8 percent attending several times a week. Nine percent of Catholics say they never attend services (Gallup and Castelli, 1987). The exact reason for the decline is not clear, but Greeley (1990) argued that disagreements over the Church's official ban on artificial birth control has been the major factor in the attendance decline.

Not only has church attendance declined but many have left the Church. Figures have indicated that individuals were leaving the Catholic Church at a higher rate than any other major religious denominations (Kosmin and Lachman, 1993). Gallup and Castelli (1987) reported figures of nearly 4 million leaving the Church. The major reasons many of these individuals reported for leaving can be summarized as follows:

1. A loss of interest in either the Catholic Church specifically or religion in general.
2. The rejection of specific teachings (for example, the teaching on birth control).
3. The belief that the Church was straying too far from the Bible.
4. The Church's emphasis on money.
5. The individual was divorced and he or she felt a separation from the Church because of that status.

I asked the respondents how often they attended church services "in a typical month" (see Table 6.2). The overall average was 5.6 times, more than once a week. The married attend, on average, 6.2 times per month. The annulled attend 5.6 times and the divorced attend 4.5 times per month.

The figures indicate that all three groups are higher on church attendance than what has been found nationally for Catholics. The figures for the annulled (9.9 percent) and the divorced (8.7 percent) for never attending, however, are similar to the 9 percent reported by Gallup and Castelli (1987). Although these three groups are higher than the national figures, the married attend more than the annulled and significantly more than the divorced. The results indicate that divorce decreases church attendance. I would argue that this is an indication of a disenchantment among the divorced (and annulled) with church policy on divorce and remarriage and/or how the Church (and its members) treats the divorced. The Church is often perceived as a place for families, not singles—especially divorced singles.

Table 6.3 presents data that show how often the annulled and divorced attended church together as a couple when they were married. The married were asked how often they currently attend church services together. Approximately one-half the annulled and one-third of the divorced reported attending services every week when they were married. Slightly more than three-fourths of the married sample reported currently attending church services every week. Approximately 1 percent of the married couples reported never attending church. The annulled and divorced groups reported nonattendance rates of 21 and 22.2 percent, respectively, or twenty times the rate of the married. The figures for the married group were significantly higher than those for either the annulled or the divorced groups.

TABLE 6.2. Monthly Church Attendance by Marital Status

Group	Frequency (Percent/per Month)			
	0	1-3	4	5+
Annulled	9.9	12.4	32.3	45.3
Divorced	8.7	22.3	40.8	28.2
Married	0.0	13.0	42.0	45.1

TABLE 6.3. Percent Frequency of Reported Church Attendance During Marriage by Marital Status

Frequency	Annulled	Divorced	Married
Every Week	50.3	35.4	75.5
Never	21.0	22.2	1.2

Gallup and Castelli (1987) cited surveys indicating that divorce and remarriage within the Catholic Church is a major area of concern for the layperson. They pointed to a national survey of American Catholics conducted by Gallup in which respondents were asked to rate how the Church was dealing with different groups or issues within the Church. Only 6 percent rated the Church's handling of the separated, divorced, and remarried as "excellent," and 31 percent placed the Church in the "poor" category. These were the lowest ratings for the thirteen groups or issues that respondents were asked to judge. The next lowest-rated category was the "marriage annulment process." Again, only 6 percent rated the Church as "excellent," and 29 percent placed the Church in the "poor" category. Gallup and Castelli (1987) write: "Beyond doubt, the area in which the Church receives its worst rating is its treatment of separated, divorced, and remarried Catholics and the related rating of its marriage tribunal system for processing church annulments" (p. 50).

Religious Homogamy

The literature on divorce and religious participation indicates that religious homogamy is extremely important. Religious homogamy refers to marriage between people of the same religious background. The statistics indicate that the divorce rates are lower for these couples. It is commonly believed that a religiously heterogenous marriage (that is, a marriage between people of different religious faiths) lessens the commitment to one particular religion (Peterson, 1986). With this lower level of commitment comes a lower level of intensity of involvement and integration into the Church. Data show that about 18 percent of Americans are in a heterogeneous marriage; for Catholics this figure is higher, at 26 percent (Gallup and Castelli, 1987).

A number of studies (Glenn, 1982; Heaton, 1984; Ortega, Whitt, and Williams, 1988) have found lower levels of marital satisfaction among these heterogenous couples. Bahr (1981) reported a higher divorce rate among religiously mixed marriages when compared to those where both spouses came from the same religion. In one study of Catholics (Shehan, Bock, and Lee, 1990), it was found that Catholics married to non-Catholics were less likely to attend church services than marriages in which both spouses were Catholic. However, no relationship was found between marital satisfaction and mixed faith couples.

In my study I found that almost 81 percent of the married respondents were in a homogeneous Catholic marriage. In contrast, in less than 60 percent of the divorced and annulled groups cases, both spouses were raised Catholic. Although the majority of the spouses raised in a different religion were Protestant, a fairly large percentage reported no religious identification as a child.

As previously noted, a fairly substantial percentage of both of the divorced groups consisted of partners who grew up in different religions. Therefore, I analyzed the data according to whether the marriage included both spouses who were raised Catholic (homogeneous marriages) as compared to those where the spouses came from different religious backgrounds (heterogeneous marriages). This lead to some interesting findings (see Table 6.4) regarding significant differences for the annulled and divorced samples. Both of these groups reported attendance "every week" at a much higher level when the marriage was homogeneous. Likewise, the percentage reporting that they "never" attended church was higher in heterogeneous marriages. However, no such differences occur in the married sample.

These findings led me to wonder if, among the married couples, the non-Catholic spouse had converted and began attending Mass

TABLE 6.4. Percent Frequency of Church Attendance by Marital Status and Type of Marriage

Frequency	Annulled		Divorced		Married	
	Homo-geneous	Hetero-geneous	Homo-geneous	Hetero-geneous	Homo-geneous	Hetero-geneous
Every week	62.1	38.6	46.2	27.0	76.9	36.42
Never	11.5	33.3	13.5	37.8	0.0	18.2

with the Catholic spouse. My analysis revealed that this was the case. When both the spouses were Catholic, 76.9 percent attended church "every week" and none reported never attending services. However, when the marriage was heterogeneous, only 36.4 percent of the couples reported attending mass every week while 18.2 percent reported never attending. These figures were significantly different from one another.

Parochial School Attendance

It can be argued that those individuals who attended parochial school would be more highly involved in, committed to, and integrated into the Catholic faith. Results were that the vast majority of all three groups had experience with a Catholic education. Seventy-one percent of the divorced had gone to a Catholic school, and 65.4 percent of the annulled and 66.7 percent of the married had done so. This is in contrast to the national figure of 49 percent for Catholics who have attended parochial school (Gallup and Castelli, 1989). However, having a Catholic education does not seem to be a factor in explaining a divorce since the married sample was least likely to have had parochial school experience. The differences among these groups were not significant statistically.

The respondents reported an average of between nine and ten years of Catholic schooling. In fact, the groups were almost identical and, needless to say, were not different from one another statistically.

The majority of all three groups had some Catholic schooling, with a range of between 9.0 years for the married sample and 9.5 years for the divorced group. The variable that separated the groups was whether the marriage was homogeneous or heterogeneous. The largest proportion of the married group did marry within their religion and, in contrast, only a slight majority of the divorced and annulled did so.

I also asked the three groups how often they currently attend church services in a typical month. The married reported an average of 6.3 hours in a typical month, the annulled reported an average of 6.1 hours a month, and the divorced reported an average of 4.2 hours. Church attendance was highest among the married respondents, followed closely by the annulled sample. Although the figure for the divorced group still represented a weekly attendance, it was significantly lower than the other two groups. This can be interpreted as an indication that there may have been some alienation from the Church when we compare the divorced with the other two groups.

Membership in Church-Related Organizations

Feelings of isolation and loneliness are common for divorced individuals. In order to deal with these feelings one often develops new interests, joins new groups, or becomes more involved in groups to which they have been a member. In the Buehler and Langenbrunner (1987) study, 86 percent of their respondents reported an increase in leisure activities.

In my study, I asked specifically about membership in church-related groups. The annulled had the highest average in terms of the number of groups to which they belong, 3.3. This figure is significantly higher than the married individuals who reported an average of 2.4 groups. This reduced number makes sense because married couples may have many other commitments, especially if they have younger children. The married sample was significantly higher than the divorced group, which averaged 1.7 memberships.

Finally, although an individual may belong to a group, it may be in name only. I asked how many hours a month were devoted to these groups. The married sample averaged 9.8 hours per week while the annulled were slightly lower at 9.5 hours. The divorced (7.1 hours) were significantly lower than both the married and the annulled groups.

Does Gender Matter?

One of the most consistent findings in the literature describing church organizations is that females are more likely than males to be active participants and to have a stronger sense of identity with their religion (Kosmin and Lachman, 1993; Paloutzian, 1996). Women appear to be more integrated into their church than are males. The Gallup organization (Gallup and Lindsay, 1999) has found numerous gender differences relevant to religious variables. They include:

1. 73 percent of females and 63 percent of males indicated that they are members of a church or synagogue;
2. 69 percent of females and 60 percent of males reported that they believe "religion can answer all or most of today's problems" (p. 20);
3. 86 percent of females and 74 percent of males reported turning to prayer when faced with some problem or crisis;
4. 35 percent of females and 24 percent of males indicated that religion is extremely important in their lives;
5. 58 percent of females and 41 percent of males have thought "a lot" about developing their faith in the last two years;
6. 66 percent of females and 49 percent of males have thought "a lot" about their relationship to God in the last two years.

Why is there is a discrepancy between males' and females' involvement in religion and religious organizations? One hypothesis states that, historically, a gender division of labor led to female dominance in the spheres of the family and religion and male dominance in the political and economic realms. Another hypothesis is that the socialization process leads women to learn characteristics that stress cooperation, empathy, togetherness, and compassion. These characteristics are more likely to be associated with religious involvement and are more compatible with female socialization (Kosmin and Lachman, 1993). No matter what the exact reason is for the difference, there is clearly a "gender gap" in terms of religiosity.

Religious Involvement Among Catholics

These general differences based on gender occur with the Catholic faith also. Davidson and his colleagues (1997) noted that approximately two-thirds of all those who attended Mass in any particular week were female. Females were also found by the authors to be more likely to engage in prayer, read the Bible, and participate in other more traditional Catholic practices.

Davidson and colleagues' study showed that, even though the participation is higher for females, when males and females who belonged to a church were compared, very few differences occurred. For example, they found no gender differences when they asked a question about whether the participants agreed with the social teachings of the Church.

If we could extrapolate from the Davidson et al. study we might predict that, although the females may have higher rates of participation, there would be no differences between male and female members on issues of commitment to the Church.

When I compared the male and female samples, I found two major differences on the measures relating to commitment to the Church. I found that males scored higher on the measures of commitment. When asked to respond to the question: "I put the Church's goals ahead of my own goals," 48.5 percent of the males either "agreed" or "strongly agreed." In contrast, only 37.2 percent of the females either "agreed" or "strongly agreed" with the statement. About the same percentage (37.9 percent) of females either "disagreed" or "strongly disagreed." For the males it was a smaller figure of 26.5 percent either disagreeing or strongly disagreeing.

The second gender difference appeared on the question: "I am to the point where I do not know if I belong to the Church." Although a small minority of both genders agreed, more than twice as many females (12.6 percent) as males (5.9 percent) agreed.

Finally, two other questions in this study were very close to achieving statistical significance. The first was: "I am committed to the Church's goals." Males were more likely to agree (78.5 percent) than females (69.2 percent). Males (5.2 percent) were also less likely to disagree than females (11.5 percent). The second question was related to maintaining the values of the Church. Males (89.7 percent) were more likely to agree than females (82.9 percent), and males (2.2 percent) were also less likely to disagree than females (8.2 percent).

I also looked at the issue of gender for each of my three samples. I was interested in determining if there was a difference on a particular question between males and females among the annulled sample, but not among the married and divorced. For the annulled and divorced only one difference appeared based on gender. The annulled females (94.8 percent) were more likely to indicate being "proud" about being in the Catholic Church as compared to the males' response of 79.4 percent.

For the divorced the significant difference existed on the question "I do not care what the Catholic Church does or says." Nearly 77 percent of the females either "disagreed" or "strongly disagreed," and only 55 percent of the males disagreed.

Petitioners versus Respondents

The findings previously presented have combined the petitioners and respondents. I believed there may be differences between these two groups, especially on the social integration questions. For example, given many of the negative experiences that I encountered with respondents (as discussed in Chapter 7), it would be natural to hypothesize that they would feel less integrated into the Catholic Church. Table 6.5 presents my findings on these six integration questions.

When asked if they felt pride in being a member of the Catholic Church, ninety-one percent of the petitioners either agreed or strongly agreed, as compared to only 60.7 percent of the respondents. The respondents' (21.4 percent) rate of disagreement was almost ten times that of the petitioners (2.5 percent).

I asked the respondents if they put the Church's goals ahead of their own interests. Although 43.1 percent of the petitioners reported either agreeing or strongly agreeing with this statement, only 17.9 percent of the respondents were in either of these two categories. A substantial majority (60.7 percent) of respondents either disagreed or strongly disagreed.

The question relating to commitment to the Church's goals also resulted in a larger percentage (71.1 percent) of the petitioners agreeing

TABLE 6.5. Comparison of the Six Religious Integration Questions: Catholics Only

	Percent Response					
	Strongly Agree/Agree		Undecided		Disagree/ Strongly Disagree	
Question	Petitioner	Respon- dent	Petitioner	Respon- dent	Petitioner	Respon- dent
Pride	91.0	60.7	6.6	17.9	2.5	21.4
Goals	43.1	17.9	23.6	21.4	33.3	60.7
Committed	71.1	34.5	19.0	27.6	9.9	37.9
Do not care	5.7	35.5	5.7	6.5	88.6	58.1
Values	87.1	64.3	7.3	17.9	5.6	17.9
Belong	9.9	37.9	5.0	10.3	85.1	52.8

than the respondents (34.5 percent). Almost 38 percent of the respondents disagreed as compared to less than ten percent of the petitioners. Less than 6 percent of the petitioners agreed that they do not really care what the Church says or does. In contrast, 35.5 percent of the respondents said this. The difference between the two groups on the next question ("It is important to maintain the values of the Catholic Church") was also large. Nearly 90 percent of the petitioners were in the two agree categories, and 5.6 percent disagreed. In contrast, approximately 64 percent of the respondents agreed while almost 18 percent disagreed. Finally, similar kinds of differences occurred when asked if they were at the point where they do not really know if they belong to the Church. The vast majority (85.1 percent) of petitioners disagreed compared to a bare majority (52.8 percent) of respondents.

To summarize, the petitioners were more likely to feel a sense of pride in being a member of the Church, to put the Church's goals ahead of their own, to be committed to the goals of the Church, and to say that it is important to maintain the values of the Church. On the other hand, the respondents were more likely to agree that they did not really care what the Church says or does and wonder if they really belong to the Church. It should be noted that, when I did the standard statistical tests, there were significant differences between the two groups on *all six* of these questions.

SUMMARY

Results from this survey strongly supported the previous research on social integration. I found that the two divorced samples had much lower rates of "normative integration." Higher percentages of both the divorced samples indicated they knew someone close to them who had obtained a divorce.

The Catholic Church speaks strongly about the family. My interviews with Catholics who had experienced a divorce indicated that they often felt as though they were outcasts. They perceived the Catholic Church and its representatives as favoring the married and ignoring the divorced. This perception manifests itself in a lower level of commitment to the Church. Even the annulled, who may be seen as having regained the "good graces" of the Church, may have lower levels of integration into the Church than do the married. Not only do the divorced and annulled show less attitudinal integration into the Church, but this extends to their actual behaviors. My results showed that both divorced groups were less likely to attend church. This was especially true for those who have married outside the Catholic faith. I also found religious homogamy to be related to divorce. The majority of those Catholics who had never been divorced were married to other Catholics.

My results also showed that I was working with samples of people who were above the national average in terms of percentage attending parochial school along with hours spent attending Mass. However, results also showed that neither having a Catholic education nor the number of years they went to parochial school was a significant factor.

Much research points to gender differences in terms of religious commitment. In this study, I was dealing with males and females who were typically members of a church; therefore, assessing commitment to such things as church membership was not possible. I should note that the majority of my respondents were female, which may give some indication that females are more likely to go to church, be members of church groups, and so forth.

When I analyzed all the measures of social integration presented in this chapter, I found very few differences based on gender. Males and females responses were identical, for example, on their numbers of church-affiliated groups, numbers of hours they spend with these groups, and numbers of years of Catholic education. I found it interesting that the differences that did appear indicated that males scored higher on commitment. As with Davidson and his colleagues (1997), I might conclude that when one compares Catholic male and female *church* members, there would be small differences; and, in fact, the males may be more committed.

The annulment process is argued by many within the Church to be a "healing" process, leading the individual back into the "fold." The findings in both Chapters 3 and 4 indicated that, to a certain extent, this may be the case. On all the measures in my study the annulled sample scored higher than the divorced. On seven of these measures the annulled had significantly different scores from the divorced. Although they did not differ significantly from the married sample on five of the measures, the annulled did on three measures. Two of these differences were general well-being questions, and the third related to belonging to the Church.

The "healing" process did seem to be the case for many of the annulled respondents, but I argued that it is not the case for all. One of the assumptions guiding my study was that there would be fundamental differences between those who petitioned for annulments and those who were respondents in terms of integration into the Church. This was the case. The petitioners were significantly more likely than the respondents to feel a sense of belonging to the Church. I would suggest that the Church's insistence upon an annulment, and the negative experiences the respondents had with the process, has had a significant impact on their sense of being Catholic.

Chapter 7

The Petitioners

I just felt that I needed to have some kind of clarification: where I stood with the church and I really wanted to find out about everything that I could about my failed relationship.

Martha, an annulment petitioner,
aged fifty-six and divorced three years

KNOWLEDGE OF AND FEELINGS ABOUT ANNULMENTS

I asked the petitioners how much they know about the annulment process, and their feelings toward annulments before they had actually gone through the process themselves. The most common response was that they knew little about annulments. This was coupled with a real lack of knowledge about what annulments involved and the process one goes through in order to obtain one. In one petitioner's words, "I had no knowledge on how an annulment worked and had no specific feelings regarding them." The primary issue for most petitioners was that an annulment was necessary in order to remarry in the Catholic Church.

A small minority wrote that they had a good understanding of what an annulment was and how to go about getting one. Most of these individuals had gained their knowledge from attending a divorce or separation group in which a leader (sometimes a priest) talked about the process. A few had attended annulment workshops.

Initial feelings about annulments were mixed. Some reported very positive attitudes: "I feel that it [the annulment] gives us a second chance in life to pick a more compatible and spiritual person to share

127

our lives with." A large percentage of petitioners initially were ambivalent or actually negative in their attitude about annulments. The following are statements made by individuals who initially were either ambivalent or negative in their view of annulments:

- I really did not understand the process and what it meant as far as the legitimacy of my kids.
- I had a rather cynical view of annulment before it was an issue of concern to me.
- Hypocritical process. I was angry that it would be easier for a murderer to get back into the Church than one divorced.

Others felt annulments were extremely difficult to obtain or cost a lot of money.

Many of the petitioners, who initially indicated neutral or negative feelings, had a different opinion when asked to give current views. For example, consider the following initial view of a sixty-three-year-old female who married at the age of twenty-one, had children, was married for thirty-five years, and obtained an annulment: "I used to think annulments were rare and, in some ways, evasive of Christ's injunctions concerning the sanctity of marriage." When asked her postannulment view, she said: "I now feel that I was too harsh in my judgments—that certain marriages can be doomed from the start and need to end."

A fifty-year-old female who had been married twenty-one years offered the following initial view of annulments:

Before I divorced I thought they [annulments] were a way of trying to make up for the decision to divorce. I don't believe in divorce and figured annulments were all right for serious problems—but were often misused by people wishing to get out of unhappy marriages and wishing to remarry.

Following the annulment, she stated: "I see them [annulments] as a healing process now—I feel everyone may be entitled to a 'fresh start' if in good conscience they decide to terminate a marriage."

These before-and-after statements were not unusual. Many petitioners initially offered cynical or negative positions but gave a positive view after going the process.

Although the majority of petitioners gave a positive postannulment impression of annulments, some did not. One petitioner, who was unsure of the process, originally "expected it to be more healing." Another person wrote: "I do not agree with annulments but they are a necessary evil if you wish to be in good standing with the Church." In fact, a number of people had at least some problem with annulments but recognized that it was required by the Church in order to remarry.

REASONS FOR SEEKING THE ANNULMENT

Approximately two years after obtaining a civil divorce the typical petitioner in my study started contemplating a religious annulment. Why did they even think about an annulment? Generally, they cited four categories:

1. Remarrying in the Church
2. Conforming to the Church doctrine
3. Being a "full-fledged" member of the Church
4. The belief that an annulment would be a "healing process"

The majority of petitioners gave a very simple reason for wanting to obtain an annulment—they wanted to remarry within the Catholic Church. For some there was only the possibility of marriage in the future; in other words, at the time they started the annulment process, there was no prospect for a future marital partner. One of the petitioners said, "if I should remarry I would like to be married in the Church." Another typical response was: "I knew I could not live alone for the rest of my life and I thought I'd want to remarry in the Church."

For other respondents, however, there was already someone in their life. One petitioner indicated that his girlfriend refused to date him if he did not proceed with an annulment. He filed, the annulment was granted, and, eventually, they married. Others indicated specifically that they were either dating someone seriously or were engaged and they wanted a church wedding.

Although remarriage in the Church was the dominant reason given, many petitioners did indicate that other factors were important. Many of these individuals were not even dating or contemplating a future marriage. They mentioned that they wanted to be in full accord with the Church and its doctrine. These people were trying to obey church law. For them, they were not "true" members unless they followed the Church's teachings. Some of my petitioners specifically mentioned the ability to receive the sacraments. These individuals were not aware seemingly of the fact that, even though they were divorced, they were still able to receive the sacrament of Holy Communion if they had not remarried (without the benefit of an annulment). What distinguished this group was the determination to obey the rules of the Church. This individual can be placed in the "extrinsic" category. Allport (1950, 1966) defined a person with an extrinsic motivation as one whose religion is used to support nonreligious ends.

A third closely related category was that of doing what the Church doctrine states in order to be, in the words of one of the respondents, a "full member of the Church community." This individual indicated that she felt outside the mainstream of the Church, that she was not "completely whole in the Church" unless an annulment was obtained. Time and time again petitioners reported that they were not a "full-fledged" member of the Church. These individuals were committed to their religion and what they wanted (and needed) was the Church's approval for their divorce. These individuals correspond to what Allport calls an "intrinsic" motivation. He defined individuals as having this kind of motivation when religion is an end in itself. Religion is a major focus and a guiding principle of their lives.

The fourth reason stated by respondents involved the healing process. As indicated in previous chapters, divorce was a very serious decision for the respondents. It affected not only the couple but had profound consequences for numerous significant others. In addition, the Catholic faith teaches that divorce is unacceptable. The combination of these factors resulted in tremendous emotional turmoil. The way in which one can return to the good graces of the Church and help resolve this emotional anguish is to go through the annulment process. The granting of an annulment could be seen as the "stamp of approval" that there never was a real marriage "in the eyes of God." One of the respondents stated: "I knew I was never really married and I wanted the verification from the Church and also to be married someday to the 'right person.' "

The Catholic Church states that the annulment process is therapeutic. In other words, by completing the often long and personal questionnaire that tribunals require, it may allow an individual to achieve a sense of closure on that experience in their lives. Presumably, once this as been achieved the individual can then go on and build a new life. This point of view was pointed out by petitioners often when asked why they sought an annulment and what affect the process had. The following is a sampling of the comments I received:

- My current feelings about annulments is that they are very helpful and insightful. During the annulment process you are forced to take a long, hard look at what happened before and during the marriage which may have lead up to the divorce.
- I believe that an annulment allows you to review your past marriage, discover the mistakes, and start over.
- It helped me to look back at history and facts that had been hidden. I learned a lot. I had done a lot to try to hold it together. I am glad I made the choice [to get an annulment]. I feel relieved.
- I saw the annulment process as a means of healing the wounds that were left after my divorce. My marriage was my whole life before the divorce. I felt like it was my fault, I went through a time when I was very insecure, and lost a lot of confidence in myself. My self-worth was zero. The annulment helped me to see that the breakdown of the marriage was not my fault.
- The process was mentally agonizing in recalling painful situations during the "marriage." The annulment served to reassure me that I had made the correct decision in requesting the divorce.
- It required a lot of soul-searching and introspection. Honest answers to the questions shed a lot of light on the relationship. It lifts a burden of guilt. It allows a person to be told by the Church that they are okay.
- Filling out the initial questionnaire (over sixty questions) helped me put all my insights from my counseling, self-examination, and recovery work into a concise, logical, organized form.
- It was a healing process. I had to recognize my contribution to the breakup and to acknowledge that there really was not a "true" marriage to begin with.

It seems evident that for these individuals, the annulment process re-affirmed their choice to divorce. For some, they needed to be told by this higher authority (i.e., the Catholic Church) that everything was now okay; that the divorce was not their fault; that they should not feel guilty about the divorce; that, indeed, the marriage never really existed. One indication of this latter point was the fact that, among the written responses, marriage was typically written in quotes, a sign that the person saw the union as, in fact, not really existing.

ROLE OF THE EX-SPOUSE

When I asked the petitioners if they thought their former spouses were aware that a petition for an annulment had been filed, approximately 75 percent of the sample replied in the affirmative. A little over 18 percent of the petitioners said their ex-spouse was not aware of a petition being filed, and the remaining 6.3 percent were uncertain.

I then asked the petitioners how their former spouse responded. Was she or he cooperative or uncooperative? Approximately 22 percent said their ex-spouse was neither cooperative nor uncooperative. Typical responses to this question were: "There was no role. I would go to visit the children and the papers would still be on the table. I think that she never filled them out." or "He was given the option to be included in the process. The only thing is that he signed the return receipt and received the paperwork and he never did anything beyond that."

A substantial number of ex-spouses played no role in the entire process. Given the often long and demanding nature of the questionnaire they were asked to complete, many chose to do nothing.

Almost 43 percent of the petitioners indicated that their former spouse was either "somewhat" or "definitely" cooperative. In fact, in one case, the former spouse actually helped by typing up the petitioner's (i.e., his ex-wife's) handwritten responses to the questionnaire.

Finally, almost 36 percent of the former spouses were described by the petitioner as being either "somewhat" or "definitely" uncooperative. The following are some of the comments from petitioners when asked about the uncooperative role of their ex-spouses in the process:

1. Well, she thought it would mean that the children would be illegitimate or something . . . which it doesn't, plus she didn't want it because it was something that I wanted, probably.
2. He didn't understand what it was. He didn't want me to get something that he wasn't going to have. He didn't realize that there is only one annulment per marriage.
3. He had a fit when he found out I was doing this. . . . He called me up cussing and swearing. He didn't want anybody to know what he had done. He said that he didn't want a record of this anywhere.
4. He told me that he had been petitioned. He was very angry that I was deserting him when he was already down. So he said: "Why should I help you out? I'm not even Catholic. This means nothing to me."

These quotes summarize the types of responses of those exspouses who were opposed to the annulment. The opposition from the first person dealt with two issues: the status of the children and a general opposition to the former spouse. The question of the legitimacy of the children came up time and again and will be dealt with in more detail later in this chapter.

The second quote described the common theme of anger and bitterness toward the former spouse. One very common effect of divorce is often strong negative feelings toward one's former spouse and, for some, they expressed clear efforts toward blocking their former spouse's efforts in anything as an indicator of retaliation.

The third quote was illustrative of a number of other respondents who stated that their former spouse was uncooperative for fear that events that occurred during the course of the marriage (e.g., an affair, alcoholism, abuse, etc.), would be exposed and he or she did not want that to be known by anyone.

The fourth response was indicative of another category of uncooperative respondents who typically had not wanted the divorce in the first place. Not only did they have to endure the breakup of the marriage, but they then had to experience the pain of an annulment. The fourth quote also embodied another type of uncooperative individual who was either not raised Catholic or only became Catholic at the urging of the former spouse. Many of these individuals wondered what the "big deal" was concerning an annulment.

ROLE OF THE CHILDREN

The majority (68.9 percent) of petitioners in the study reported that they had explicitly informed their children about the decision to seek an annulment. When asked why they did or did not talk to their children about this process very few gave any specific reasons. For those individuals who said they did not discuss it with their children the most common reason given was the fact that the children were too young to understand.

Those who responded in the affirmative identified two reasons. First, they indicated that as parents they had always been open and honest with their children. As a consequence, they chose to inform their children. One respondent felt very firmly that the children should be included: "They were directly affected by the marriage, could understand the situation, and had a right to know."

The second and most prevalent reason for discussing the annulment with the children concerned the issue of legitimacy. Many of the petitioners wrote that they needed to reassure their children that they were not illegitimate. One respondent reported a need to discuss the issue because her ex-spouse had told their children that, by having the marriage annulled, they were "illegitimate."

In the interviews with the petitioners, I actively pursued this issue of legitimacy. And, as with the questionnaire respondents, they had little to say. Some of the petitioners who had discussed this with their children reported receiving strong support from them. Some children, however, even though they had supported the decision to divorce, questioned the annulment. One petitioner, who had been married almost thirty years, said that her daughter supported her when she decided to divorce her father: "Go for it, Mom. You should have done this years ago." However, the daughter objected when she was told that an annulment was being sought. She asked the question that many children of petitioners asked: "What does that make us?" She was, of course, concerned about her legitimacy. Her mother went on to say that they discussed the ramifications of the annulment and that her daughter was satisfied with the fact that she was not illegitimate.

Other petitioners said that the children would "just not be interested" or, similar to the questionnaire respondents, that they were too young to understand. Although the annulment may have happened ten or fifteen years ago, some had never discussed it with their children even though they were now adults.

My impression was that although the children were said to be informed about the annulment, they were clearly not an integral part of the process.

THE ANNULMENT PROCESS

In Chapter 3, I described the typical process that dioceses go through when considering an application for an annulment. However, in my interviews with the petitioners I found considerable variation.

The Interview and Use of Questionnaire

The process typically began with the petitioner, discussing the possibility of getting an annulment with his of her parish priest.

Next, he or she contacted the tribunal, which sent a questionnaire for completion (use of the questionnaire was common). Sometimes the petitioner received a preliminary questionnaire that was followed by a more extensive one. The following were one respondent's comments concerning the nature of the questionnaire:

> Golly, it was like a made-for-TV movie. Oh, Lord! They asked me about sixty different questions. They told me to get a notebook and take it easy. It started out with the courtship. It started with the early years of the marriage. What would a typical day be like? Did he work? Did you work day or night or the opposite shift? Just things like that. It talked about the children. Then it talked about what finally started to break this up.

The petitioners always mentioned that there were questions dealing with the courtship, dating, their home life, and so forth. A sample version from one diocese appears in Appendix A.

Many of the petitioners found it to be useful, but some found the questionnaire painful. For example, the same person quoted previously continued:

> Even though it was extremely painful for me to have to think about this and go to bed with this and think about this all night long, it was really a very healing thing for me. Because once I had written it down I would go back and reread it. I could see from the very beginning this was doomed. This was doomed from the beginning. Truly, twenty-five years was more or less an endurance. It never really was a marriage.

Another petitioner had this to say: "It was an emotional thing. I couldn't handle more than two or three questions at a time. I'd get so emotional. It was ten years after the divorce. Those questions just brought everything back."

These quotes were typical. Most were able to deal with only a few questions at a time because they either required a lot of thought or were very painful.

The Hearing

Although completing a questionnaire was necessary, attending a hearing was not. Of the petitioners in my sample, only 24.1 percent indicated that they attended the hearing. For most of these individuals, attendance was required. The majority, then, did not attend the hearing. There were four typical responses for not attending:

1. They were either not aware that one was being held or, if they were aware, they did not know when it was being held.
2. They were informed it was not necessary to attend.
3. The location of the hearing was too far from where they lived.
4. They feared opening up "old wounds."

I would like to comment on the first and fourth reasons. The first reason seemed to indicate that the tribunal did not clearly convey this information to the petitioner. A sampling of quotes included:

- Did not tell me I could.
- I wasn't informed about the hearing.
- Did not know I could; it wasn't explained that I could.

This kind of response was by far the one most frequently mentioned and indicated a more general feeling on the part of the petitioners that they were not kept fully abreast of their case and what stage it was in.

In the fourth category of response the petitioners were very apprehensive about what the hearing would involve and how they would react. In the words of one respondent: "I think that I had been through so much pain going before the judge (i.e., the civil judge in the divorce case) that I just did not want to delve up anymore pain."

Would You Do It Again?

I was interested in whether the petitioner, following the completion of this process, would have still gone through the process. They were also asked to explain their answer. In contrast to many of the questions for which the respondents did not write anything or, at least, very little, everyone wrote something when asked this question and many of the answers were quite extensive.

Over 83 percent of my sample gave an affirmative response when asked if they would go through the process again. Only 10 percent reported they were uncertain. There were actually a few respondents who, after having gone through the process, became advocates for others. One petitioner, for example, a female who had been married for twenty-nine years, wrote that she needed "a lot of help and understanding" when she was getting her annulment. Appreciating the assistance she received, she decided to do the same for others. Another, a male who had been married for twenty-two years, recognized a "calling" and became a facilitator in the Beginning Experience program.

A large majority of petitioners had no serious problem with the process and indicated they would definitely repeat the procedure, knowing what they currently know. When asked to explain their responses, the reasons could be classified into three major groups.

1. It is required by the Catholic Church.
2. It is a healing process.
3. It is important to their current partner.

Petitioners typically pointed to the belief that an annulment is something that is required if one is to be a "good" Catholic. These individuals were typically born and raised Catholic. Catholicism, with all its teachings, had been thoroughly internalized by these petitioners, many of whom had spent part of their learning years in a Catholic school. The hold that the Church has with these people was very evident. Being Catholic was an integral part of their lives and they said they wanted to remain in the Church and receive its sacraments.

The following is a sampling of what some of these respondents had to say:

- I believe the annulment process is valid, and—though painful— it is the only process by which a person can continue to practice a "Catholic" faith if that person chooses or should wish to choose to be married again.
- I was born a Catholic and will die a Catholic (I hope). I believe and respect the teachings of the Church, although I, like others, sometimes try to pick and choose what I believe, what I want to believe. Basically, however, I believe in the Church and intend to follow its practices, including annulment.
- I would go through whatever the Church required of me to end my marriage. I am Catholic to the bone.
- Since the Church's stand remains that marriage within the Church is not possible without an annulment, it is still necessary if one is to "move on," as a Catholic.

Although many stated that an annulment was necessary to remain in good standing with the Church, it was not the most popular explanation. The dominant reason reported was one we have already encountered—it provided a sense of healing. Time and again people wrote, often quite extensively, about how they were required to look closely at their lives and their former marriages. The process was a catharsis for them, allowing them to think about the past and, although it was painful at times, to confront their demons and move on. One female petitioner spoke extensively about this:

By going through the annulment process I was able to take a look at where I was coming from when I picked the person I married and why the relationship did not grow. Taking a look at this helped me see the areas in my life I needed to work on. It also helped with the guilt I felt for my marriage failing, and helped me see there is nothing else I could have done to make my marriage work. I think going through the annulment process gives a person a big chance for personal growth.

Other petitioners stated:

- First, this process helped me to understand why my marriage was a bad one. I could understand my mistakes and my spouse's. It helped me to work through my grief process. It also taught me to be a better person and to use my knowledge in future relationships with my son, with other children, with friends of both sexes, and in another love/marriage.
- The annulment was a closure for me. The tribunal affirmed my belief that our marriage should never have taken place. I felt more at peace with the divorce and more reconciled with my Church as a result of the annulment.
- The process, especially answering the long questionnaire, sort of provided an opportunity to remember why I obtained the divorce. I remembered things I had put out of my mind.
- It is a very healing experience. It was like working through the grief process. You were able to look at the whole experience/ marriage and see what happened.
- The annulment process made me take a good look not only at myself and my family background, but also why I do certain things, like jumping into a marriage. It became evident that I did not know what marriage is about.

The third classifiable reason was the fact that they would go through it again because it was important to their current partner/ spouse. The following quote was given by a woman who was born and raised Catholic, had some Catholic schooling, and still identifies herself as Catholic:

My current husband is Catholic also and has never been married before and he wants the annulment so we can be married in the Church. I feel like the Catholic Church is out of touch with the modern world on this issue and I don't feel I need permission to marry when it's an issue between me and God. *But* I would do it again because it is so important to my husband.

Ten percent of the respondents were not sure whether they would have even started the process. One wrote that she taught "a divorce and beyond class. I hear the pain, anguish, and anger. I don't believe they are healing. That's what we're told to believe. It's basically a mandatory rule to remain Catholic if you want to marry."

Other petitioners offered more comprehensive reflections:

- If the Catholic Church can forgive other sins so readily by going to confession, I think it is hypocritical to say a person cannot join the Church or fully participate if they are already Catholic simply because they are divorced. I know people who are divorced because their spouse left them, filed, and received the divorce, although the other party did not want a divorce. The person not wanting the divorce has to prove church-accepted grounds to get an annulment. The whole process is too difficult, too long, and too painful.
- I went through the process hoping it would "prove" to me that there never was a "true marriage" with my former spouse. One of the reasons it took me so long to begin the process is I was not sure I would believe or agree with the decision they made. I am still not sure. The process was good; I grew through it, but I have still not fully accepted the annulment and have not moved on as I thought I would.

Less than 7 percent of the sample said they would not have started the annulment process if they had known what it would be like. The dominant reason was the pain and anguish caused by the entire process. One individual added that he thought it placed an undue burden upon the witnesses.

However, some of my petitioners indicated an actual pride in getting an annulment. In one individual's words, "I am extremely proud of being granted an annulment. I would do whatever it takes to get one." However, this person was in a distinct minority. Even for those who said they would still go through the process again there were feelings of ambivalence about either the concept of the annulment itself or the process they went through. One petitioner indicated that it was important to "obey" the rules of the Church—"even if I believe they are outdated, cause hardship, and pain and misunderstanding as well as alienation for many." Another felt that the process took too long and made people "feel as if they're waiting to get permission to come back into a church they love and respect."

CASE STUDIES

The following are four case studies which will illustrate the experiences that many petitioners had. Some of these typify the petitioner, and others are unique. Most of the sample who started the annulment process saw it through to the finish, but one did not. We start with her case.*

Joan

Joan was in her mid-sixties and was married for over thirty years. She was raised as a devout Catholic and acknowledged that religion was probably the most important thing in her life when she was growing up. Her mother was also a devout Catholic and Joan believed that her mother's faith was the "greatest gift that she [her mother] ever gave to me."

When asked if other faiths could provide the kinds of things she had learned in the Catholic faith, Joan gave an emphatic "NO." She had tried other religions but found them wanting: "Something, a real ingredient, is missing, like if you left the salt or seasoning out of the soup."

As might be expected, the divorce was extremely difficult, given the length of the marriage. She filed for the divorce because of various psychological problems that her ex-husband displayed. He had also been physically abusive on different occasions. Despite this situation, she agonized with the decision of proceeding with a divorce. She stated that he was "the only man that I have ever loved. It wasn't a decision that I wanted to make. It was a decision to stay alive or not."

Before the divorce she found herself living in a shelter for about a month. In the shelter she was not able to eat, sleep, or make any kind of major decision. However, as time went on, she believed that what she had to do became clearer. She filed for divorce.

When she was married she was very active in her church. Many of her fellow parishioners were far from supportive, however, when they

---

*In order to preserve their anonymity I have changed names along with any specific information which might inadvertently identify the respondents in the study.

learned about the divorce. Joan stated that after her divorce fellow parishioners would shun her when they saw her in public: "The people at church, especially the women, would see me in the store and would turn their backs and walk away. There are still a lot of them who won't talk to me."

In addition, her children were not supportive of the divorce. One of her children felt she should go back to her husband. Her son said he did not want to see or hear from her again unless she went back to her husband.

As a devout Catholic and family member, she was extremely hurt by the events that took place after divorcing her spouse. Indeed, the hurt was so intense that she "felt like the price to stay alive was too high." She went on to say she just could not take it any longer. What she did was talk to a friend who was also a therapist. Taking the advice of the therapist she entered a hospital. Her ex-husband wrote her letters during her stay, but she tore them up.

Prior to their divorce, Joan spent time in an abuse shelter. In the shelter, she called a priest. He talked to a fellow priest in the area who ministered to the divorced. This priest visited Joan in the shelter and provided both spiritual assistance and help with practical matters. He also suggested that she apply for an annulment.

Annulments were not new to Joan. She had heard about them long before her divorce. Her opinion, however, was very negative. She heard that annulments were a "cop-out for people who had a lot of money." Joan was raised a strict Catholic and did not believe in divorce, let alone annulments. A friend had gotten an annulment and Joan was disapproving. The topic of annulments had also come up with her children and they were opposed. From their perspective it made them illegitimate. Joan remarked that not only did her children feel that way, but "to a small extent" so did she.

Despite her initial resistance, Joan went ahead and applied for the annulment. I asked her to explain what an annulment is. She stated:

> It means that back in the beginning of the marriage that there was some reason why the marriage was not valid. Because of either emotional, physical factors, one person is not mature enough, that there is not a legitimate marriage because of some reason . . . for some reason there is something lacking that keeps it from being

valid. It's made with good intentions, but the ingredients to make for a good and healthy marriage are not there.

She completed the paperwork and consulted with the priest but went no further. When asked why she stopped the process, Joan said there were many reasons. First, she stated that she was not dating anyone. In her words, she was "still afraid of men." Second, she did not want others to become involved in the annulment. She did not feel it was appropriate that others should have to testify about her, her ex-husband, and their marriage. Joan felt that she had a good case for declaring the marriage null and void (listening to the specific circumstances of her marriage and the events before the marriage, I believe she would have no difficulty in getting an annulment, even in a diocese where very strict guidelines are used), but stopped at least partly because she did not want others to get involved.

The third major factor in halting the process was the belief that it would make her children illegitimate. She maintained that this was the crucial factor: "I guess the biggest factor is that I don't want them [her children] to feel illegitimate. They were definitely not illegitimate and I don't want them to feel that way . . . the whole outlook on the annulment needs to be changed."

I asked her further questions on her position on divorce and how she thought the Church should deal with this issue. The following is the dialogue on these issues.

RJ: You mentioned a moment ago the *Baltimore Catechism* and "death do us part." What is your view of the Church's stance on divorce?

JOAN: I think that the pope is not realistic. I think that he speaks like his head is in the sand. He is staying in the dark, and this is the way I want it to be and not really the way it is. The Church, uh, Father [the priest who suggested the annulment] was talking once about when so many things were made, the life span was not as nearly long as it is now. People change so much and they live longer. It isn't realistic to have till "death do us part."

When I was in divorce groups, the majority of women—in fact, every woman that I knew except one left because of an abusive situation; they had to get away. They didn't want to leave. It tore their life apart in every way. It destroyed my life. It took everything away from me that I loved. They [the women] don't divorce because they want to. The Church is not realistic. We don't want it this way and we don't accept it. This is reality. This is the way it is. I don't think that you change the basic structure of the Church. It is time to take a look at this, the way it is, and the situation needs to be changed.

RJ: What would you do if you were head of the Church? What would you say about divorce? Would you do away with annulments?

JOAN: The annulment process, the first part (of course I haven't been through the second part) I would make mandatory. That is so healing. I would have people there for free counseling with people going through divorce, going through separation, someone there if you have to leave in a dangerous situation. Someone who would help them. . . . If I was the Church I would look at the whole marriage, especially toward the end. I wouldn't put the emphasis on the beginning. I would change the whole outlook toward annulment. Over the life of this marriage, it has died. As though the spouse is dead. I have trouble with going back with my marriage. For twenty-five years it was beautiful. I have trouble with saying it never happened.

RJ: Can you understand why some people would want an annulment? Or be in favor of annulments?

JOAN: Well, they get the Church's blessings and they can get remarried in the church. That is the biggest reason for me to go through an annulment. . . . Maybe if no children were involved I could see an annulment process. I could see it if someone wanted it but not mandatory. If you get married in the Church and accepted in the Church, then you have to have an annulment to remarry.

Joan went on to identify some problems she saw with the Catholic Church. She believed the Church did not really allow for change:

If some people want to go with the Latin mass, then make it available. Don't say that you can't do it. They aren't taking the people into consideration and they are losing people—young people because of divorce and the older people because they have changed so much that it isn't their church. You are losing people that are my age, an awful lot of people. . . . You don't meet their needs. . . . I was in a small group that was reaching out to people going through divorce. I had no idea at the time that I was going to be divorced. I went to two meetings. They didn't want to deal with divorce. They don't want to deal with reality. They don't want to hear our needs and meet them. That is where the Church will eventually be destroyed. . . .

Joan's views were quite unique among the petitioners with whom I spoke. She obviously had thought about her marriage, getting a divorce, and obtaining an annulment very seriously. However, although she was able to file for a divorce despite the enormous impact it had, she was not able to follow through with the annulment. She believed the questionnaire process was very helpful in contrast to some who said it was too long or too intrusive. Her major reasons for not completing the process were unselfish—she did not wish for her children to consider themselves illegitimate and she did not feel it was right to get others (i.e., witnesses) involved in taking a stand on her marriage.

Joan has remained single, was working part-time, and, despite some of her experiences from fellow parishioners after her divorce and some problems she saw with the Church, she remains a devout Catholic.

Margaret

Margaret was in her mid- to late fifties, had a master's degree, and was born and raised Catholic. She and her ex-husband dated for two years and were married for more than twenty-five years. The last five years, however, found them living, in her words, "apart in the same house." She felt herself "basically dying." When one of their children experienced some problems, they sought counseling. The counseling provided "new insights" for her. Margaret sought a divorce.

The decision to divorce was not made lightly. She had struggled with it for a number of years, but "could no longer endure the unhappiness." When thinking back about whether to seek a divorce, she stated:

At that time while I was agonizing over the decision, I felt that my spouse and I were good people. . . . We both openly committed to marriage and the institution of marriage of being forever.

We had children. We believed at the time we married that marriage was for the procreation of children and for the lifelong commitment. We were married in the Catholic Church and we were going to do everything humanly possible that would work. There was a point in time that the marriage began to die and it did die. . . . Even though my spouse and I tried counseling and programs offered through the Church nothing brought us closer or to a mutual understanding of our roles and a mutual relationship in marriage anymore. I had to face that it had ended.

As with many other women her age, Margaret encountered dramatic changes after the divorce. She had been working for five years prior to the divorce and she continued to do so after the breakup. Her children were now older and out of the home and she often felt alone. She commented:

It was painful for me to become single again. I came from my mother's home to living with my spouse and I was in the real world at fifty years old and now a single woman. I found that I could not expect support from my children. I did not get it from friends. My faith community was not there. I was rejected. . . . I was in this position of being a divorced woman.

Margaret said that she was "always aware" of annulments but did not really know what one entailed. After the divorce she started investigating the process and finally applied for an annulment. She worked with someone in the Church over a three-month period and often experienced strong emotions during this stage: "I did a lot of crying. I was opening a lot of wounds. I uncovered more pain than I had realized that I had been through before."

Margaret was one of the few who actually attended the hearing. There were two priests who asked her various questions. One, she felt, was very kind and understanding, and the other was more formal. She believed that the hearing was extremely fair and was done in a "kind and respectful manner."

Her ex-husband did not really participate in the proceedings, but essentially gave his blessing to her. She asked him to read what she had written for the tribunal, and he only changed one word in the entire document. When the annulment was granted, he removed his wedding ring, called all the children, and said that the marriage was now over. Margaret believed this had a tremendous impact on the relationship between her and her ex-spouse:

> The tensions between us disappeared. At this present time we are friendly with one another, communicate about the children, and get together during the major holidays. I think that there has been healing for both of us. A nice relationship has continued.

Margaret received no information as to the grounds for the annulment being granted. She believed that the reasons could be found in the childhood experiences and emotional deprivation that both she and her husband experienced. She felt their backgrounds precluded the ability to form a loving marital bond as adults.

Margaret reported very positive feelings about the entire annulment process and indicated a number of times that she found the experience extremely healing, with no negative consequences. At the same time there were a number of unexpected positive aspects. She gained new insights into herself; this, she believes, has led to a better relationship between herself and her ex-husband.

Margaret did see why some people would be opposed to annulments. She believed that some individuals might not want an institution telling them what they did or did not do wrong in their marriage. Others, she felt, may believe that the marriage was valid, especially when children were brought into the world as a result of the union. Still others may think that the annulment process is degrading and fails to recognize their own dignity. Although she had very positive experiences, she stated that an annulment was not the best way for the Catholic Church to deal with divorce. When asked what she would do, she remarked:

> I guess that I would go back and help prepare our young people for marriage in a much better way. We need to change our views. Things do happen. We need to get in touch with reality. Whatever process that we can use to help us achieve that reality, we should do it. I don't have a specific vehicle or procedure to do that. With the good hearts and minds of our people in the Church, we could figure it out.

Margaret has remained a strong Catholic throughout her life, as has her ex-spouse. She is grateful for the guidance that the Church has given her, but does see problems within the Church. In addition to rethinking annulments as a way of dealing with divorce, she felt that the Church needs to reassess its position on divorce:

> I think that the Church needs to open up to the reality of the situation of divorce. I am using the experience in our country of 50 percent of the marriages ending in divorce. . . . We as a church must be more understanding, compassionate, and forgiving with those who have gone through an extremely painful experience in life. We seem to be able to do that with widows and widowers but we can't do that for the separated at the institutional or the official level. There are good people in the Church and they can show compassion, but the teachings do not show that kind of compassion.

Margaret stated that she saw the Church as very patriarchal and felt that, "as a woman my righteous rage is being ignored by the Church." She would allow priests to marry, democratize the Church, and continue ways to serve the downtrodden.

Despite seeing these problems, she currently did not feel that she would leave the Church. Although the Church had its "ups and downs," she had not been able to find any other church that gave her "the Eucharist or the opportunity to share the scriptures, that homily, that community, and that sense of being together and uniting in prayer."

Frank

Frank and his ex-wife dated for only a few months, but were married for over twenty years. They were separated for approximately five months and, when I talked with him, he had been divorced a little over one year. He indicated that his ex-spouse had filed for the divorce, telling him that she was not able to live "life to its fullest" if she continued in the marriage. According to Frank, there were significant problems in the marriage that originated with one of the children. The family dynamics among the three were such that even with family therapy, the situation seemed hopeless. The situation improved almost immediately, he stated, when his ex-spouse left the marriage.

Unlike most divorces, the children remained with Frank. This was due to the fact that his ex-wife did not want custody. The children (teenagers) rarely saw their mother even though she lived close by; but, as Frank said, "she does try." When they did see their mother it typically was for only a few hours. They spent their time together doing such things as going to a movie or dinner. Although they have stayed all night with her only a handful of times, she does call them regularly.

Frank indicated that the divorce was not only difficult because they were married for so long but because they were very active in the Church during their marriage. Both he and his ex-wife helped prepare engaged couples for marriage. On World Marriage Day, they had even given a talk about marriage. Given these experiences it was not difficult to see how a divorce would not only be personally devastating but embarrassing.

Frank and his ex-wife moved around quite a bit because of his job. She dealt with the moves quite well until their last move. He said there had been a history of depression in her family and that it had manifested itself in her. Despite having an advanced degree, she was not able to work outside the home because of severe headaches. After their last move she received psychological counseling and went on medication. Things improved and she became able to work outside the home. Only two months after she started working she wanted a separation; five months later she sought a divorce.

Almost the entire time they were married she had stayed at home, cooked, cleaned, ran errands, and took care of the children. Once the divorce occurred he became responsible for these activities. As most single parents soon discover, daily life can be overwhelming:

> My ex-wife was a gourmet cook and a stay-at-home mom so that she could keep the house looking neat and clean. She cooked; she ran all the errands for the kids—if they had a doctor's appointment or any activities after school—and now all of a sudden I had to do it all. I had to learn to cook. . . . But the errands, gosh! I didn't know if I was coming or going. It's unbelievable. You cannot imagine how difficult it is to be a single

parent. I was always wondering how the kids were and making decisions about taking them to therapy and just what is going on in their minds and trying to communicate with them. I tried to put my own life together. It is very difficult and unbelievable.

Their older child, along with Frank, was in counseling. Both had the same therapist. Frank's ex-wife also started seeing a therapist at the same counseling center. Her disclosure of wanting a divorce not only was a shock to Frank but to her therapist as well. Frank stated: "When she announced that she wanted a divorce her therapist took it so hard that afterward she told me, 'I was not prepared for this.'" Frank indicated that he thought his ex-wife was not being truthful with the therapist and that her depression was a major factor in their divorce.

When I moved from the divorce to the topic of annulments, Frank said that annulments were not new to him. Given the fact that he was active in the Church and gave presentations on marriage, he was much more conversant with them than most of my respondents. In addition, he became active in a divorced and separated Catholics group. Once a year they would have a priest come and talk about annulments. Through these talks he also became very aware of what the acceptable grounds for an annulment were in his diocese.

Frank spoke to the parish priest and discussed the marriage and what he thought the grounds for the annulment should be. He argued that the predisposition for depression had existed before they were even married. Remember, he stated that others in her family had problems with this condition. He even stated that his former in-laws were willing to state this in a letter to the marriage tribunal. Furthermore, he had other witnesses willing to testify about the long history of depression.

The grounds, as Frank stated, seemed beyond question. However, the petition for annulment was turned down before it was even sent to the tribunal. His parish priest took the petition to the tribunal and, only nine days later, he was informed that the case had no merit. What was the reason for turning down this petition when so many others which may seem so questionable are not? Frank stated it this way:

> The Church rejected my petition outright without submitting it to the tribunal. The judicial vicar rejected it outright because the depression was not manifested on the day of the marriage. They

said that genes don't count. . . . Your marriage is still seen in the eyes of the Church as valid. End of discussion.

Frank was dumbfounded. He then proceeded to apply to the local tribunal and was told the same thing. Failing there he applied to the tribunal in the diocese where they were married. He was again told the same thing. He even went so far as to ask his ex-wife to apply for an annulment, thinking that the Church might pursue other grounds with her. She told him she would consider it but, at the time of our interview, had not done anything about it.

I asked what his reaction was to being turned down. Frank responded: "Shock! It's bad enough to be rejected by one's wife. Now, I felt that my church was rejecting me. Amazingly, so many things went through my mind: Well, I'll become an Episcopalian."

Frank was engaged and felt that the church was wrong and being unfair in this matter: "The Church is telling me that I am not entitled to a best friend and the Church is telling me that I'm not qualified to a full-time mother." He seemed very concerned about the children and providing them with two parents. At another point he stated:

I think that it is so cruel to tell a mother or father that their children are not entitled to a stepparent. . . . Children need a mom and a dad. To say that you cannot remarry because you don't have valid grounds for an annulment is just forcing the children to live in an environment that is less than ideal.

He also said that he thought he had grounds for an annulment and that he had many people who were be willing to testify that depression was inherited: "I thought the Church would be more progressive with recognizing that. These tendencies are inherited. . . . The Church wasn't willing to accept that argument."

For Frank, getting an annulment so that he could remarry in the Church was crucial:

The thought of having to remarry outside the Church is very painful. Do we go to a Protestant denomination or do we go a justice of the peace? We would not have the involvement of God in our marriage vows, and that is not acceptable.

What made this case even more interesting was that there was a priest who was a relative of Frank's new fiancée. His advice was to keep appealing so that the judicial vicar would be forced to submit it to the tribunal. Others also told him to appeal it, to Rome if necessary. He believed, however, that the psychological toll that this would create would be too much.

Given the fact that Frank was so active in the divorced and separated group, I asked if he was aware of other cases in which a petition had been filed and the case was denied. He stated that he certainly was aware of other cases but did not know of even one where the petition was denied. He even gave an example of someone who had gotten two annulments and was currently seeking a third.

I asked him how he felt about this, especially regarding the person had already been granted two annulments. He responded that, after hearing about the first two marriages, an annulment was understandable and that they made sense in both instances. However, he said, "I think mine makes sense, too."

Frank strongly believed that the Catholic Church "should not go in the same direction as Protestant churches" in terms of recognizing all divorces as legitimate. "We cannot make it that easy. I do believe that we do have to have an annulment process." He went on to state that the Church needs to consider changing the doctrine that an annulment be granted only if there was some defect prior to the marriage:

> I think that the Church has to look at how the people have changed during their marriage and look at the state of the marriage at the time of the divorce. Marriage is a process, a continuing journey. This is not applicable to me. I think that the Church should change, that the Church needs to look at the marriage at the time of divorce. Not just the marriage at the time of the marriage.

Frank was born and raised a strict Catholic. As a child he went to parochial school and attended Mass six times a week. When he married, he and his former spouse, who was also raised Catholic, attended Mass every week. Despite having his annulment petition rejected he still continued to attend Mass twice a week and saw Catholicism as an essential part of his life. The possibility of leaving the Church had entered his mind, but this thought lasted less than a month. He saw some problems with the Church, especially with the laws: "I believe that the Church is not as compassionate as it needs to be. Again, I find that the priests are compassionate, but church laws are not." When asked if he felt that the Church had let him down, Frank responded in the affirmative. He felt that he had given a lot to the Church and the Church did not reciprocate. But, in the end, he was a devout Catholic and there was really nothing he could imagine that would lead him to leave the Church.

Judy

Judy was a lifelong Catholic. She attended parochial school and went to Mass almost daily. She was currently in her mid-forties and worked at a Catholic university in the West. Although her financial condition suffered after the divorce, she expressed the strong belief that her life changed almost immediately for the better. Judy's ex-spouse had problems with alcoholism, often berated her, and sometimes became violent. She discovered after the divorce, which she initiated, that she was not the "stupid bitch" that he kept telling her she was. She became very active in the Church and discovered she was competent and a "good, caring person."

Prior to her divorce she worked with a program in the Church that introduced adults to the Catholic faith. As a part of this program, annulments were discussed. Because of this Judy had a good knowledge of annulments and the process involved in obtaining one. Prior to this, however, her only knowledge or impression of annulments was that you could essentially buy one for yourself.

About eighteen months after the divorce was finalized she initiated the annulment process. The procedure she went through was very typical. She first met with a church deacon who helped her file the case. The deacon had her tell her story from the time she and her ex-husband started dating. Judy completed a short questionnaire followed by a longer one. She followed a strict plan for completion of the longer questionnaire. She had as a goal the completion of three questions a night starting with the easiest and then working her way up to the harder questions. She also provided the names of witnesses to be contacted.

Judy discussed the annulment with her ex-husband. Since he was non-Catholic he had very little interest in or sympathy for the whole matter. He told her that the tribunal had contacted him and that he did not respond. He also said that he was very angry and felt as though she was deserting him when he was already down. Judy said that he told her: "Why should I help you out? I'm not even Catholic. This means absolutely nothing to me."

She and her ex-husband had two young children who were probably not able to fully understand the concept of annulment. Judy indicated that she discussed the matter with them and they had a number of questions about it. She talked to them about the need to "get these things off my chest" and the legal divorce did not meet this need. She discussed the matter of illegitimacy and the myth that you cannot receive Holy Communion if you are divorced.

Judy said that she had to disclose very intimate details of her life. This, of course, was very difficult to do, especially at a very vulnerable time in her life. She also wondered if they would accept her case and what they would think of her as a person. She did not have to worry about the former question; her petition for the nullity of the marriage was granted on the grounds of lack of due discretion.

Despite some minor problems, Judy had a very positive opinion about annulments and their effects. In her words, an annulment was a "very freeing experience." In contrast to most of the petitioners who sought an annulment because they wanted to remarry, Judy had no such plans. In fact, at the time of the interview, she was not even dating. Her major reason for going through the process was to learn about herself, what went wrong with the marriage, and how to avoid those same pitfalls in any future relationship. She indicated that the entire process was very healing:

> After I finished answering all of the questions and I turned all of my information in, I made an appointment with a priest to go through Reconciliation. I was able to really basically put the marriage behind me and to forgive a lot of the things that happened with him [her ex-husband]. I have no problem communicating with him now at all. He still does. When I address him, I look directly at him. When he communicates with me, he looks

directly at the floor. He can't look at me. He can't discuss our children or things that are happening.

The only problem she reported with the entire procedure was that it tended to be a "very cold process." At least this was what she perceived in her diocese.

I still have some qualms over the fact that respondents . . . get this letter and only get sixty days to turn their testimony in. I think that takes a longer length of time for them just to adjust to the shock of it. Because most of them have not been warned by their former spouse that this was going to take place.

She said that the way in which her archdiocese conducted the process was appealing. The petitioner was offered the name of an advocate and was encouraged to contact that person to assist in the process. The advocate then went over the procedures, heard their story, and answered any questions that the petitioner had.

Judy felt that the Church needed to educate people about its real position on divorce and remarriage. She said that many people felt that the Church was not accepting of the divorced person, but that was not the case. Individuals felt that "if you get divorced you are sinning against the Church. There's a lot of people who are alienated and hurt by that who don't need to be alienated and hurt because it's just not true." She firmly believed that the divorced person was still welcome in the Church and that it was only the case where a person remarried without obtaining an annulment where a problem existed.

Judy is currently an advocate for anyone who might be involved in the annulment process. In order to be an advocate one must be appointed by the archbishop and go through special training. Typically, a letter is sent from the director of advocate services at the tribunal to the petitioner indicating that the advocate has been assigned to help in the process. It is up to the petitioner to then contact the advocate. If the petitioner has not done this in approximately two to three weeks, then the advocate contacts the petitioner.

At the initial meeting Judy hears the petitioner's story. After this, they review the questionnaire that the petitioner will need to complete. In this particular archdiocese the questionnaire consists of three sections: one for the marriage, a second for oneself, and the third for the ex-spouse.

After the petitioner has completed the questionnaire Judy meets with him or her again, looks over the questionnaire, and, if necessary, makes suggestions for changes. Judy then writes an advocate's brief. This brief includes the divorce decree, both the short and long questionnaire, an impression of the petitioner, and the grounds for which Judy thinks the annulment should be sought.

Although she probably deals more often with the petitioner she did state that she may also work with the respondent. Judy indicated that a lot of advocates do not work with them because respondents are very angry when they receive the letter from the tribunal indicating that a petition has been filed. She stated:

> They [the respondents] are opposed for many different reasons. One is out of sheer anger to begin with. Usually they are not the one who initiated the divorce. They believe that the sacrament was what the priest performed at the wedding ceremony. They don't see the sacrament having been the commitment between the two people.

Judy's case was unique in that she not only saw the need to bring some kind of closure to her own marriage through the annulment process, but she personally witnessed some of the problems with the process and chose to become an advocate in order to get people through the "cold" aspects. Not only does she put in long hours performing this role but retraining is expected every year. In addition, she does this strictly on a volunteer basis; there is no pay involved.

SUMMARY

The petitioners in this study came from throughout the country. I noticed that there was considerable variation in the annulment procedure from diocese to diocese. Although all required a questionnaire to be completed, there seemed to be little else that was consistent. I was also struck with the variation in the impressions that these individuals had with the process. For some petitioners the process, or at least parts of it, seemed cold; for others it was not. Some of the respondents felt their parish was welcoming, others thought their divorce made them second-class citizens in their church.

Finally, I cannot help but be baffled by Frank's case. If any case seemed clear, it was this one. Yet of all the people I talked with, his was the only case that was turned down. Certainly it would seem that the tribunals he was appealing to were far more restrictive in their grounds for an annulment than are most in the United States.

.

Chapter 8

The Respondents

. . . then I go seek an annulment and then I try to create this case in front of the Catholic Church that makes it sound like it wasn't a marriage to begin with. I mean, you can write up a case, you know, for anything. So, I pick out all these things and I live the rest of my life with an annulment and a lie, because I want an annulment. So the rest of my good standing with the Catholic Church is really a lie.

> Sally, aged fifty-seven,
> a lifelong Catholic

The vast majority of individuals in my study were petitioners. However, I asked the sample if they would provide the name and address of their ex-spouse so that I could include them in my study. Unfortunately, very few did this. As a consequence I sought a sample of respondents, that is, people who did not initiate the annulment, from other sources. During the course of my study, *Shattered Faith,* written by Sheila Rauch Kennedy (1997), was published. She received numerous letters from people who were also respondents in annulment cases. Ms. Kennedy responded to these people and was kind enough to include a card describing my research and how to contact me. As a result I was able to obtain a sample of respondents. This was a highly select group of individuals that represented those who not only cared enough to write to Ms. Kennedy, but also did not support the concept of an annulment. Because of these people, however, I do know that some individuals disagree with the concept of annulment and, through their questionnaire and interview responses, what the disagreements entail.

QUESTIONNAIRE INFORMATION

About one-fifth of the respondents were first informed of the petition for an annulment either by a letter or phone call from their former spouses. In the remaining cases the marriage tribunal informed them by way of a letter. I did have one unusual case in which a respondent learned that the former spouse intended to initiate annulment proceedings as part of the divorce decree.

Table 8.1 presents the responses to the relevant annulment questions. When asked if they knew why their former spouse had petitioned for the annulment the vast majority (80 percent) replied in the affirmative. The reason given by almost all the petitioners, according to the respondents, was to be able to "marry in the Church." Only two respondents gave other reasons. One said that she believed her ex-spouse petitioned to go along with the rules of the Church and to be a good Catholic, and the other indicated that he thought his ex-wife filed for an annulment to justify the divorce and "her adultery."

How did these respondents feel about annulments before the process started? The plurality reported that they had no real idea about or knowledge of annulments. Some of those who did report some familiarity with annulments had a favorable opinion of them. One respondent, who said that he was conversant with annulments, wrote that he was hopeful that one would be granted even though his former wife was the petitioner. Another wrote: "I had always staunchly defended the Church against accusations that annulments could be bought or gotten capriciously." A third thought the process could be a healing

TABLE 8.1. Responses to Five Annulment-Related Questions: Respondents Only

Question	Percent Saying "Yes"
Do you know why your ex-spouse sought an annulment?	80.0
If you have children, were they informed?	89.7
Did you attend the hearing?	14.6
Did your ex-spouse attend the hearing?	14.3
Did you ask witnesses to write a letter?	53.3
Was the annulment granted?	81.3

one. Some felt annulments were permissible in certain circumstances. One individual wrote: "I believed before my experience that they were only given for very *grave* reasons, not for reasons that could perhaps be worked out with proper counseling."

Of those respondents who had children, almost nine out of ten told their children of the annulment. This figure is somewhat higher than that given by the petitioners (68.9 percent). Of those who told their children, a common theme was: "They have a right to know," "they were old enough to understand," and "I have always been open with them."

Less than 15 percent of the respondents attended the tribunal hearing. Of those who did attend, the primary reason was to argue in favor of the marriage and against the annulment being granted. One person called it a "kangaroo court," another referred to it as an "interrogation," and a third stated that she went to hear her "sentence" being read. For the majority who did not attend, the major reasons were, in order of frequency mentioned,

1. they were not invited to attend (26.1 percent),
2. they were not allowed to attend (17.4 percent),
3. they lived too far away from where the hearing took place (17.4 percent),
4. they were not aware of the fact that they could attend (13.0 percent), and
5. they were opposed to annulments and did not want to participate in any way (8.9 percent).

Some of the respondents showed their opposition to the annulment by going before the tribunal and arguing for the marriage, and others demonstrated their opposition by staying away. As might be expected, the majority of the respondents did not know if their ex-spouse had attended the hearing or not.

Slightly over one-half of the respondents asked witnesses to write letters for them. The letters were written primarily by friends and relatives and, in some instances, a counselor. The process took a little over a year and 81.3 percent said that an annulment was granted. However, in 9.4 percent of the cases no decision had been reached yet. If only half of these are granted (which is probably low), that would mean that in 86 percent of the cases an annulment was granted. Almost all those who originally could be placed in a neutral category in terms of knowledge about and feelings toward annulments had an opinion after having gone through the process. One respondent saw an annulment as a good source of closure to the marriage. A second viewed an annulment as permissible when there was a "real impediment" to the marriage. The overwhelming majority reported very negative attitudes. Some of the comments were: "annulment is an insult to injury"; "it is hypocritical, biased, disgraceful, laden with injustice"; "they are extremely hurtful and make the healing process take longer."

Among those who initially had negative feelings, only one person changed to a positive stance. This individual originally had a "rather cynical view of annulment." This respondent attended an annulment seminar and afterward reported that it "can help in the growth process. . . . The annulment process was a closure for me. The tribunal affirmed my belief that our marriage should never have taken place. I felt more at peace with the divorce and more reconciled with my church as a result of the annulment. . . ."

Almost all the respondents who initially held a negative attitude toward annulments before they went through the process kept that opinion when it was over. One respondent wrote that annulments were "a complete and unmitigated farce. . . . I felt raped by the tribunal. No one seemed to grasp anything I was writing (and I wrote plenty)." Another individual who had converted to Catholicism left the Church after the annulment experience. She stated that her Catholic friends had told her that she "will burn in hell. . . . I already have been through hell with the divorce and annulment circus. So let it be."

Very few respondents originally were in favor of the annulment process. Of those who were, most maintained this positive view. One, however, who had "staunchly defended" the Church's position on annulments, became adamantly opposed. This person wrote quite extensively on her current opposition:

Now I see that the Church has no care at all for children or for their parents. It is vile to say that people have not been married at all.

I realized that I had been used. I would not have gone to that hearing or whatever it was and allowed the monsignor to tape my response to irrelevant and absurd questions. But they had been hassling me for a couple of years and I thought I would just put an end to it. As it was, I was like a criminal in some place where you are judged on something you are not even told, and you have absolutely no say.

. . . I used to be a very sincere and devoted Catholic, as I believed my husband to be. I often went to daily Mass. . . . We did not practice birth control, accepting the Church's teaching in that matter, absurd as it may seem from the vantage point of the present. In spite of being an educated person, I totally accepted the authority of the Church. . . .

Because of the above, it was a great shock to me to discover that "the Church," this great holy institution that I had accepted to be sort of overseen and protected from error by God Himself (!) would, in order to be consistent with its teaching that divorce can never be allowed, simply deny the facts of my life and that of my children. . . .

And so a great veil was torn from my eyes. It was terrible. For many years I grieved over my loss (not only my marriage, my wonderful large happy intact family, but the Church itself and all I had believed in) and eventually (after close to thirty years) I realized that the lesson life had taught me was valuable (albeit painful) and that my children were just as well off to have been spared those lies.

CASE STUDIES

The following are the stories of six individuals who went through the annulment process and were very much opposed to having their former spouses petition for an annulment to have their marriages declared null and void.

Jane

Jane was a very bright and articulate female approximately fifty years of age. She and her ex-husband John, the parents of three children, were married almost twenty years and dated for several months before they were married. Jane was born and raised Catholic and still remains in that faith despite her struggles with the Church over the annulment issue. When asked why she remained Catholic, she really could not explain it. She stated that it is, for her, "a mystery. . . . Why am I here? I'm mad; I'm mad. I can't walk away. I wish I could. I think in many ways that would be the authentic thing to do." What led this lifelong Catholic to reach this point?

After two decades of marriage, a divorce was granted. When asked for the reasons for the divorce Jane declared that it was a basic incompatibility: "We never learned how to fight and fight fairly and get over it. He would go into great pouting fits that would last for weeks. And it just wore us both down." She went on to state that the marriage reached the point where almost anything would precipitate an argument, and she and her husband did not know how to disagree with one another and then resolve issues amicably.

However, they still continued to see one another for two years after the divorce. Although John had a separate residence he was often at her house. Jane stated that she and John had a lot in common in that they still shared the children and participated in common hobbies. In fact, she stated that she honestly believed that they would get back together one day. She felt that the divorce would not only enable them to confront but to resolve the issues that originally separated them. Eventually, she felt that, "we probably would remarry and that we'd live happily ever after."

Her hope was abruptly shattered when John met another woman— in Jane's words, "a soul mate." This occurred approximately two years after they had divorced. In the beginning Jane did not know about the relationship. Given the belief that she and John would get back together, she reported that this discovery was devastating for her. In addition, Jane had also learned that she had breast cancer and underwent a mastectomy. Frightened for her physical self, and trying to deal with her emotional self, she stated: "I thought emotionally that I had died. I never dreamed that there would be anybody else." She felt that, if anything, John would live as a "hermit." John remarried and, according to Jane, seemed very happy.

Having faced the end of this chapter in her life, she then had to struggle with the fact that her marriage was going to be declared null by her church. I started our conversation with the question of how she first learned about annulments in general. Jane indicated that she had known about them all of her life. She had not known anyone who had actually received an annulment and she believed they were granted in very limited circumstances: "that either the wife or husband were alcoholics or they had never consummated the marriage." She said that belief remained with her until her twenties. It was around that time that she started to become aware of the fact that annulments were being granted for various psychological reasons: "Maybe there is some validity, because if you are living in a hell of an emotional turmoil, how can this go on? And maybe it would be better" if the marriage ended. It would be reasonable to annul the marriage on those kinds of grounds.

Once their marriage had ended, John filed for an annulment so that he could remarry in the Church. In addition, John's fiancée was seeking her own annulment.

Jane had a great deal of knowledge about the process that her ex-husband went through to get the annulment. In her words, he made "all the right moves." These moves included a witness list "of an arm's length." Among those he listed were a number of priests who knew both of them and every therapist they had seen previously.

She was very outspoken about some of the aspects of the process. For example, she indicated that someone was appointed to defend the marriage. She described this person in extremely negative terms:

> . . . what a jerk. Oh, . . . this . . . priest who told me within, I'd say, five minutes, "Well, there's nothing that I can do for you. You threatened your husband with divorce throughout the marriage and as far as I'm concerned that wasn't a good marriage. I never saw my parents do this." And I said, "congratulations. It sounds like you are a real normal person coming from a normal background. Congratulations." He was the biggest creep that I have ever met in my life. I mean just a weird, weird, weird person; no personality whatsoever, and that was my defender.

When asked if either she or John had attended the hearing, she stated that there was none. She felt that she was very naive and that, being very good with words, she thought she "would stun them [the tribunal] with my logic." Taking the whole matter very much to heart, she proceeded to write a letter of between sixty and seventy pages reviewing their entire marriage, including the most intimate details. She indicated that she probably should not have been as forthcoming as she was in the letter because the tribunal used this against her. She went to the tribunal and, although she was not able to read the letters written by the priests or counselors, she was given permission to see what she had sent the tribunal after it had been marked by those who had read it. She continued:

> I don't know how this happened, but I saw what they were marking. It was just my own fault and any time I had mentioned that there had been a fight or anything we'd gone through, you could just see the yellow highlighter . . . they were skipping all of the reconciliation we'd gone through. You could see from their markings . . . what their line of thinking was.

I asked if the annulment was granted and she said that it had been. The reasons given in the annulment were a lack of "due discretion" and a "psychological immaturity." She remarked that both she and John were somewhat immature in that they both wanted things "their own way," but she firmly believed that they were no more immature at the time of their marriage than any other individuals at their age. I asked if she felt that "wanting it your own way" could have been interpreted by the Church as a sign of immaturity, to which she replied:

> Absolutely. Oh, any way I go, any way I express it they have me. It's like my rudimentary chess against Kasparov or somebody. Any way I move the pieces they would have me. If I admit that we fought, that was immaturity. Anything that I would say . . . I mean, it was just anywhere you turn, their logic has you pinned down. Yeah, it showed immaturity and, yes, we did not grow together. In any marriage I think that fails ultimately it ends with divorce and could be annulled on those grounds.

Many parents do not discuss the annulment process with their children; Jane, however, reported that she did. One of her children was too young to understand it fully, but Jane believed that he still knew "a little about what was going on."

Her two older children had a very difficult time dealing with the annulment. Although Jane thought that it might lead the oldest child to leave the Church, she did not. The other child, who happened to be living with her father at the time, was extremely upset that the Church ruled that her parents had not really been "married in the eyes of God." Jane tried to explain to her daughter that they were, indeed, married when she and her father had become parents. Jane went on to state that this "did not make any sense to them; it doesn't to most people."

When Jane asked if her second oldest daughter was going to church, the daughter typically responded in a sarcastic manner: "I don't think so." According to Jane, the effect of the annulment upon the children had the biggest negative impact. This seemed especially evident with the second oldest child.

An irony was that Jane was born and raised Catholic, but John had converted at the time of their marriage. In fact, Jane felt so bound to the Church and its teachings that she would not marry John unless he converted. Thus, the Church granted her ex-husband, a former non-Catholic, an annulment so that he might remain in the Church, and Jane, the staunch Catholic from birth and defender of the marriage, viewed the annulment as telling her that her marriage "did not exist in the eyes of God." I asked her how she felt about this. She responded:

> I think I felt totally abandoned. It was bad enough when [her ex-husband] found somebody else and declared his commitment to her within six weeks to two months ignoring the fact that we had been in a relationship for twenty-three years.
> . . . To go through this horrifying procedure of letters, not telling me that I could or should be meeting them face to face . . . To be sent these cool letters and to be told when I would phone: one nun told me—I think it was a nun, it might have been a psychologist, "Well, sweetheart, we can tell you this: it doesn't look good for you and you might better get on with your life." To which I said, "Thank you very much, but I don't need your psycho babble today." Oh, the hurt; I couldn't express it at the time.

I asked Jane if there would be any circumstances under which she believed that an annulment might be acceptable. She replied that there were conditions where it would be acceptable: "If a couple were to marry and soon after they discovered that they were not sexually compatible," or if conditions such as alcoholism or being a compulsive liar were present.

Jane had thought about the Church's position on divorce and remarriage and believed that the doctrine needed to be changed. She felt that the Church should recognize marriages such as hers and John's, but she doubted that recognition would ever occur, at least in her lifetime. She continued:

> I have no problem with [John's] marrying and being in the Church. My bitterness is not toward him. My bitterness is that *they erased my life.* Call me divorced; I'm perfectly fine with that. I don't know if I'll remarry in the Church. I can't even see that far down the line. But I'll be damned if I ask for their permission or kiss their butt.

I asked what she would have done if she were in John's shoes. She stated that she did not know what she would have done but did say that she hoped she would not have proceeded as her ex-husband did, playing what she called "this hypocritical game." She stated that there were, indeed, bad times and that a divorce came to be the only way out, but there were also some "tremendously good times."

Jane is still an active Catholic. She stated that the Mass and the sacraments were the glue that kept her in the Church. She still attended Mass and, in her words, "I am still very faithful within my little private world of worship." She added that she wanted nothing to do with the "organized Church" and she could imagine leaving the Church. This could happen if she "met somebody who was spiritually mature and was very happy in the Episcopal Church."

One of her regrets was that she did not appeal the annulment decision to Rome. She thought about it but was told that not only did she have to have $1,000 to proceed, but also that she had no grounds for an appeal.

Jane was perhaps the most outspoken and articulate critic of the annulment process. Just reading her words does not convey adequately to the reader the emotional despair and resignation that she indicated in our interview.

Joyce

Joyce was in her sixties and had been married for twenty-five years after dating for about two years. Her marriage produced three children, all of whom were now in their thirties, and six grandchildren. Joyce was born and raised in the Catholic tradition. Her ex-husband, Eric, had a father who was Catholic but his mother belonged to a Protestant denomination, and Eric was raised in his mother's faith.

Eric initiated the divorce because he met another woman. The other woman was, in fact, their next-door neighbor and a long-time friend of Joyce's. As one might imagine, this became a very painful experience for Joyce. She stated that she "went into shock for about three days," and that the first year after the divorce was "just horrendous" for her. She made it very clear that if it were her decision there would have been no divorce.

It was a difficult time emotionally and financially. She had not been in the workforce and initially received alimony. However, when that stopped, to make ends meet and keep her house, she invited one of her married children and her spouse to move in with her.

Joyce first learned of annulments in general at the Church that she had been regularly attending. She decided to attend a talk on the subject and took a friend. Joyce did not like what she heard. The priest, in her mind, seemed to be "selling annulments like M & Ms." The priest went on to say that psychological factors were the main reason annulments were now granted and that "most Catholics shouldn't have ever gotten married because of psychological reasons." Joyce was very angry, especially at this latter statement, and became so upset with what she heard that she left the meeting.

Shortly after this informational meeting Joyce received a letter from the archdiocese indicating that Eric had petitioned for an annulment. She recognized one of the priest's names in the letter as the one who spoke on the topic of annulments at the church. After receiving the letter Joyce called her priest who told her to try and calm down and that the Church "takes this very seriously." Joyce proceeded to write to the tribunal stating, among other things, that she did not understand how an annulment could be granted considering both the length of the marriage and the fact that the union produced children and grandchildren. To make matters worse, Joyce reported that she was also engaged in a civil case with Eric at the same time over the fact that he had stopped paying alimony.

Joyce recalled contacting Eric about the annulment petition and was very sarcastic in her conversation with him. She told him: "You know, you married me in the Presbyterian Church, you married me in the Catholic Church; why don't you take her and marry her in a synagogue? That would cover all three religions . . . if she said she was a Buddhist, you'd be Buddhist. . . ."

Joyce continued by saying that the priest did not like the letter she wrote and called her about it. She stated that she was told by him that "eighty or ninety percent of all marriages in and outside the Catholic Church should have never taken place because of psychological reasons." In response, Joyce asked: "What is your alternative, fornication?" How did the priest respond to that, I asked? Joyce stated that he only laughed, thinking that it was "a very funny statement." The conversation, as one might detect, was fraught with tension. Joyce admitted not acting nicely on the phone, but she also said that she had no respect for him.

Joyce recalled that she wrote continually to the tribunal. She also mailed a copy to the office of the cardinal. A total of twenty-five letters were sent by Joyce to the tribunal. These letters were written by Joyce, her friends, and people from the Church. Eric had only two witnesses write letters: a sister and an ex-girlfriend. Joyce stated that she met the ex-girlfriend two weeks before Joyce and Eric married, and then she never saw her again. Joyce did not meet the sister until six years after she and Eric were married. Joyce felt that neither of these women had any relevant information to present in terms of the courtship.

Joyce also sent copies of articles on annulment that she had collected from different periodicals. One of these articles, which she sent the tribunal, stated that Rome was even questioning the large number of annulments being granted in the United States. She remarked that, at one point in the article, it stated that "if all these people are psychologically unbalanced then they are having a hell of a problem in the United States."

According to Joyce the tribunal process was "fraught with faults." For example, she gave testimony at the hearing that was tape recorded. However, the tape turned out to be inaudible. She did not discover this fact until much later. Her ex-husband, she says, thought the judge was his advocate. When Joyce finally was appointed an advocate of her own, he did not speak English! To make matters even worse, the priest who was helping Joyce died of cancer during the proceedings. She reported encountering tremendous frustration every step of the way.

The annulment was granted on the basis of Eric's immaturity at the time of the marriage. Joyce stated: "How can you tell that retroactively after thirty-three years unless he's still emotionally immature? And then he shouldn't be able to be married in the Catholic Church again." She was able to read some of the testimony and claims that Eric made many assertions that she believed to be lies.

I asked her "Why do you think the Church is doing this?" She replied: "They're doing it because a great percentage of American Catholics get divorced. And they want to bring them back into the Catholic Church." I then asked her if she felt there were any circumstances in which an annulment would be appropriate. She reported that her son-in-law had obtained an annulment. He had been married only a very short time and discovered that his wife was pregnant with another man's baby: "That was a deception on the part of this woman. . . . He got an annulment and I think it was rightfully so." She also saw mental illness as a legitimate reason for granting an annulment. However, she drew the line at "psychological reasons." She talked at length about this:

> But psychological is fuzzy. It's a fuzzy reason. Give me a legitimate, logical reason and I'll go along with it but . . . everybody has some psychological thing in their past somewhere. Growing up alone has psychological problems. . . . Marriage has got to cause psychological problems and stress.
> . . . The year before you get married and all the planning and everything like that is stressful. . . . Believe me I spoke to psychologists and they all laughed at this whole thing.

After the annulment was upheld with the court of the Second Instance, Joyce wanted to appeal to the Rota in Rome. She was strongly discouraged from proceeding, however. She was told that it could take years for the case to be decided if it went to Rome. She was also told that more proof was needed demonstrating that the marriage was valid. She was dumbfounded: "I said how much proof do I need? I can't resurrect people who are dead." She asked one of the tribunal judges about the days when marriages were arranged by the parents and the children did not even know one another:

> What about those marriages? They lasted for fifty years. The Church didn't annul those marriages and they didn't even know each other when they got married. Oh, but he gave me the biggest runaround. And, finally with his back against the wall, he just threw up his hands and said: "I'm not talking as a priest now, just as an average person—I think the Church should stay out of the marrying business." And that's when I brought up the fact that it was a sacrament. . . . So I said are you telling me you don't believe marriage is a sacrament? And he just laughed at me. I walked out of there crying. And I said I would never go to church with him as the priest. I thought he was a phony. Every time he got up in the pulpit he started talking about family values, blah, blah, blah . . .

Joyce was also told that there would be a $1,000 fee requested if she wanted to appeal to Rome. She said that she did not have that kind of money and even offered to show them her financial records. She also was aware of the fact that, despite being told that she was responsible for paying the fee, she was not required to have the money in order for the appeal to proceed to Rome. The appeal did go to Rome. She received a letter in Latin (evidently from the Rota in Rome) along with a letter from the Archdiocese stating that more information was needed in order for her case to proceed. She decided that she had done enough to state her case and that she had invested so much of herself in the process that she did not respond to the letter. She did not hear from Rome and she assumes that the case was dropped since she did not provide the additional information.

I asked her, "What kinds of things would you change within the Church if you had the power?" As might be expected, she focused on annulments:

> Well, I would like them to be honest about annulments. If you are going to grant annulments don't put people through a ringer. Don't just talk about psychological reasons. If you are going to

give a person an annulment do it and get it over with. . . . Call it something other than an annulment. The word annulment means obliterated; it's not there, gone. It's not there; it never was. And it makes this sound like you didn't get married in the eyes of God. I don't feel that way personally.

Again, Eric was originally Protestant. Actually, they were married both in the Protestant Church and the Catholic Church. Her Catholic friends were able to attend the Catholic ceremony but, at the time, were not allowed to attend the Protestant one. I asked her how she felt about the Church granting an annulment to Eric, who originally was not Catholic. She said she was very upset and that the biggest impact of all this has been that it led her to leave the Church: "I'm no longer a practicing Catholic. I still consider myself a Catholic, but I am not a practicing Catholic."

Her children were trying to get her to attend other churches but she had resisted. Joyce wanted to go back to the Catholic Church but felt as though she could not:

I feel betrayed; I feel double betrayed; and triple betrayed. I've been betrayed by my best friend, my husband, and my church. And I know I'm supposed to be forgiving and I'm supposed to say forgive me. You know, I can forgive my ex-husband and I can forgive his wife but it's hard for me to forgive the Church. Because it's really the one that should have backed me up one hundred percent. I didn't do anything wrong. . . . I was a wife, a mother, and a grandmother, and I felt wronged by the church.

Cathy

Cathy was married nineteen years. In addition, she and her ex-husband, Bill, dated for four years prior to their marriage. They had two children, both of whom were in the twenties. Bill was not Catholic, but Cathy was. When they were married Cathy went to Mass occasionally with members of her family rather than with Bill.

Cathy was the one to initiate the divorce. Bill had trouble with alcohol abuse. In contrast to most of my respondents, she stated that the divorce was not particularly difficult for her. A legal settlement was reached out of court. She did say that it was emotionally trying. She had thought about proceeding with a divorce for many years. In her mind there was no reason to continue in the marriage.

Cathy attended Catholic schools all her life but indicated that, to the best that she can remember, the topic of annulments was never discussed. She said that annulments were "the best kept secret of the Catholic Church and still are as far as I am concerned." When asked how she, a respondent, would define an annulment, she explained that it was a "decision by the Catholic Church to dissolve my marriage completely, so the world can know that it never existed."

After their divorce Bill remarried a Catholic, but the wedding did not take place in the Catholic Church. The reason he sought the annulment, then, remains unclear. When she received a letter from the marriage tribunal stating that Bill was seeking an annulment, she was asked to complete an enclosed questionnaire. Although quite lengthy she completed it and returned it to the tribunal office. She stated that she strongly believed that the annulment would never be granted. She said that she thought that would be the end of it and she would not hear about it again. Much to her disbelief, the annulment proceeded and it turned out to be, in her words, "a two-year battle."

Once she discovered that Bill's annulment application was going to be taken seriously by the tribunal, she met with a priest from the parish where she was married. Accompanied by her parents, she wanted to find out more about annulments. At this meeting she first received the impression that the annulment would go through because the priest really focused on the fact that Bill was an alcoholic and that he was not capable of making mature decisions.

Next Cathy received a letter asking if she would like to testify before the tribunal. She was eager to do this believing that once they heard her testimony the annulment would not be granted. She reported that the meeting started out pleasantly but, in her words, "quickly disintegrated." She was essentially told that the petition for annulment would be granted.

She followed this meeting with letters and telephone conversations with the tribunal judge. It was then Cathy decided, from that point on, she would respond to the tribunal only by certified mail: "There was no talking to them and, besides, I can say so much more in a letter."

Cathy stated that it would be logical to assume that substance abuse would be the grounds for the annulment but this was not the case. Originally, the grounds were to be based upon the lack of ability to enter into a valid marriage due to a background of alcoholism, but the cause was changed at a later point in the proceeding to a "lack of due discretion," that is, the inability to take on the basic requirements of marriage due to "causes of a psychic nature." Cathy opposed both of these grounds and the fact that the grounds were changed, but was told only that if she wished to speak with someone she should contact the tribunal office.

She was asked to provide a list of witnesses who would support the validity of the marriage, but did not do so because she felt that there was no need to. Bill did provide witnesses who wrote letters. Finally, she went to the tribunal office where she was allowed to review the testimony. A priest was there all the time who she said watched her "like a hawk." She was neither allowed to take notes nor to make copies of the testimony.

Cathy also met with a person who was in charge of defending the validity of the marriage—that is, the defender of the bond. He spent about an hour with her trying to talk her out of proceeding any further. She asked him what the next step in the process was and what her source of appeal was when the tribunal nullified the marriage. According to Cathy, he became very upset with her.

Once the annulment was granted, Cathy wrote a letter to the tribunal, which reviewed what had happened to date along with her feelings about the entire process. The following are some excerpts from that letter:

> My first reaction [to Bill's petition] was to laugh. I couldn't imagine why he wanted an annulment nor did I think for a moment that the Catholic Church would grant him an annulment. After all, I was a Catholic and Bill was a Protestant and we had received the sacrament of matrimony that was an eternal bond, or so I thought, and my church would stand behind me. Little did I know that I was about to embark on a journey where I would encounter the lies, deceit, corporate practices, bias, hypocrisy, betrayal, and a process laden with injustice. . . .
>
> Under no duress Bill and I attended marriage instruction sessions conducted by [name of the priest], whose sole responsibility was to be certain that Bill and I understood fully the responsibilities of the sacrament of matrimony. . . .

Now the question remains: why after twenty-eight years does Bill want to annul our marriage? He is not a Catholic and stands to gain no spiritual benefits from this. Could it be that his wife wants to receive the sacrament? Could it be that he has been coerced by his wife for her own personal gains? Clearly, there is a hidden agenda here. There could be no other possible reason for this and, if this is true, as we all know that it is, then there can be no annulment. I read nothing in canon 1095 [the church law relevant to "defective consent"] regarding the spiritual benefits of second wives. [Name of the priest] kept suggesting that I am opposing this annulment out of anger and resentment toward Bill and/or his wife. I assure you that this is not the case. . . .

My anger lies with this entire inquisitorial process. I am opposed to this annulment because it goes against everything I have ever believed regarding the sacrament of matrimony. . . . It is hypocrisy and I will stand up for what I believe is right.

Cathy continued to read her letter to the tribunal. She went into great detail about the procedures. In her report to the tribunal she suggested that Bill may have made up various things in his testimony to qualify for an annulment. She also disputed the idea that he lacked the ability to understand the basic rights and obligations of marriage (i.e., a lack of due discretion): "He was twenty-five years old. If he lacked due discretion then exactly at what age did he become a responsible adult capable of making decisions about his future?" She stated that they had been engaged for two of the four years they dated and he had "plenty of time to back out of the engagement." She added that Bill did not leave his parents' home to get out of a bad situation, that she was not pregnant, and that no one forced him into the marriage. She also expressed her anger and frustration with not having her questions answered and not having been granted any basic, human rights throughout the entire proceedings.

The thing that troubled Cathy the most was that her ex-husband, a non-Catholic, was granted an annulment. In addition, she was raised to be a faithful Catholic, and he had very little interest in her religion. She felt hurt and betrayed by the Church. The process, she stated, was both intolerable and unfair: "Nobody, not once, showed any kind of sympathy for the fact that my marriage was going to end. Nobody. They were only in favor of my husband."

Cathy believes that the Church really has a long way to go when it comes to matters relating to divorce. She stated that she would like to see annulments become "a thing of the past." She felt that if people make a decision to divorce then they should live with the consequences even if it entails not being able to receive the sacraments. She saw divorce as solely a civil matter and did not think that "the Church needs to step in and say, okay, the marriage never existed."

Cathy, who is now in her early fifties, has been divorced from Bill for eleven years. She was employed and single. Religion was still important to her but not the Catholic Church. She attends only occasionally and said she was considering becoming an Episcopalian.

OTHER STORIES

There were many other individuals I interviewed worthy of having their stories told. Charles, Susan, and Jack are three such people who shared their strong feelings about annulments.

Charles

Charles and his former spouse, a Catholic, were married for more than thirty years and had four children, all of whom attended Catholic schools. They were now grown and out of the house. Although Charles was in his seventies and retired, he was still physically active.

His ex-wife filed both for the divorce and annulment. He said that she filed for the divorce because of her "lust for money" and the annulment in order to remarry in the Church. Although Charles was a lifelong Catholic, he had not heard about annulments. When he learned that his former spouse had filed, he contacted a priest who informed him about annulments. His first reaction was that of shock.

Since his ex-spouse had moved to another state, the annulment process was handled entirely through the mail. He received the standard questionnaire and, with the assistance of a priest, he completed and returned it. He indicated that no hearing was conducted.

Not only was the annulment granted (on psychological grounds), but he was informed that he needed to see a psychologist before he could remarry in the Church. This stipulation was interesting in that, although some indicated that the tribunal recommended counseling, none of the other petitioners or respondents said this was required of them.

Charles was bewildered by the entire matter. As a youth growing up in the Midwest he attended Mass every week. When he married he and his former spouse continued to attend Mass on a regular basis. He indicated that he no longer attended church services regularly. He said that the reason is that he is "confused" because of the annulment: "I just don't understand how the Catholic Church can grant an annulment after thirty-four years. . . . I just can't buy the theory of it." Elsewhere, he stated:

> I feel that they're being two-faced when they tell me that I don't know how to raise a Christian family. That's what's bugged me all this time. Civil divorce—it's black and white. But tell me that I don't know how to raise a Christian family when I worked hard to educate four children in the Catholic Church and they come along and tell me that I'm kicked out. That's about the extent of it. That's the theory I get from the whole thing.

I asked Charles if he felt any bitterness toward his former spouse for seeking an annulment. He replied that his negative feelings were not with her but with the Church:

> I have no bitterness toward her. . . . She's just another human being on this earth and you have to go by the laws, but I don't understand the laws of the Church when it comes to annulment. . . . When I have faithfully done my utmost and worked hard for forty years in . . . , which is hard work, putting four kids through college and to get kicked in the face . . . by the Church.

Charles is now retired and still considers himself Catholic. He commented that to continue to attend Mass would be too "hypocritical."

Susan

Susan was unique among the sample because she opposed the annulling of her marriage and the tribunal supported her. She had been married thirty-three years, having married when she was twenty-five and her husband, Max, was thirty-one. They had three grown children. Susan was not Catholic. However, Max came from a large Catholic family. When they married, she went to Mass with him. In fact, she actually signed a promise to raise the children in the Catholic faith.

Max tried to seek an annulment before they were officially divorced, but was told by the tribunal that a civil divorce was first required. This prompted him to accelerate the divorce in order to get an annulment. Susan was puzzled as to the exact reason why he sought the annulment so quickly. She does not know, for example, if another woman had entered his life to prompt his actions.

She became aware of her ex-husband's intentions when she received a letter from the tribunal. She proceeded to protest the annulment. When asked about witnesses, Susan listed a friend who knew her as a child, her mother, and two of her ex-sisters-in-law. Her mother died during the proceeding and, as it turned out, Max had also listed his two sisters that Susan had listed. Consequently, her only witnesses were the friend and the two former in-laws who only "half testified for me."

Susan indicated that two people were "lifesavers" in the process. One of them was actually the woman who originally wrote to Susan from the tribunal. She had received a letter giving Susan the name of the defender of the bond. Thinking the defender of the bond would contact her, Susan finally, after a period of months, called and spoke with him. Susan was told by him that he would appoint the woman who originally contacted her and had been guiding her through the annulment process as her defender of the bond. Susan also said that her defender had spoken with a priest in the archdiocese and this priest had asked her whose "side" she was on, Susan's or the archdiocese's. Susan stated that the priest was very much in favor of annulments and, in effect, accused her defender of the bond of "being unfaithful to the cause." Beth, her defender, provided, according to Susan, a lot of information about annulments and the process.

The second "lifesaver" came from reading *Shattered Faith* (1997). At one point, for example, the tribunal suggested that she see a psychiatrist. Having just read this book she decided to ignore the request. She also learned from the book that she could appeal the decision, if it ruled for annulling the marriage, to the Rota in Rome. She also learned that she would not have to pay for an appeal. This was not the impression she had received from the tribunal. The payment was very important to Susan because she was having medical problems and much of her income was going toward these bills.

Susan not only made numerous phone calls to the tribunal office, but sent letters stating that she had every intention of pursuing the case, even to Rome, if a decision for nullity was made. She also indicated that she would not pay the fee and that she felt it should be the responsibility of the archdiocese to pay the required fee to Rome. The fact that the Catholic Church ruled on her Protestant marriage made her furious: "That is why I opposed it so strenuously." She stated firmly that if two people were Catholic and they both agreed on an annulment then that would be fine, but not when there is opposition or where one of the spouses is not a Catholic. She said she had not really thought much about the Church's position on divorce and remarriage, stating that she is not even sure what the current position is.

I asked why she thought the annulment was not granted. She said she thought it had to do with two practical issues: money and appeals, but not the three children and the length of the marriage. In other words, Susan believed because she made it very clear that she would fight the annulment all the way to Rome and that the archdiocese would have to provide the fee, this led the tribunal to refuse the annulment petition. I asked if she thought Max might appeal. Susan said she had asked him and he said "no." She was shocked at his response, given the fact that he was an attorney and "loves lawsuits."

Jack

Jack, who was seventy-four at the time of our interview, was another unusual case in two ways. First, few of the respondents were male; second, Jack was gay. He was married for approximately twenty-five years and had two children who were now in their thirties. Although he stated that the marriage had no emotional content, he wanted to keep it.

During the 1950s Jack read a book about a homosexual relationship and began to feel that it may apply to him. He proceeded to "come out" and, for the next two years, engaged in several relationships with other men. One day he received an invitation from an old friend to attend a party. He went. It was at that party that he met a woman whom he started to date, and they eventually married. Jack was a very strictly raised Catholic and felt that "if you are homosexual and you don't practice it, then it was acceptable." He and his ex-wife married and, in his words, "it was really quite delightful in many ways." He stated that he never had a relationship with a man in all the years he was married.

Jack did not state exactly why he married. One possibility was the Catholic view on marriage and homosexuality. He stated that he was "interested in having a successful marriage. That was very important to me because my parents were married for fifty years."

After the divorce his ex-wife anticipated remarrying and so she sought an annulment. He really did not protest the annulment petition but he was angry when he learned that the annulment had been granted on the basis that he was incapable of marriage. I asked him if the homosexuality was at the center of the petition being granted and he said that he did not really remember; the annulment had been granted approximately fifteen years ago. He did not recall if there was a specific reason cited, but it would be safe to assume that his sexual orientation was central to the decision.

Jack's current view was that annulments did not deal with "reality." He said that he was indeed married and it was a successful marriage in many ways. When asked if he thought an annulment could be justifiable in any circumstances, he said "No, not if it's going to say the marriage didn't exist." I asked if he was angry that his ex-wife sought an annulment. He said that his anger was not so much with the annulment petition itself, but with his former wife. In his view the annulment was just another instance that allowed her to abdicate any responsibility for what had occurred in their marriage.

Jack had long since left the Catholic Church. He indicated that the homosexuality issue was a major factor for his leaving the Church. He said that he had lapses in his faith and deeds but that he tried to "do the right thing." He tried to live up to his religion but ultimately decided that he was essentially a persona non grata in the Church and so quit going. When I asked if there was anything that might cause him to return to the Church he responded with a definite "No."

SUMMARY

I believe the stories told by these individuals illustrate and even dramatize many of my findings. Although a few respondents felt annulments were a good thing, the vast majority did not. These individuals reported very different views from the petitioners in the previous chapter.

Most of the respondents, as with the petitioners, had little knowledge or experience with annulments. Many believed that they were granted only in extraordinary circumstances. However, for most of the respondents, unusual circumstances were not present and yet an annulment was granted. This fact no doubt made it harder for the respondent to deal with his or her own situation.

As these case studies demonstrate, a lot of anger and anguish was created by annulment petition. Many reported extremely negative encounters with priests and tribunals, a "very cold process," and a sense of alienation from the Catholic Church. A number of cases were ironic in that the respondent had been born and raised Catholic, and the petitioner, their former spouse, had been raised in another faith.

Chapter 9

Conclusion

The church should call this [an annulment] "permission to re-marry" instead of saying the marriage never existed.

Linda Christiansen

Our culture is one that emphasizes the individual over the group. One only has to look at the titles of songs: "I Gotta Be Me" and "I Did It My Way," or sayings such as: "I owe it to myself" and "Do your own thing" (Myers, 2000). This individualism can be seen in other areas. Go into any bookstore and you will find a huge section on self-improvement. A casual perusal of a local bookstore revealed these titles: *Cutting Loose: Why Women Who End Their Marriage Do So Well* (Applewhite, 1997), and *Honoring the Self: Self-Esteem and Personal Transformation* (Branden, 1985), which is broken down into three major sections—"The Dynamics of Self-Esteem," "The Struggle for Individuation," and "Egoism." Professional sports in America also demonstrates our stress on individualism, often at the expense of the group and/or nation. Consider tennis: the Davis Cup consists of worldwide competition among nations. The top players from Australia, Sweden, Germany, and most other countries consider it an honor and a privilege to represent their respective countries. American players such as Jimmy Connors, Pete Sampras, and Michael Chang have often been reluctant to play. Instead, they have opted to rest for their next tournament or play an exhibition match in exchange for a large fee.

David Myers (2000) addressed this issue of individualism versus collectivism in his book, *The American Paradox*. He discussed the emphasis on the self-esteem movement along with the typical therapeutic position that whatever helps the individual is paramount. He quoted a "prayer" by Fritz Perls, a Gestalt therapist:

I do my thing, and you do your thing
I am not in this world to live up to your expectations,
and you are not in this world to live up to mine,
You are you and I am I,
And if by chance we find each other, it's beautiful.
If not, it can't be helped. (p. 168)

Myers also quoted a therapist who stated, "We are in the business of saving individuals, not marriages" (p. 184).

Although individualism has made America great it has also exacted a toll. Myers (2000) stated that along with the emerging individualism has come increasing rates of "loneliness, homicide, thefts, eating disorders, and stress-filled disease such as heart attacks" (p. 178). Another cost is divorce. America is the most individualistic, he argued, but also the most divorce prone. Cultures that stress collectivism (e.g., Japan) have lower divorce rates.

It is against this backdrop that the American Catholic Church exists. The dilemma for the Church is that our society is individualistic and divorce prone, but Catholic doctrine is promarriage and against divorce. For better or worse, the Church's way of dealing with this dilemma is by granting annulments.

As I delved into the area of annulments I found it to be, at times, very murky. Not only was the average non-Catholic almost totally unaware of what annulments were, but I found many Catholics, and even priests, to be largely nonconversant in the area. As I indicated in an earlier chapter, Ronald Vasoli, a lifelong Catholic and a sociologist who teaches courses in the family and the sociology of law, admitted his ignorance about annulments until his former spouse applied for one.

One goal in writing this book was to enlighten Catholics and non-Catholics alike as to what annulments are, the process for receiving one, the extent to which they are granted, and the argument both for and against annulments. I sought to frame annulments within a social, cultural, and religious context. I wanted to determine if those who had an annulment were different attitudinally or behaviorally from those who were divorced but did not have an annulment and/or from those Catholics who were married and never divorced. Finally, I wanted to determine if there were any differences between those who had sought the annulment (the petitioners) from those who were the object of the annulment petition (the respondent), and to make these people "real" by presenting case studies.

SUMMARY OF FINDINGS

My samples came primarily from Family Life groups located in different parts of the country. The majority of the respondents were female and had a higher level of education than did the typical Catholic. The vast majority were white, middle-aged, and had moderate incomes. Although the married sample had higher incomes the demographic differences among the three samples were small and statistically insignificant.

When I considered factors relating to marriage and the family I found differences, as would be expected, on their perceptions of their marriages. The annulled and divorced groups were more likely to see their former marriages as worse than what they expected them to be. They also perceived their marriages as worse when asked to compare them with other couples they knew.

A majority of all the groups believed that divorce was justifiable in some instances. Physical abuse, infidelity, drugs, and child neglect were most often listed as justifiable reasons, and problems with in-laws were seen by both the divorced groups as the least justifiable. For the married sample, financial problems ranked last. Immaturity proved to be an important reason for the annulled. Although 45.2 percent of the annulled group felt this was a legitimate reason for divorce, only 23.4 percent of the divorced and 9.8 percent of the married sample cited this as a justifiable reason. When studies look at the reasons people give for their divorce, rarely does one find immaturity mentioned. As I indicated in Chapter 4, immaturity is currently stressed by tribunals as a determinant in whether the marriage "really existed." It would therefore be logical to assume that the annulled individuals would be "primed" to cite this reason.

Divorce has been shown to be a very devastating event. My findings reinforced this. Both the annulled and divorced individuals scored lower on measures of well-being. The divorced were most likely to feel a sense of failure, and least likely to be satisfied with their life and health. The married sample scored highest on all measures, and the annulled were in between. As I expected, the divorced and annulled groups, compared to the married group, had higher percentages who had seen a therapist.

When I focused solely on the divorce experience, I found high percentages of both the divorced and annulled groups undergoing various negative conditions after the divorce—poor appetite, feeling blue, feeling depressed, and so forth. Again, these are very common feelings, especially right after a divorce. When I considered those respondents who had been divorced less than a year, along with two years or less, I found that the annulled scored better on various psychological measures.

I was also interested in the respondents' level of integration into the Catholic Church. Previous research has found that, similar to marriage, those who have higher levels of integration display higher levels of well-being. I argued that those who are married, by virtue of their marital state, would be most integrated into the Church, and the divorced would be least integrated. The reason for this is that marriage is a sacrament within the Church. It not only is a highly idealized state but makes one a "full-fledged" member of the Church. I tested this idea by giving the three samples six attitudinal questions relating to the Church. The predictions were strongly supported. On all the measures the married had the highest score (i.e., gave the most integrated response), and the divorced scored the lowest; the annulled sample was in between. It could be argued that the annulment helps provide the person with the feeling that, even though they have been divorced, the Church has accepted the fact that they, unlike the divorced-only individual, are in the good graces of the Church.

When I analyzed various behavioral integration measures I found that (1) the married sample had the highest frequency of Mass attendance, and the divorced but not annulled had the lowest; and (2) less than three in five annulled and divorced marriages were homogeneous, (both partners were born and raised Catholic). In contrast, both partners in the married sample came from Catholic backgrounds. Less than one-third of the divorced and half of the annulled attended Mass together every week when they were married; in contrast, the figure for the married was approximately three-fourths. More than one-fifth of the two divorced groups never attended when they were married.

Generally, we could conclude that the annulled, as compared to the divorced only, scored higher on measures of well-being, adjustment, and attitudinal and behavioral integration. One could ask if the annulled were originally different from the divorced only or if the annulment actually led to better adjustment and integration. As to the former, it is possible that the annulled wanted to be better Catholics and more integrated and therefore they sought an annulment, whereas the divorced only were already less committed to the Church, had lower feelings of well-being, and so forth. The latter possibility is that the annulment process actually led to better adjustment, fewer psychological problems, and higher integration. For those who advocate the annulment as a "healing process," the latter argument would make sense.

Future research in this area might investigate these two alternatives. The best scenario would be to follow a sample of married Catholics over a period of time in a longitudinal study. Questionnaires measuring well-being and so forth would be given at various stages in their lives. Some of these individuals would eventually divorce. Furthermore, some of these divorced individuals would go through the annulment process (either as petitioner or as respondent), and others would not. We would then be able to answer this "chicken or egg" problem.

As we have seen, those who have had their marriages annulled can be placed into two categories: (1) those who petitioned for the annulment, and (2) those who were the respondent. The findings indicated that these two groups were unique and often very different from one another. When I compared the two groups on the various measures the largest differences occurred with the Church integration measures. Significant statistical differences existed on all six questions.

Finally, the case studies revealed many differences between the petitioner and the respondent. Although many of the petitioners indicated that they saw problems with various aspects of the annulment process, they agreed that the annulment process had more positive than negative aspects. The belief that annulments are a "healing process," that they are the "law" and are required to remarry in the Church, and that they enable one to become a member in good standing all stood out as reasons petitioners sought an annulment.

On the other hand, the respondents were typically not so positive about annulments; in fact, many were openly hostile. Some of the respondents had been married for up to thirty-five years and could not believe that the Church would go back that far and determine that there was some impediment existing that made the marriage not valid. Others expressed disbelief that the marriage could be declared null but any children that may have resulted from the marriage were legitimate. Others had not even been raised, or married, in the Catholic Church who had their marriages declared null because the former spouse wanted to marry a Catholic in the Church. Particularly upsetting for others was the fact that they had been raised in the Catholic Church and their spouse had converted. However, after divorcing, the converted spouse sought an annulment. "Betrayal" was how most of these respondents characterized how the Church treated them.

THEORY

The main thrust of this book is on those whose marriages have been annulled. Believing that there are crucial differences between petitioners and respondents or, more specifically, those who were positively disposed to annulments versus those who were opposed, I sought an explanation for the differences. I feel that two social psychological theories can be used. For the petitioners I apply Festinger's (1957) theory of cognitive dissonance, and for the respondents Linville's (1985, 1987) model of self-complexity is applicable.

The Petitioners: Cognitive Dissonance Theory

It is not difficult to understand the reason(s) for a divorced Catholic, male or female, to seek an annulment. The doctrine of the Catholic Church is very clear when it comes to remarriage—if one wants to remarry in the Church and continue to receive the sacraments, the previous marriage has to be declared null. This often represents a serious dilemma for not only the divorced person, but no doubt for many priests who minister to this population. It was quite typical to encounter not only respondents but petitioners in the study who were not especially fond of having to go through the annulment process. Others found it to be wanting in one way or another. On the other hand, the petitioners felt they had to do this in order to remain a Catholic in good standing. To face the future, not only without one's spouse but also without the Church, which they typically had been born and raised into, was both frightening and unwanted. Equally scary and unwanted was the potential of having to spend life alone if the individual wanted to remain within the Church but not seek an annulment. These individuals solved the dilemma through the annulment process.

I theorize that these people experience a feeling of cognitive dissonance. Cognitive dissonance is a result of an inconsistency of one's attitudes and/or behaviors. Let us start our discussion of this theory with a hypothetical case. Assume that two people have been married a number of years and the wife (Ann) decides that she is no longer happy in the marriage. Furthermore, part of her unhappiness stems from emerging sexual feelings toward other females. Ann, raised in a Baptist home, is taught that both divorce and lesbianism are against "God's law." But she cannot deny these feelings. What does she do? If she stays in the marriage she is miserable; if she files for a divorce or acts on her sexual feelings she undermines her lifelong beliefs.

Cognitive dissonance theory states that Ann experiences conflict before she reaches a decision. She is torn between staying in the marriage and her emerging sexuality. Now consider that Ann decides to divorce her husband, James. It is at this point that she experiences dissonance, or a state of inconsistency. Having engaged in a behavior (i.e., divorce) that is inconsistent with her attitude (opposition to divorce), she is now in a dissonant state. Ann now must reduce her dissonance. Cognitive dissonance states that two methods of reducing the dissonance are to (1) change her attitudes toward James and/or divorce and lesbianism, and (2) seek out information consistent with her decision and avoid information inconsistent with her choice (Festinger, 1957). Let us consider both of these alternatives.

The first method of dissonance reduction would specifically involve developing negative attitudes toward James and positive attitudes toward divorce and lesbianism. The theory also holds that the more important the decision the greater will be the dissonance and, as a consequence, the greater the need to reduce the dissonance. Ann makes the very difficult decision to divorce James. Are there any valid reasons to end the marriage because of James? Does he physically abuse her? Is he an alcoholic? A workaholic? If she is not able to answer "yes" to these types of questions, the decision becomes extremely difficult. To justify the divorce James becomes in *her mind* a "monster"; his silence is interpreted as anger toward her, an innocent remark becomes a "put-down." He starts to becomes a horrible husband, an abusive father. Divorce becomes her only option. Her attitude toward divorce becomes less negative. She now tells herself things such as "Everybody does it," "It is impossible to live a lifetime with the same person," and so forth.

Ann can also reduce her dissonance by seeking out people and information that support her decision and avoid situations or people who would contradict her decision. Ann might seek out good friends who have little knowledge of James and who tell her: "Yes, you had no other choice but to divorce the bum!" She might avoid individuals who know James and know that he is not a "monster." If she comes into contact with these individuals, she is careful to act as if nothing has happened and carefully avoid any discussion of the divorce or James.

How does she deal with her emerging lesbianism? She might conclude that men in general are "bums." They are irresponsible, abusive, and adulterers. Her only alternative is to seek the love and companionship of another woman. Whereas she grew up and continues to attend a more traditional religious denomination she now may seek out a church that is supportive of gays and lesbians.

Having applied the theory to Ann and James we can now begin to see how it can be applied to the case of annulments. Again, one way to alleviate an inconsistency is to change one's attitude. In other words, if a person has experienced dissonance over being divorced (especially if that person has been the one to file for the divorce) and being a Catholic (which teaches "till death do us part"), a way to resolve the imbalance is to file for an annulment. In obtaining an annulment it, in a sense, is giving the Church's approval for the divorce because it never was really a marriage from the beginning. Some of the respondents who opposed the annulment even alluded to this idea. In the end, the annulment resolves the dissonance, providing for the petitioner a reduction of stress, a way to deal with a situation which the Church disapproves of but remain within the good graces of the Church.

Although I did not survey priests on their attitude on annulments, I believe that there are some who also experience feelings of dissonance. With the growing numbers of Catholics who are either divorced or divorcing, priests must deal with this segment of their parishes. It is probably safe to say that most priests look at the high incidence of divorce with dismay. Many undoubtedly believe in, and/or support, the Church's teachings concerning divorce. On the other hand, they see some of their own flock, whom they may know quite well, experience a bad marriage and, oftentimes, divorce. They do not want their parishioners to suffer, nor do they want to alienate them from the Church either. Pastorally, the way to deal with the situation is the annulment. In their eyes this is the compassionate answer.

The Respondents: Self-Complexity Theory

Females made up the majority of respondents in this study. In my interview with Sheila Rauch Kennedy, she made the relevant point that older women are less likely to be able to find a marital partner. This is especially true if the woman is more highly educated since females may be less willing to marry someone who has less education or is generally lower in social status (Wu, 1994). In contrast, men typically marry someone younger than themselves. In addition, there are many more women than men at older ages; in short, men have more females available than females have males to marry (Macionis, 1999). As discussed in Chapter 7, a prime motivator for seeking an annulment was to remarry.

Not only were older women more likely to be respondents, my belief is that they are more likely to oppose the annulment. The question becomes: Why is this so?

An answer may be found in the research and theory on self-esteem, especially the area of self-complexity. Self-esteem refers to how we feel about ourselves. Although there are people who have negative self-concepts and feel badly about themselves, most individuals indicate positive self-evaluations (Smith and Mackie, 1995). Consequently, any negative blow to the individual's psyche represents a blow to the self-esteem. Linville (1985, 1987) argued a theory of self-complexity, a perspective that relates to how an individual perceives himself or herself.

Linville argued that individuals vary with respect to how they deal with events in their lives. Some, she stated, have a tremendous response to life's "ups and downs," and others show very little response. Why should this be so? According to Linville it was because they vary in self-complexity. Self-complexity refers to the number and diversity of aspects of the self. Consider, for example, a person who has a number of roles in life: accountant, wife, mother, tennis player, and member of the local Audubon society. This person's life consists of a number of different aspects. Although mother and wife may be linked psychically, the others are largely independent of one another. This person, then, would be said to be high in self-complexity.

Now, consider that this person loses her job. Although traumatic, Linville hypothesized that the person still has other independent roles to fall back on. She still can see herself as a good wife and mother, a good tennis player, and so forth. The fact that she was fired from her job should have little impact on these other roles.

However, let us consider that another woman, also an accountant, has few, if any other, roles. Her work is her life; it is how she identifies herself. If she were to lose her job it would result in a major blow to her identity. As a consequence, there should be a tremendous impact on her self-esteem given the fact that she is low in self-complexity.

In one study, Linville (1987) had undergraduate students attend two separate sessions two weeks apart. Their task on each occasion was to complete questionnaires measuring stressful events, self-complexity, depression, and illness. She predicted that those respondents who were high in self-complexity would be less vulnerable to negative consequences (e.g., depression and physical ailments). That was exactly what she found. Subjects in the study who were high in self-complexity displayed lower levels of depression, perceived stress, and physical illness after experiencing stressful events.

I argue that this model can help us understand the hurt that many of the female respondents expressed. Many of these women spent ten, twenty, or even thirty years in a marriage. Much of their lives was based upon the role of wife and, typically, mother. The roles of wife and mother are intertwined or, as Linville states, the roles are related closely in memory. In other words, wife and mother are not totally independent of one another as are wife and accountant, for example.

Therefore, there is less complexity with the former than with the latter, although both consist of two roles.

When something such as a divorce occurs the impact would likely be greater for the woman who has less complexity, that is, whose life is defined by being that of a wife and mother. In contrast, the woman who gets a divorce is still an accountant and has that to help bolster her self-esteem. This may also help explain why women have typically experienced higher levels of depression: their lives, until recently, have had less complexity. Therefore, a stressful event such as a divorce can have more of an impact than for the typical male who has had other roles to make up his identity.

What about an annulment, however? As I stated earlier, the respondents most affected by their ex-spouse's applying for an annulment were older females. In my sample the average age of this type of respondent was sixty years, had been married almost twenty-two years, and over 39 percent had at least three children. For these women much of their lives had been defined by their roles of wife and mother. These were women who had typically been born and raised Catholic. They had often gone to Catholic school and believed very strongly in their faith.

For these women, their lives may be said to be low in self-complexity. The Catholic Church has emphasized the roles of wife and mother. In other words, although wife, mother, and Catholic are three roles, they are overlapping roles. Again, they are "connected in memory." These women have lived the life of a good Catholic and tried, as the Church dictates, to be a good wife and mother.

Now the Church says that the marriage they "thought" they had is null and void because of an impediment that existed long ago that kept the marriage from being a valid one. Here is a woman who has been married, for example, twenty years; has four children; and is a faithful church attender and now is told that the marriage is null. In one interviewee's terms, the declaration of nullity "erased my life."

To make matters even worse let us say that a woman, a lifelong Catholic, married someone who was originally Protestant. He converts to Catholicism at her request and they marry in the Catholic Church. The two divorce and he then asks the Church for an annulment in order to remarry. This scenario may be seen by the wife as the ultimate betrayal on the part of the Catholic Church. She has trusted this "grand" institution to stand up for her and instead it has "sided" with the ex-spouse. This could be extremely hurtful. Since this woman's level of self-complexity is low, she is more likely to experience depression as a result of the event. Indeed, I witnessed this chain of events when I interviewed respondents whose ex-husbands had filed for the annulment. The result was anger, hurt, bitterness, a sense of betrayal, and depression.

What about those males who have fought long and hard against having their marriage declared null? One thing these respondents shared with their female counterparts was a lengthy marriage and children.

As I noted, however, the probabilities for a man finding another spouse are greater than for a woman. Why then should the fact that their ex-wife sought an annulment be troublesome? After all, if the husband were Catholic, as most were in the sample, this would free him to remarry in the Church. One answer may be that he has no plan to remarry. Beyond that, however, I argue that a similar kind of mechanism may be at work for the males as for the females. Therefore, the Linville model remains applicable.

A commonality shared by most of the males who were respondents was a strong sense of being a husband and a father. Although almost all these men had jobs, I had the sense that when I spoke to them about their jobs and their family, their occupational roles were less important. Specifically, the roles of Catholic, husband, and father surfaced as clearly important to them. Although they may have had more roles than their female counterparts they still were low in self-complexity by virtue of their overlapping religious and familial roles.

RECOMMENDATIONS

I spent over four years on this study, surveying those who had experienced an annulment and those who had not. I interviewed at length both petitioners and respondents, and I spoke with people in the Catholic Church. Based on the results, I now conclude with some recommendations for all those concerned: petitioners, respondents, and those within the Church, whether they be clerics ministering to the divorced or those people within the tribunals who act as advocates, defenders, and judges.

How should the Catholic Church respond to the divorced? One alternative, although one that may not receive widespread acceptance, is for it to take a "hard-line" approach not only in its doctrine decrying divorce but in its actions. The importance of marriage and that it is a lifelong commitment would be emphasized along with the position that an annulment will be granted only in certain, rare cases (that is, *clearly proven* impediments that existed *prior* to the marriage or abuse). For example, the Church can say that the deserting party has to demonstrate clearly and without a reasonable doubt that his or her life was in danger.

It is possible to interpret the annulment process as an indictment of the premarital counseling that takes place in the Church. When couples undergo Pre-Cana or other kinds of church-related counseling programs and are declared "fit" to be married and then ten or twenty years later the marriage is annulled, it does not speak well of either the premarital counseling or the annulment process. If the priest saw no reason for the couple not to be married then, how can a marriage tribunal come along years afterward and say "without a doubt" that there were preexisting circumstances that prevented a "valid" marriage? Why not make a marriage "annulment proof?" In other words, through premarital counseling and extensive meetings with a priest who has been trained in marriage and the family, along with counseling experience, the marriage could be declared as valid, with no chance for annulment. This could be the Church's equivalent of the covenant marriage that now exists in Louisiana and Arizona.

This stance would strongly reaffirm the Catholic Church's position against divorce and send a clear message to its members and the world that divorce simply will not be tolerated unless there are some overpowering reasons. Although this might not be a popular position it might help to herald a new age where other religions become less tolerant of divorce.

Galston (2001) stressed the influence that religion can play in discouraging divorce:

For the overwhelming majority of Americans, marriage remains a sacrament and still takes place under the aegis of religion. If every church and synagogue took as one of its principal tasks the thorough preparation of young people for marriage, it could make a significant difference. There is some evidence that this strategy works best when all the religious institutions within a community unite around this objective in a mutually reinforcing way. (p. 55)

Why not let the Catholic Church lead this movement? For the Church to take a position where it can be perceived that it is "giving in" to divorce by the granting of annulments, is analogous to parents saying that it is alright to use drugs, have premarital sex, and so forth, because many other teenagers are engaging in those activities. To say that something occurs frequently does not mean that it is right and just. The Church can say "no" to divorce and annulments, that certain rigid standards must be maintained.

If the Catholic Church takes the lead, ultimately society and its values and laws relevant to divorce would change. We are starting to see this change in many states already. But if the Catholic Church, along with other denominations, treat the divorced as "victims" rather than persons who decide, for one reason or another, just to walk away without trying to make the marriage work, then the divorce rates will continue to be high.

A second alternative, one that is probably more "palatable" to most people, is to treat the divorced and separated with compassion and kindness no matter what the reasons for the divorce were. Although many within my study experienced this, many others did not. Some indicated feeling similar to an outcast. Many felt they had been deserted by the Church that they had known and loved. If I learned one thing from this study it was that even most of those who filed for the divorce did so with great regret and were very concerned about the Church's response. The Church is certainly aware of this but needs, if it is to take this compassionate stance, to implement programs at each and every parish to minister to the divorced.

The Church might be advised to provide seminary training to all prospective priests in the matters of the family, including divorce. In an interview, Irene Varley (1999), executive director of the North American Conference of Separated and Divorced Catholics (NACSDC), stated that priests from the nearby seminary could do something such as an internship with various organizations. She stated that very few sign up with her group believing that it would act as a kind of acknowledgment and acceptance of divorce. Priests need to be sensitized to this issue if they are going to properly minister to the needs and concerns of the divorced Catholic.

If the Catholic Church is to continue with the granting of annulments on the scale that it is, it needs to reform the process. Even the many petitioners who strongly favor annulments noted that they were not fully informed or, at times, were even baffled by the whole process. Often the Church does not provide clear information individuals need. Tribunals might also consider informing the respondent about the petition for an annulment in a more humane way. If a letter is used it might be followed up with a phone call. They should provide information (either in the letter or verbally) about what the process entails and their rights and options. Respondents should be allowed more time to complete what is often a long and emotionally draining questionnaire. Once all the materials have been received a quick decision should be made.

The Church should establish clear and uniform guidelines to be used by all tribunals. From my interviews I discovered a wide variation in how tribunals dealt with the annulment process. Some kept the parties informed throughout the entire process; others did not. Some were careful to see that the petitioner had an advocate and the respondent a defender of the bond; however, others did not. Although some of the petitioners and respondents were made aware that the judgment could be appealed, some tribunals failed to inform the individuals of this possibility. In an interview with Father Andrew Greeley (1999), I asked about this variation. He believed that there would be resistance to imposing a strict uniformity in terms of how the archdioceses and tribunals dealt with such matters. Although developing complete uniformity may not be possible, it would certainly be beneficial to have all tribunals develop some standardized operating procedures.

Marriage tribunals might also consider using women more extensively in the process. Criticisms sometimes arose from women who saw the process as a totally patriarchal one. To have a "bunch of celibates," in one respondent's words, decide on whether her marriage was valid, "demeans marriage and women."

Finally, the Church needs to address the three major arguments used by those respondents opposed to annulments. These three are (1) the question of legitimacy of the children, (2) the belief that the Church is in the "business" of annulments to make money, and (3) that the granting of an annulment allows the petitioner to abdicate his or her responsibility for the divorce. These three issues are "public relations" problems for the Church; they make the Church look bad.

The Church must realize that many people are not convinced that, if the marriage is declared to be null, the children are no less legitimate. Time and again I heard about the effects on the children and whether they became illegitimate. Save Our Sacrament (SOS) is very emphatic in its belief that children are affected by the process: "This statement [that there is no effect] underscores a denial and ignorance intrinsic to the entire annulment procedure . . . there are many reports of devastating reactions in the children" (Leary, 1999, p. 3). The Church states emphatically that the children are still legitimate, but it needs to address this issue on a level that individuals can understand and *accept.*

Second, many people expressed the view that annulments are a way to make money. This does not seem to be the case, however. The costs for the Church go well beyond that which is charged to the petitioner, especially if a case is appealed to the Rota in Rome. One estimate is that it costs the Church approximately $10,000 to appeal to Rome (The Respondents' Appeal to the Vatican Rota, 2002). The Church would do well to publicize the cost of a typical annulment case or, at least, the range that currently exists across dioceses. Dioceses, and their tribunals, could put out a brochure itemizing the costs along with the average cost to the petitioner. The fact that an individual can seek an annulment as a hardship case needs to be emphasized. This allows the individual to petition for an annulment at either a reduced cost or at no charge at all. To my knowledge this is not done.

Third, and very important, the Catholic Church needs to adequately address the argument that an annulment is the individual's way of not taking any responsibility for the marriage and divorce. Many of the respondents made this argument in one way or another. Probably the most forceful came from a woman who felt that the biggest impact of an annulment was to enable Catholics to deny that they ever made a commitment and therefore relieve themselves of the responsibility for the divorce. In this person's view an individual needed to take responsibility for one's actions; annulments, she stated, allowed one to "undo what they have done." She also said:

> For instance, if you murder somebody and the state decides that you can have a murder annulment (Oh, I didn't really mean to kill that person). So let's get that stricken from the record. That would be a terrible thing on society. . . . I think that it grants people the option to not follow through on their agreements thus cheating themselves and their partners of life's lessons. . . .

This respondent saw annulments as entirely "self-serving" instruments: "There are people who want to deny responsibility about everything in their lives. The same people who file for bankruptcy and put too much on their credit cards and don't want to take responsibility for that."

This viewpoint is one that is not without merit. It is easy to see an annulment in this way. Unlike the criticisms surrounding the children and money, the argument that an annulment relieves one's responsibility for the divorce is one that the Catholic Church will probably find more difficult with which to deal. However, in order to be more receptive to the individual who is opposed to annulments, the Church needs to address it in some way.

For the individual contemplating petitioning for an annulment, there is much cause for optimism. The Catholic Church has become very receptive to a divorced individual seeking an annulment. A vast majority of petitions for an annulment are granted. Church doctrine indicates that although one was married for a long duration or that the marriage produced children, this should not deter the individual from seeking an annulment. As far as the petitioner is concerned the place to start is with the parish priest. Also, many dioceses and their tribunals have become part of the World Wide Web. For those with access to the Internet, one can merely type in "annulment" and be greeted with a wealth of information. As I indicated in Chapter 3, the Philadelphia diocese answers numerous questions about annulments and gives a step-by-step procedure for the process. We might conclude that for one who truly believes that his or her marriage was never valid, the odds are very good that the petition will be accepted.

What about the respondent, especially one who believes the marriage was a legitimate one? Fortunately for this individual the organization called Save Our Sacrament exists to address the "problem" of annulments within the Catholic Church. This organization was founded in 1997 by Dr. Jan Leary, a pastoral therapist. Save Our Sacrament has six support goals (SOS Goals, 2002).

1. To provide counseling to respondents
2. To work with respondents who want to appeal to the Rota in Rome
3. To provide information and other kinds of resources that might not be given by the tribunal
4. To encourage and support the reopening of past annulment cases on the part of respondents who so wish
5. To "give voice to the children of annulled marriages which decree that children are NOT part of a sacramental marriage!" (SOS Goals, 2002)
6. To provide assistance for "the reopening of past annulment cases by those who have experienced the 'tribunal-abuse' of having their marriage declared 'null.'"

In addition, this organization seeks six reform goals:

1. To call attention to the bias by tribunals against both the respondent and the marriage and the "hypocrisy permeating the U.S. tribunal system."
2. To call attention to the "devastation" that the annulment process has upon the children.
3. To call the Vatican to the realization that God's grace is present in marriages that may end in divorce. "SOS calls the Vatican to the reality that annulment is 'Catholic divorce,' although poorly done."
4. To make the public aware that not only Catholics but non-Catholics married in other churches are having their marriages ruled upon by the Catholic Church.
5. To call upon Rome to replace the external forum (that is, the annulment process) with the Internal Forum.

6. To institute regional conferences which would present work-shops "regarding respondent empowering ways of dealing with the annulment system." (SOS Goals, 2002)

Many of the respondents admitted almost a total ignorance of the process and what options (e.g., the fact that they can have an advocate to see that their rights are protected), if any, they had. For those who want to challenge an annulment petition, then, this organization should be the starting point.

It was pointed out earlier that an annulment case is a heavy financial burden on the diocese and, as a result, the Catholic Church. One tactic that a respondent who is convinced that his or her marriage was a valid one can undertake is to make it clear that the case will be taken all the way to Rome if necessary. Very few cases are appealed to the Rota, but if dioceses are aware that respondents will pursue this line of action the tribunal may be less likely to judge a marriage invalid on the basis of the more "ambiguous" reasons (such as psychic impairment).

The Catholic Church is in somewhat of a bind. If it continues to grant annulments on the scale that it currently does, more publicity will be generated, some will become alienated from the Church, and organizations such as SOS will grow. In addition, almost all of those individuals from other religious traditions with whom I spoke not only cannot understand the concept of an annulment, but also look at the process derisively. This reflects against the Catholic Church. Certainly the Church is not run by popular opinion, especially that of non-Catholics, but in this age of increased ecumenism the Catholic Church does risk damage to its image.

On the other hand, if the Church grants annulments only in certain limited circumstances (as is the case of the court of Third Instance in Rome) there could be massive defections from the Church.

Many people within the Church with whom I have spoken believe that divorce should be handled pastorally, with kindness and a forgiving attitude. The internal forum, which SOS favors, would seem to make sense for the divorced person and many priests. From the Church's perspective it would eliminate much of the workload for marriage tribunals, not to mention the money that would be saved. However, any movement toward this would no doubt be met with objection not only from many church scholars but the Church hierarchy itself.

Father Orsy (1986) concluded that marriage tribunals have such a long history in the Church that it would be inconceivable to eliminate them. He advocated that the tribunal move toward a more pastoral emphasis. He stated:

> As it is, the institution [tribunal] is still very legal in character; the only qualification the judges must possess is an academic degree in canon law. But there is much more to a marriage case than the norms of the Code. Perhaps the church should think of special schools where future judges could get an all-around training, with less law and more human sciences. The art of forming a legal judgment, *ius dicere,* is not the art of healing. (p. 287)

Indeed, Father Orsy is correct. In the final analysis, marriage tribunals are dealing with human beings; human beings who have suffered the pain of divorce; human beings who have sought to understand why their marriages failed; human beings who act, think, and feel. The Catholic Church and its marriage tribunals, if they take the compassionate route, *must* do all they can to make those experiencing a divorce as welcome as possible. If the Church is to keep the annulment process within the jurisdiction of the tribunal, it must do all it can to include both the petitioner *and* the respondent in such a way that neither become alienated from the Church.

In order to keep these people, the Church must confront the important issues of the legitimacy of the children, the length of the process, oftentimes the lack of information, and the argument that an annulment is a "Catholic divorce." One thing seems certain: divorce will not disappear. If the Church is to keep all its members, it must face the fact that the annulment process needs to be modified. In my discussions with those Catholics who felt hurt and betrayed by the Church for granting an annulment I learned one thing: most *wanted* to remain within the Church.

The future of annulments appears to be murky. In an interview with Father Andrew Greeley (May, 1999), he predicted that fewer annulments will be sought. He said this would result from younger Catholics, especially those with little respect for church authority, ignoring annulments. He also indicated a very simple way of dealing with the divorced and remarried Catholic—allow them to receive the Eucharist without the turmoil of the annulment process.

In a panel session at the Annual Meetings of the Society for the Scientific Study of Religion, Sheila Rauch Kennedy (1999) presented the following analogy:

> Imagine for a moment that a pharmaceutical company discovers a cure for an uncomfortable and embarrassing but not life threatening disease such as acne. Although the market potential is clear, the treatment is so painful and time consuming that despite a strong advertising program only 10 percent of those who could be cured are willing to try it. Of that 10 percent, 20 percent find the program too painful and drop out but the 96 percent of the 80 who complete the program are now acne free and pleased with the results. Four percent of the 80, however, experience negative life altering experiences such as severe depression and emotional breakdowns.
>
> While this case is imaginary, consider for a moment these three questions: 1) Do you think the FDA would approve such a program with the overall success rate so small? 2) If a pharmaceutical company withheld information about the potential negative side effects, could it be held legally and financially liable for the experiences of the 4 percent? 3) Given this scenario do you think the company would move forward with its program or perhaps seek a different cure?

People such as Sheila Rauch Kennedy, a non-Catholic, along with people such as Jan Leary, a Catholic, are the start of a possible movement to change Catholic policy surrounding divorce, remarriage, and annulments. They, along with some clergy, feel that the internal forum process or changing to something along the lines of the Orthodox position is a practical solution to the problem.

Allen (1999) stated that Cardinal Godfried Daneels, among others, feels that the Orthodox position is a good one. The Orthodox position is that people make mistakes and, therefore, divorce and remarriage is permitted. Matusiak (2000) stated that what is crucial is whether the marriage has quit functioning. If the two parties no longer do things together, have sexual relations, like or love each other, and so forth, the marriage no longer exists. Once a civil divorce is granted the parties may marry again within the Church. The Church will marry an individual up to three times. According to Matusiak the marriage ceremony for a second or third marriage is a little different than if it were the first marriage for both parties, but the differences are so subtle that no one typically notices.

The Catholic Church, according to Matusiak (2000, personal communication) has "painted itself into a corner." Indeed, this does seem to be the case. To take the position that divorce is never acceptable means alienating thousands of Catholics. On the other hand, admitting that divorce is a fact of life and dealing with it the way it currently has (through the annulment process) is creating dissension within the Church. The Church needs to recognize this fact and develop a way of dealing with divorce in a way that *all* will see as honorable, humane, and healing.

APPENDIX A:
TRIBUNAL QUESTIONNAIRE

ARCHDIOCESE OF INDIANAPOLIS
METROPOLITAN TRIBUNAL
P.O. Box 1410
Indianapolis, Indiana 46206

BASIC DATA FOR INTRODUCTION OF A MARRIAGE CASE

INSTRUCTIONS: *Please type or print clearly. It is important that each item have a response. If a question is not applicable to your situation, write "NA." If you do not know an answer, write "Unknown." If Items are left blank, this Data Sheet may be returned for completion.*

PART I. *Please give the following information about* **yourself.**

1. My full name

     Last Name   First   Maiden

2. My complete address

    City, State, Zip Code

3. My phone number   (   )   Home   (   )   Work

4. My father's full name

     Last Name   First   Maiden

    4a. He is   ☐ Living   ☐ Deceased

5. My mother's full name

     Last Name   First   Maiden

    5a. She is   ☐ Living   ☐ Deceased

6. Check one: My parents   ☐ never divorced   OR   ☐ divorced as I was growing up   OR
     ☐ divorced during my courtship

7. My date of birth is

     Month   Day   Year

8. Location of my birth

     City   State

9. Date & church of my baptism

     Month   Day   Year

10. Location of church

     City   State

11. My religion is

    11a. I practice it   ☐ Yes   ☐ No

12. My occupation/employer is

PART II. *Please give the following information about your* **former spouse.**

1. Former spouse's full name

     Last Name   First   Maiden

2. Complete address

    City, State, Zip Code

     (   )   Home   (   )   Work

3. Ex-father-in-law's full name

     Last Name   First   Maiden

    3a. He is   ☐ Living   ☐ Deceased

4. Ex-mother-in-law's full name

     Last Name   First   Maiden

    4a. She is   ☐ Living   ☐ Deceased

5. Check one: These parents   ☐ never divorced   OR   ☐ divorced while my former spouse
     was growing up   OR ☐ divorced during our courtship

6. Former spouse's date of birth is

     Month   Day   Year

7. City and state of birth _____

8. Check one: ☐ I believe my former spouse was baptized. Date _____

                    Name and location of church _____

              ☐ I am sure he/she was never baptized before or during our marriage.

9. Former spouse's religion _____

  9a. He/She practices it   ☐ Yes ☐ No

10. My former spouse's occupation and employer   ☐ at the time of the divorce   ☐ presently

---

PART III. *Please give information about the **marriage** you wish the Tribunal to review.*

1. Date of Marriage _____
                     Month   Day   Year

2. Place of the Marriage _____
                     Name of Church or Other Facility

3. Location (City/State) _____

4. Our ages at the time of this marriage: I was _____ years old; My former spouse was _____ years old

IMPORTANT: *The situation described in No. 5 below does not pertain to all marriages. Please read it carefully and make the appropriate responses.*

5. If at least one of the parties in the above marriage is Catholic and the marriage did **not** take place before a Catholic priest, did the Catholic Church grant permission for the marriage?
☐ Yes (Complete 5a)   ☐ No (Complete 5b)   ☐ Does not apply *(Skip to No. 6)*

  5a. If "Yes" in No. 5, please give the following information:
    Name of the Priest _____
    Name & Location of the Church where marriage preparation occurred _____

  5b. If "No" in No. 5, was this marriage later convalidated before a Catholic priest?
    ☐ Yes *(Please complete the following)*   ☐ No *(Please complete 5c)*
    Date of Convalidation _____ Name of Priest _____
    Name and Location of Church _____

  5c. Has the Catholic wife or the Catholic husband joined another church publicly?
    Catholic Wife: ☐ No ☐ Yes ____ Catholic Husband: ☐ No ☐ Yes ____
                       Date   Date

6. How many children were born of this marriage? _____

7. Please name the children and give dates of birth for each.

_____   _____   _____   _____

_____   _____   _____   _____

8. Date and location of divorce _____
                           Date   City   State

9. Was this your first marriage?   ☐ Yes ☐ No

10. Was this your former spouse's first marriage?   ☐ Yes ☐ No

11. If this was NOT *your* first marriage, please identify previous spouses, dates and locations of marriages and dates of divorce.   ☐ Not applicable to me

Name of Previous Spouse   Date of Marriage   Place: Church/Other   Date of Divorce

_____   _____   _____   _____

_____   _____   _____   _____

  11a. If any of your previous spouses listed above was married to someone else before marriage to you, place an asterisk (*) to the left of their name(s).

12. If this was NOT your *former spouse's* first marriage, please identify any of his/her previous spouses, dates and locations of marriages and dates of divorce.

☐ Not applicable to my former spouse *(the one identified in Part II)*

Name of Previous Spouse	Date of Marriage	Place: Church/Other	Date of Divorce
_____	_____	_____	_____
_____	_____	_____	_____

12a. If any of the previous spouses of your former spouse listed above was married to some- one else before they married your former spouse, place an asterisk (*) to the left of their name(s).

13. How many times have you been married *(include present union if you are now married)?* Number of marriages ⎯⎯⎯⎯⎯

PART IV.

1. Please check which of the following statements best describe your intention and what you believe to have been your former spouse's intention *prior* to marriage.

Myself	Former Spouse	
☐	☐	A. I am open to having children when they come.
☐	☐	B. I prefer not to have children right away, but I am open to the possibility of children immediately.
☐	☐	C. I feel that it is up to me to decide if and when there will be children.
☐	☐	D. I definitely do not want children right away and I will not compromise on this.
☐	☐	E. I definitely do not want children at all and I will not compromise.

2. If you checked either C, D, or E above as either your or your former spouse's intention, please explain why.

_____

_____

3. Please check which of the following statements best describe your intention and what you believe to have been your former spouse's intention *at the time of the marriage.*

Myself	Former Spouse	
☐	☐	A. I intend to enter a permanent and life-long union.
☐	☐	B. I intend to get married, but if the marriage is unhappy or if my expectations of marriage are not met, I reserve the right to leave the marriage with the option of marrying somebody else.

4. If you checked B above as either your or your former spouse's intention, please explain why.

_____

_____

5. Please check "Yes" or "No" for yourself and your former spouse in response to the following statement:

Myself	Former Spouse	
Yes ☐	Yes ☐	At the time of the marriage we believed that we had an obligation to be
No ☐	No ☐	faithful to each other.

6. If you checked "No" for either yourself or your former spouse, please explain.

_____

_____

7. My former spouse and I were related by blood or legally. ☐ No ☐ Yes ⎯⎯⎯⎯⎯⎯⎯⎯

Relationship

8. How long was your marriage happy? _____

9. Please check the appropriate boxes for yourself and your former spouse.

Myself	Former Spouse	
☐	☐	A. Continued education after high school and before marriage.
☐	☐	B. During childhood/adolescence a family member or someone in the household had a drinking/drug problem.
☐	☐	C. During childhood/adolescence a family member or someone in the household suffered from an emotional/mental problem.

10. My former spouse and I had sexual intercourse prior to marriage. ☐ Yes ☐ No

11. A pregnancy was involved in our decision to marry. ☐ Yes ☐ No

12. Briefly summarize the problems in your marriage. Indicate with a * any of these problems which were present **before** marriage. *(You will have the opportunity to discuss these problems in detail later in the process.)*

_____

_____

_____

_____

_____

_____

PART V. *Please check the appropriate box below.*

☐ A. I have plans to marry.

☐ B. I have already remarried. _____

Date

☐ C. I have not remarried and I do not presently have plans to marry.

If you checked A or B above, please complete the following information which pertains either to: your intended spouse or your present spouse.

1. Name _____

2. Address Last_____First_____Maiden

3. Was this person ever baptized? ☐ Yes ☐ No ☐ I don't know

4. Has he/she been married before? ☐ Yes* ☐ No

***N.B.** If your intended spouse or your present spouse has been married before, you should know that his/her previous marriage must also be investigated by the Tribunal to determine whether he/she is free to marry you in the Catholic Church. If you have such a situation, he/she may begin his/her marriage case now by requesting a copy of this Data Sheet.*

5. Have you ever presented a marriage case to this Tribunal or any other church court?

☐ No ☐ Yes Date: _____ Location: _____

Month   Year   City   State

I hereby swear that the information that I have given is true and complete to the best of my ability.

_____   _____

Signature   Date

Please identify the priest/pastoral minister whom you have consulted and/or who may be contacted by the Tribunal if necessary.

_____   _____

Priest/Pastoral Minister   Parish

APPENDIX B:
QUESTIONNAIRE—DIVORCE
AND RELIGIOUS ANNULMENT SURVEY

DIVORCE AND RELIGIOUS ANNULMENT SURVEY

INSTRUCTIONS: Please place a check mark in the box next to the appropriate response, or write in your response to the open-ended questions. (Please feel free to attach sheets if you need extra space.) Please return the completed questionnaire in the enclosed paid envelope.

FAMILY AND MARRIAGE

First of all, we'd like to ask some questions about your former marriage. Please answer the following questions thinking about that marriage.

Q1   How old were you when you first married? ☐ years old

Q2   How old was your former spouse when you married? ☐ years old

Q3   How long were you married to your former spouse? ☐ years

Q4   Did you and your former spouse have children?

  1 ☐ No; Go to Q5
  2 ☐ Yes; Go to Q4b and Q4c

  Q4b   What is the current age and sex of these children?

   1 Sex: ☐ Male; ☐ Female; ☐ Age

   2 Sex: ☐ Male; ☐ Female; ☐ Age

   3 Sex: ☐ Male; ☐ Female; ☐ Age

   4 Sex: ☐ Male; ☐ Female; ☐ Age

   5 Sex: ☐ Male; ☐ Female; ☐ Age

  Q4c   Who has custody of the child(ren)?

   1 ☐ I have custody.
   2 ☐ My former spouse has custody.
   3 ☐ We have joint custody.
   4 ☐ Children are living independently.

Q5   Before you married did you have counseling as a couple with:

1   ☐   a priest
2   ☐   a minister or preacher
3   ☐   a counselor or therapist
4   ☐   NONE. We did not have counseling.
5   ☐   I can't remember.
6   ☐   Other, Please describe: _____

Q6   Who filed for the divorce?

1   ☐   I did.
2   ☐   My former spouse did.

Q7   How long have you been divorced?   ☐ months **OR**   ☐ years

Q8   Briefly state the reason(s) for your divorce: _____

Q9   Do you consider there to be *any* justifiable grounds for divorce?

1   ☐   Yes; Go to Q9b
2   ☐   No; Go to Q10
3   ☐   Not Sure; Go to Q9b

   Q9b   Which of the following would you consider acceptable reasons for getting a divorce?
          (Check all that apply).
          1   ☐ No longer loved each other
          2   ☐ Physical abuse
          3   ☐ Alcoholism or substance abuse
          4   ☐ Infidelity
          5   ☐ Financial problems
          6   ☐ Sexual problems
          7   ☐ Neglect of children
          8   ☐ Emotional problems
          9   ☐ Problems with in-laws
          10   ☐ Immaturity
          11   ☐ Other (please list or describe) _____

Q10   If you filed for the divorce, how difficult a decision was it? If your former spouse filed, how
      difficult was the divorce for *you*? (Check one)

1   ☐   Very difficult
2   ☐   Difficult
3   ☐   Neither Difficult Nor Easy
4   ☐   Easy
5   ☐   Very Easy

DIVORCE/ANNULMENT SURVEY   PAGE 3

Q11   Which of these periods would you say was most *difficult* for you? (Check one)

1 ☐ Before the decision to divorce
2 ☐ After decision to divorce but before final decree
3 ☐ The period just after the divorce was final
4 ☐ Now

Q12   Which of these periods would you say was *best* for you? (Check one)

1 ☐ Before the decision to divorce
2 ☐ After decision to divorce but before final decree
3 ☐ The period just after the divorce
4 ☐ Now

Q13   Which of the following would you define as the major reason(s) your marriage ended
(please select as many as apply; place a 1 in the box by the most important reason, a
2 by the next important, and so on).

1 ☐ No longer loved each other

2 ☐ Physical abuse

3 ☐ Infidelity

4 ☐ Financial problems

5 ☐ Sexual problems

6 ☐ Neglect of children

7 ☐ Emotional problems

8 ☐ Problems with in-laws

9 ☐ Alcoholism or substance abuse

10 ☐ Immaturity

11 ☐ Other (specify _____)

Q14   Compared with other couples you have known, how would you rate the degree of overall satisfaction that you *felt* with your marriage? (Check one)

1   ☐ Much less satisfied
2   ☐ Somewhat less satisfied
3   ☐ About the same
4   ☐ Somewhat more satisfied
5   ☐ Much more satisfied

Q15   Compared with your expectations of marriage *before* you were married, how did your marriage turn out? (Check one)

1   ☐ Much worse than I expected
2   ☐ Somewhat worse than I expected
3   ☐ About as I expected
4   ☐ Somewhat better than I expected
5   ☐ Much better than I expected

Q16   Approximately what percentage of your family and close friends approved of your decision to divorce? (Check one)

1   ☐ None of them
2   ☐ Less than 25%
3   ☐ 25-50%
4   ☐ 51-75%
5   ☐ More than 75% but not all
6   ☐ All of them

Q17   How many of your close friends are divorced? (Check one)

1   ☐ None
2   ☐ A few
3   ☐ Most of them
4   ☐ All of them

Q18   Which of the following do you see as things that influenced you to actually seek a divorce? (Check all that apply)

1   ☐ Parent's desire
2   ☐ Children's desire
3   ☐ Divorced friends
4   ☐ Ease of divorce laws
5   ☐ Opportunity of alternative financial support
6   ☐ Non-divorced friends
7   ☐ Children grew up and left home
8   ☐ Approval of religious leader
9   ☐ Individual or family counseling
10 ☐ Other (specify: _____)

DIVORCE/ANNULMENT SURVEY   **PAGE 5**

Q19 Were your parents ever divorced?

   1 ☐ Yes
   2 ☐ No

Q20 Were your former spouse's parents ever divorced?

   1 ☐ Yes
   2 ☐ No

Q21 Were any brothers or sisters divorced before your divorce? (Check one)

   1 ☐ Yes
   2 ☐ No

Q22 Did you or did your former spouse seek an annulment?

   1 ☐ I sought the annulment.
   2 ☐ My former spouse sought the annulment. Go to Q27.
   3 ☐ Neither I nor my spouse have sought an annulment.

   Q22b. Briefly explain why you chose *not* to seek an annulment: _____
   _____ Go to page 8, Q38.

Q23 How long after you were divorced did you start thinking about seeking an annulment?

   ☐ months **OR** ☐ years

Q24 How long ago did you start the process of seeking an annulment?

   ☐ months **OR** ☐ years

Q25 Briefly explain why you chose to seek an annulment: _____
_____

Q26 Did your former spouse know you applied for the annulment?

   1 ☐ Yes. Go to Q26b
   2 ☐ No. Go to Q27
   3 ☐ Not sure. Go to Q27

   Q26b When your former spouse became aware of the request for annulment did s/he cooperate?

      1 ☐ Yes, definitely. Go to Q29
      2 ☐ Yes, somewhat cooperative. Go to Q29
      3 ☐ Was neither cooperative nor non-cooperative. Go to Q29
      4 ☐ No, somewhat non-cooperative. Go to Q29
      5 ☐ No, definitely non-cooperative. Go to Q29

Q27   Do you know *why* your former spouse sought an annulment?

    1   ☐ Yes. Go to Q27b
    2   ☐ No. Go to Q28
    3   ☐ Not sure. Go to Q28

    Q27b   If yes, briefly explain the reason(s): _____

_____

Q28   How did you find out that your former spouse was seeking an annulment? (Briefly describe)

_____

_____

Q29   If you have children, did you inform them about you or your former spouse seeking or getting an annulment? (Check one)

    1   ☐ Yes
    2   ☐ No
    3   ☐ No children. Go to Q30.

    Q29b   Why or why not? (Briefly explain) _____

_____

Q30   Did you attend the tribunal hearing?

    1   ☐ Yes
    2   ☐ No

    Q30b   Why or why not? (Briefly explain) _____

_____

Q31   Did your former spouse attend the tribunal hearing?

    1   ☐ Yes
    2   ☐ No
    3   ☐ Don't Know

    Q31b   Do you know why your former spouse attended or did not attend? (Briefly explain) _____

_____

Q32   Did you have witnesses write letters of support for you?

    1   ☐ Yes; Go to Q32b
    2   ☐ No

    Q32b   What was their relationship to you (i.e., counselor, relative, friend, etc.)? _____

DIVORCE/ANNULMENT SURVEY   PAGE 7

Q33   Was the annulment granted?

1 ☐ Yes; Go to Q33b and Q33c
2 ☐ No; Go to Q34
3 ☐ No decision yet; Go to Q34

> Q33b   How long did the annulment process take from the time you turned in your papers (or first knew about it) until a decision was made? ☐ months **OR** ☐ years
>
> Q33c   How much did the annulment cost? _____ I don't know ☐

Q34   Please explain, as best you can, your knowledge of, and your feelings toward, annulments before you started the process (briefly explain):

_____

_____

Q35   Please explain your current feelings about annulments (briefly explain): _____

_____

_____

Q36   Knowing what you know now, would you go through the process again?

1 ☐ Yes
2 ☐ No
3 ☐ Uncertain

Q37   Would you please explain why you just gave the answer you did?

_____

_____

_____

_____

_____

_____

_____

_____

PERSONAL OPINIONS AND BELIEFS

Q38   Have you felt so sad, discouraged, hopeless, or had so many problems (during the past month) that you wondered if anything was worthwhile? (Check one)

    1 ☐ Extremely
    2 ☐ Very much so
    3 ☐ Quite a bit
    4 ☐ Some
    5 ☐ A little
    6 ☐ Not at all

Q39   How happy, satisfied, or pleased have you been with your personal life during the past month? (Check one)

    1 ☐ Very Happy
    2 ☐ Fairly Happy
    3 ☐ Satisfied
    4 ☐ Somewhat Dissatisfied
    5 ☐ Very Dissatisfied

Q40   Have you been bothered by any illness, bodily disorder, pains, or fears about your health during the past month? (Check one)

    1 ☐ All the time
    2 ☐ Most of the time
    3 ☐ A good bit of the time
    4 ☐ Some of the time
    5 ☐ A little of the time
    6 ☐ None of the time

Q41   Have you had severe enough personal, emotional, behavioral, or mental problems during the past year that you felt you needed help? (Check one)

    1 ☐ Yes, sought help
    2 ☐ Yes, did not seek help
    3 ☐ Severe problems, did not seek help
    4 ☐ Few, personal problems
    5 ☐ No personal problems

Q42   Have you ever seen a counselor, psychologist, etc. about any personal, emotional, behavioral or mental problems concerning yourself? (Check one)

    1 ☐ Yes
    2 ☐ No

DIVORCE/ANNULMENT SURVEY   **PAGE 9**

Q43   Approximately how many times have you seen a therapist in the last year? ☐

Q44   Approximately how long ago did you *first* see a therapist?

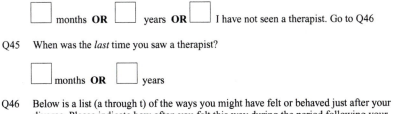

☐ months **OR** ☐ years **OR** ☐ I have not seen a therapist. Go to Q46

Q45   When was the *last* time you saw a therapist?

☐ months **OR** ☐ years

Q46   Below is a list (a through t) of the ways you might have felt or behaved just after your divorce. Please indicate how often you felt this way during the period following your divorce using the following responses: None of the time, Some of the time, Occasionally, or All of the time.

	None of the time	Some of the time	Occasionally	All of the time
Q46a I was bothered by things that usually don't bother me. . . .	☐	☐	☐	☐
Q46b I did not feel like eating; my appetite was poor.	☐	☐	☐	☐
Q46c I felt that I could not shake off the blues even with help from my family or friends.	☐	☐	☐	☐
Q46d I felt that I was just as good as other people.	☐	☐	☐	☐
Q46e I had trouble keeping my mind on what I was doing.	☐	☐	☐	☐
Q46f I felt depressed.	☐	☐	☐	☐
Q46g I felt that everything I did was an effort.	☐	☐	☐	☐
Q46h I felt hopeful about the future.	☐	☐	☐	☐
Q46i I thought my life had been a failure.	☐	☐	☐	☐
Q46j I felt fearful.	☐	☐	☐	☐
Q46k My sleep was restless.	☐	☐	☐	☐
Q46l I was happy.	☐	☐	☐	☐
Q46m I talked less than usual.	☐	☐	☐	☐
Q46n I felt lonely.	☐	☐	☐	☐
Q46o People were unfriendly.	☐	☐	☐	☐
Q46p I enjoyed life.	☐	☐	☐	☐
Q46q I had crying spells.	☐	☐	☐	☐
Q46r I felt sad.	☐	☐	☐	☐
Q46s I felt that people disliked me.	☐	☐	☐	☐
Q46t I could not get "going".	☐	☐	☐	☐

Q47   The questions below (a through j) refer to your feelings about the quality of your social relationships. Indicate how often you have felt the way described in each of the statements *during the past year* using the following responses: Never, Rarely, Sometimes, Often, Very Often.

	Never	Rarely	Sometimes	Often	Very Often
Q47a I am bothered by things that usually don't bother me. . .	☐	☐	☐	☐	☐
Q47b Most everyone around me seems like a stranger.	☐	☐	☐	☐	☐
Q47c I get a lot of satisfaction from the groups I participate in.	☐	☐	☐	☐	☐
Q47d There are good people around me who understand my views and beliefs.	☐	☐	☐	☐	☐
Q47e I have a romantic partner who gives me support and encouragement.	☐	☐	☐	☐	☐
Q47f I belong to a network of friends.	☐	☐	☐	☐	☐
Q47g There are people I can count on for compansionship. . .	☐	☐	☐	☐	☐
Q47h I don't have one specific relationship in which I feel understood.	☐	☐	☐	☐	☐
Q47i I am an important part of the emotional well-being of another person.	☐	☐	☐	☐	☐
Q47j I don't have a special love relationship.	☐	☐	☐	☐	☐

Q48   We would like to get your beliefs on a number of issues. For each statement, please indicate whether you would approve or disapprove.

	Strongly Agree	Approve	Undecided	Disagree	Strongly Disagree
Q48a Premarital sex between an engaged couple. . .	☐	☐	☐	☐	☐
Q48b Abortion after a woman has been raped.	☐	☐	☐	☐	☐
Q48c Abortion as a means of birth control.	☐	☐	☐	☐	☐
Q48d Homosexual relations between consenting adults.	☐	☐	☐	☐	☐
Q48e Extramarital sex.	☐	☐	☐	☐	☐
Q48f Divorce and remarriage when no children are involved.	☐	☐	☐	☐	☐
Q48g Divorce and remarriage when children are involved.	☐	☐	☐	☐	☐
Q48h Divorce with no remarriage.	☐	☐	☐	☐	☐
Q48i Marriage to a divorced person who has never been married in the Catholic Church.	☐	☐	☐	☐	☐

DIVORCE/ANNULMENT SURVEY

Q49 For the remaining questions (a through kk) we would like to get your personal opinions on a number of different issues.

	Strongly Agree	Agree	No Opinion	Disagree	Strongly Disagree
Q49a I feel a sense of pride in being a member of their Catholic Church.	☐	☐	☐	☐	☐
Q49b I put the Church's goals ahead of my own personal interests.	☐	☐	☐	☐	☐
Q49c I am committed to the Church's goals.	☐	☐	☐	☐	☐
Q49d To be perfectly honest, I don't care what the Catholic Church says or does.	☐	☐	☐	☐	☐
Q49e It is important to maintain the values of the Catholic Church.	☐	☐	☐	☐	☐
Q49f I'm to the point where I don't know if I belong to the Church.	☐	☐	☐	☐	☐
Q49g Women should be allowed to become priests.	☐	☐	☐	☐	☐
Q49h I often wonder what the meaning of life really is.	☐	☐	☐	☐	☐
Q49i The end often justifies the means.	☐	☐	☐	☐	☐
Q49j Everything is relative, and there just aren't any definite rules to live by.	☐	☐	☐	☐	☐
Q49k With so many religions abroad, one doesn't really know which to believe.	☐	☐	☐	☐	☐
Q49l The only thing one can be sure of today is that s/he can be sure of nothing.	☐	☐	☐	☐	☐
Q49m If you don't watch yourself, people will take advantage of you.	☐	☐	☐	☐	☐
Q49n No one is going to care much what happens to you, when you get right down to it.	☐	☐	☐	☐	☐
Q49o I have little control over the things that happen to me.	☐	☐	☐	☐	☐
Q49p There is really no way I can solve some of the problems I have.	☐	☐	☐	☐	☐
Q49q I can do just about anything I really set my mind to do.	☐	☐	☐	☐	☐
Q49r What happens to me in the future mostly depends on me.	☐	☐	☐	☐	☐
Q49s This is the dreariest time of my life.	☐	☐	☐	☐	☐
Q49t I am just as happy now as when I was younger.	☐	☐	☐	☐	☐
Q49u Most of the things I do are boring or monotonous.	☐	☐	☐	☐	☐
Q49v The things I do are as interesting to me as they ever were.	☐	☐	☐	☐	☐
Q49w As I look back on my life, I am fairly well satisfied.	☐	☐	☐	☐	☐
Q49x Things are getting worse as I get older.	☐	☐	☐	☐	☐
Q49y I feel like a failure.	☐	☐	☐	☐	☐
Q49z I like myself.	☐	☐	☐	☐	☐
Q49aa My life is on the right track.	☐	☐	☐	☐	☐
Q49bb My future looks good.	☐	☐	☐	☐	☐
Q49cc I wish I could change some part of my life.	☐	☐	☐	☐	☐
Q49dd I am satisfied with my life as a whole.	☐	☐	☐	☐	☐
Q49ee I feel I have no control over my life.	☐	☐	☐	☐	☐
Q49ff Overall, I am satisfied with my physical health.	☐	☐	☐	☐	☐
Q49gg Overall, I am satisfied with my emotional and mental health.	☐	☐	☐	☐	☐
Q49hh People should be guided more by their feelings and less by rules.	☐	☐	☐	☐	☐
Q49ii Obedience and respect for authority are the most important virtues children should learn.	☐	☐	☐	☐	☐
Q49jj Atheists and others who have rebelled against the established religions are no doubt every bit as good and virtuous as those who attend church regularly.	☐	☐	☐	☐	☐
Q49kk Marriages are stronger when the wife does not work outside the home.	☐	☐	☐	☐	☐

BACKGROUND

Q50   If you had to choose one word or phrase to describe your political beliefs, which of the following would you use?

    1 ☐ Very Conservative
    2 ☐ Conservative
    3 ☐ Moderate
    4 ☐ Liberal
    5 ☐ Very Liberal

Q51   What is your current denominational affiliation?

    1 ☐ Roman Catholic
    2 ☐ Protestant. What Denomination? _____
    3 ☐ Jewish
    4 ☐ Other. Please describe: _____
    5 ☐ None or no preference. Go to Q52

    Q51b   How often would you say you currently attend religious services in a typical month? ☐

    Q51c   Has your participation in your parish or congregation increased, decreased, or remained about the same since getting a divorce?

        1 ☐ Increased
        2 ☐ Decreased
        3 ☐ Stayed the same

Q52   What was your former spouse's religious affiliation when growing up?

    1 ☐ Roman Catholic
    2 ☐ Protestant. What Denomination? _____
    3 ☐ Jewish
    4 ☐ Other. Please describe: _____
    5 ☐ None or no preference.

Q53   When you were married how often did both you and your spouse attend church together? (Check one)

    1 ☐ Every Week
    2 ☐ Two to Three times month
    3 ☐ Once a month
    4 ☐ Less than once a month
    5 ☐ Never

Q54   How many church affiliated groups do you belong to? ☐ number of groups

    Q54b   Approximately how many hours a month would you say that you devote to these groups? ☐ hours

DIVORCE/ANNULMENT SURVEY   PAGE 13

Q55   How many years of education do you have? ☐ years

Q56   Did you attend a Catholic school?

    1 ☐ Yes
    2 ☐ No

    Q56b   For how many years? ☐ years

Q57   In what year were you born? 19☐

Q58   Are you. . .
    1 ☐ Male
    2 ☐ Female

Q59   What is your race or ethnicity? (Note: if more than one, check the one you consider the most important part of your background.)

    1 ☐ American Indian or Alaskan Native
    2 ☐ African American, African or Black
    3 ☐ White
    4 ☐ Asian American, Asian or Pacific Islander
    5 ☐ Hispanic or Latino/a descent
    6 ☐ Other: Please specify: _____

Q60   What is your family status currently? (Check all that apply)

    1 ☐ single, never married
    2 ☐ in a committed relationship (not legally married)
    3 ☐ divorced or legally separated
    4 ☐ widowed
    5 ☐ married (first marriage)
    6 ☐ remarried after divorce
    7 ☐ remarried after widowhood

Q61   What is your current job or occupation? _____

Q62   What is your **total family income** before taxes in 1997?

    1 ☐ Under $15,000   5 ☐ $40,000-54,999
    2 ☐ $15,000-19,999   6 ☐ $55,000-69,999
    3 ☐ $20,000-24,999   7 ☐ $70,000-84,999
    4 ☐ $25,000-39,999   8 ☐ $85,000 and over

APPENDIX C:
INTERVIEW OUTLINE

1. Length of marriage: _____ yrs.

2. Age when married: Self _____ Ex _____

    a. How long did you date before you were married? _____

3. How long have you been divorced? _____ yrs.

4. Do you have children from that marriage? Yes _____ No _____

    a. How many? _____

    b. Age of each: _____ _____ _____ _____ _____ _____ _____

5. Who initiated the divorce? Self _____ Ex _____ Both _____

    a. List the reason(s) for the divorce:

6. Was it difficult to get a divorce?

    a. What were the pros and cons?

    b. How did your life change after the divorce?

7. How (or from whom) did you first learn about annulments?

    a. What was your first impression?

    b. What is an annulment, or what does it mean to you?

8. Who sought the annulment? Self _____ Ex _____

9. Why?

10. Describe the procedure you went through:

11. Were there any negative aspects to this process?

12. Describe the role your ex-spouse played in the process:

13. (if applicable): Did you talk to your children about getting an annulment? Yes _____ No _____

    a. If yes, what did you tell them?

    b. If no, why not?

    c. Have you discussed it with them since? Why or why not?

    d. If you were to discuss it, what would you say?

    e. If too young, at what age would you consider them able to understand? _____ yrs.

14. Was the annulment granted? Yes _____ No _____

    a. What were the reason(s) given by the tribunal for granting (not granting) the annulment?

15. Any negative effects of having sought an annulment?

16. Any positive effects?

17. What has been the biggest impact of getting an annulment?

18. (if applicable): Knowing what you know now, would you go through this process again? Yes _____ No _____

    a. Why or why not?

19. Can you see why some people would object to annulments? Yes _____ No _____

    a. Why or why not?

    b. How would you respond to those objections?

20. With which religion did you identify with when growing up? _____ Ex-spouse? _____

21. With which religion did you identify with when you were married? _____ Ex-Spouse? _____

22. With which religion do you currently identify with? _____ Ex-Spouse? _____

23. How often did you attend church services in a typical month when you were growing up? _____ Ex-Spouse? _____

24. How often did you attend in a typical month when you were married? _____ Ex-Spouse? _____

25. How important would you say that religion was to you when you were growing up? Ex-Spouse?

26. How important would you say that religion is to you currently? Ex-Spouse?

27. What meaning does it have for you to be Catholic, and why are you Catholic?

28. What do you see, if anything, as some of the problems with the Church?

29. What would be the one thing within the Catholic Church that you would change if you had the power?

    a. Why?

30. Is there anything that would lead you to leave the Church?

    a. Why or why not?

31. Age: _____   Years of Education: _____

    Sex: _____   Occupation: _____

32. Is there anything that I might not have asked that you would like to say?

33. Request consent form.

References

Allen, John L. (1999). Reopening the divorce question. *National Catholic Reporter* October 29: 6.

Allport, Gordon W. (1950). *The individual and his religion*. New York: Macmillan.

Allport, Gordon W. (1966). The religious context of prejudice. *Journal for the Scientific Study of Religion* 5: 447-457.

Amato, Paul R. and Alan Booth (1991). A prospective study of divorce and parent-child relationships. *Journal of Marriage and the Family* 58: 356-365.

Amato, Paul R. and Bruce Keith (1991a). Parental divorce and adult well-being—A meta-analysis. *Journal of Marriage and the Family* 53: 43-58.

Amato, Paul R. and Bruce Keith (1991b). Parental divorce and the well-being of children. *Psychological Bulletin* 110: 26-46.

"American Catholics Still Seek Greater Role" (1999). *National Catholic Reporter* October 29: 11-20.

Anson, Ofra (1989). Marital status and women's health revisited: The importance of a proximate adult. *Journal of Marriage and the Family* 51: 185-194.

Applewhite, Aston (1997). *Cutting loose: Why women who end their marriages do so well*. New York: HarperPerennial.

Bahr, Howard M. (1981). Religious intermarriage and divorce in Utah and the mountain states. *Journal for the Scientific Study of Religion* 20: 251-261.

Barbash, Fred (1995). Divorce bitterly divides Ireland. *Detroit News* November 19: <http://www.detnewscom/menu/stories/25372.html>.

Benokraitis, Nijole V. (1999). *Marriages and families: Changes, choices, and constraints* (Third edition). Saddle River, NJ: Prentice-Hall.

Berkman, Lisa F. and Lester Breslow (1983). *Health and ways of living: The Alameda County study*. New York: Oxford University Press.

Blake, Nelson (1962). *The road to Reno: A history of divorce in the U.S.* New York: Macmillan.

Blazer, Dan G. (1982). Social support and mortality in an elderly community population. *American Journal of Epidemiology* 115: 684-694.

Bloom, Bernard L. (1975). *Changing patterns in psychiatric care*. New York: Behavioral Publications, Inc.

Bohannan, Paul (1971). The six stations of divorce. In Bohannan, Paul (Ed.), *Divorce and after* (pp. 33-62). Garden City, NY: Anchor Books.

Book of Discipline of the United Methodist Church (1996). Nashville, TN: The United Methodist Publishing House.

Booth, Alan and John N. Edwards (1985). Age at marriage and marital instability. *Journal of Marriage and the Family* 47: 67-75.

Booth, Alan, John N. Edwards, and David R. Johnson (1991). Social integration and divorce. *Social Forces* 70(1): 207-224.

Booth, Alan and D.R. Johnson (1994). Declining health and marital quality. *Journal of Marriage and the Family* 56: 218-223.

Branden, Nathaniel (1985). *Honoring the self: Self esteem and personal transformation.* New York: Bantam.

Brodbar-Nemzer, Jay (1984). Divorce in the Jewish community. The impact of Jewish commitment. *Journals of Jewish Communal Service* 61: 150-159.

Brown, Gerald Lee (1979). The rhetoric of divorced Catholics groups and the founding of a national organization. PhD dissertation, Temple University, Philadelphia, PA.

Brozan, Nadine (1998). Annulling a tradition. *The New York Times* August 8: B5-B6.

Buehler, Cheryl and Mary Langenbrunner (1987). Divorce-related stressors: Occurrence, disruptiveness, and area of life change. *Journal of Divorce* 11: 25-50.

Burr, Jeffrey A., Patricia L. McCall, and Eve Powell-Griner (1994). Catholic religion and suicide: The mediating effect of divorce. *Social Science Quarterly* 75(2): 300-318.

Clark, Leslie F. (1993). Stress and the cognitive-conversational benefits of social interaction. *Journal of Social and Clinical Psychology* 12: 25-55.

Clarke, Sally (1995). Advance report on final divorce statistics, 1989 and 1990. *Monthly Vital Statistics Report 43(9) (Supplement).* Hyattsville, MD: National Center for Health Statistics.

Cleary, Paul D. (1987). Gender differences in stress-related disorders. In Barnett, R.C., L. Biener, and G.K. Baruch (Eds.), *Gender and stress* (pp. 39-72). New York: Free Press.

Cockerham, William C. (1989). *Sociology of mental disorders* (Second edition). Englewood Cliffs, NJ: Prentice-Hall.

Colasanto, Diane and James Shriver (1989). Middle-aged face marital crisis. *Gallup Report*: no. 284(May): 34-38.

Coleman, Gerald D. (1988). *Divorce and remarriage in the Catholic Church.* New York: Paulist Press.

Comin, Paula Ripple (1996). The early years: The divorcing person in a responding church. North American Conference of Divorced and Separated Catholics.

Comstock, George W. and Kay B. Partridge (1972). Church attendance and health. *Journal of Chronic Diseases* 25:665-672.

Cooney, Teresa and Peter Uhlanberg (1989). Family-building patterns of professional women: A comparison of lawyers, physicians, and post-secondary teachers. *Journal of Marriage and the Family* (51): 749-758.

Cott, Nancy F. (1983). Divorce and the Changing Status of Women in Eighteenth-Century Massachusetts. In Gordon, Michael (Ed.), *The American family in social-historical perspective* (Third edition) (pp. 347-371). New York: St. Martin's Press.

Crawford, Mark E., Paul J. Handal, and Richard L. Wiener (1989). Relationship between religion and mental health/distress. *Review of Religious Research* 31(1): 16-22.

Davey, Theodore (1997). The internal forum. In Kelly, Kevin T., *Divorce and second marriage* (pp. 178-182). Kansas City: Sheed and Ward.

Davidson, James D., Andrea S. Williams, Richard A. Lamanna, Jan Stenftenagel, Kathleen Maas Weigert, William J. Whalen, and Patricia Wittberg (1997). *The search for common ground: What unites and divides Catholic Americans.* Huntington, IN: Our Sunday Visitor Publishing Division.

Devall, Esther, Zolinda Stoneman, and Gene Brady (1986). The impact of divorce and maternal employment on pre-adolescent children. *Family Relations* 35: 153-159.

Dillon, Michele (1993). *Debating divorce: Moral conflict in Ireland.* Lexington, KY: University Press of Kentucky.

Donnelly, Denise and David Finkelhor (1992). Does equality in custody arrangement improve the parent-child relationship? *Journal of Marriage and the Family* 54: 837-845.

Doyle, James A. and Michelle A. Paludi (1995). *Sex and gender: The human experience.* Madison, WI: Brown and Benchmark.

Durkheim, Emile (1951). *Suicide: A study in sociology.* J.A. Spaulding and G. Simpson, trans. New York: The Free Press.

Dwyer, Jeffrey W., Leslie L. Clarke, and Michael K. Miller (1990). The effect of religious concentration and affiliation on county cancer mortality rates. *Journal of Health and Social Behavior* 31: 185-202.

Dyer, Everett D. (1983). *Courtship, marriage, and family: American style.* Homewood, IL: The Dorsey Press.

Eels, Laura Workman and Kathleen O'Flaherty (1996). Gender perceptual differences in relation to marital problems. *Journal of Divorce and Remarriage* 25: 95-116.

"Fall festival of marriage" (1994). *Home Life* July: 62.

Feldberg, Roslyn and Janet Kohen (1980). Family life in anti-family setting: A critique of marriage and divorce. In Henslin, J. M. (Ed.), *Marriage and family in a changing society* (pp. 415-427). New York: The Free Press.

Festinger, Leon (1957). *A theory of cognitive dissonance.* Stanford, CA: Stanford University Press.

Fishman, Sylvia Barack (1996). American Jewry: Families of tradition in American culture. In Airhart, Phyllis D. and Margaret Lamberts Bendroth (Eds.), *Faith traditions and the family* (pp. 100-113). Louisville, KY: Westminster John Knox Press.

Foster, Michael S. (1999) *Annulment: The wedding that was.* Mahwah, NJ: Paulist Press.

Fox, Greer Litton and Robert F. Kelly (1995). Determinants of child custody: Arrangements at divorce. *Journal of Marriage and the Family* 57: 693-708.

Fox, Thomas C. (1993). U.S. Catholics loyal, choose moral terms. *National Catholic Reporter* October 8: 22-29.

Gallup, George Jr. and Jim Castelli (1987). *The American Catholic people: Their beliefs, practices, and values.* Garden City, NJ: Doubleday and Company, Inc.

Gallup, George Jr. and D. Michael Lindsay (1999). *Surveying the religious landscape.* Harrisburg, PA: Morehouse Publishing.

Galston, William A. (2001). Divorce American style. In Tischler, Henry L. (Ed.), *Debating points: Marriage and family issues* (pp. 51-58). Upper Saddle River, NJ: Prentice-Hall.

Garfinkel, Irwin S., Sara S. McLanahan, and Philip K. Robins (Eds.) (1994). *Child Support and Child Well-Being*. Washington, DC: Urban Institute Press.

Garrity, Robert M. (1991). Shame, dysfunctional families, and the lack of due discretion for marriage. *The Jurist* 48: 364-389.

Gartner, John, Dave B. Larson, and George D. Allen (1991). Religious commitment and mental health: A review of the empirical literature. *Journal of Psychology and Theology* 19(1): 6-25.

Geiss, Susan and K. Daniel O'Leary (1981). Therapists' ratings of frequency of marital problems: Implications for research. *Journal of marital and family therapy* 7:515-520.

Glenn, Norvall D. (1982). Interreligious marriage in the United States. *Journal of Marriage and the Family* 44: 555-566.

Glenn, Norvall D. (1997). A reconsideration of the effect of no-fault divorce on divorce rates. *Journal of Marriage and the Family* 59: 1023-1026.

Glenn, Norvall D. and Michael Supancic (1984). The social and demographic correlates of divorce and separation in the United States: An update and reconsideration. *Journal of Marriage and the Family* 46: 563-575.

Glenn, Norvall D. and Charles N. Weaver (1988). The changing relationship of marital status to reported happiness. *Journal of Marriage and the Family* 50: 317-324.

Glick, Paul (1984). Remarriage: Some recent changes and variations. *Journal of Family Issues* 1: 455-478.

Goode, William J. (1993). *World changes in divorce patterns*. New Haven: Yale University Press.

Goodstein, Laurie (1997). So the marriage was never actually valid. *The Washington Post* April 25: A1, A9.

Gordon, Michael (1978). *The American family: Past, present, and future*. New York: Random House.

Gray, Paul (1995). The Catholic paradox. *Time* (October 9): 64-68.

Greeley, Andrew (1990). *The Catholic myth: The behavior and beliefs of Americans*. New York: Charles Scribner's Sons.

Greeley, Andrew (1999). Interview by Richard Jenks. May 11.

Grief, Geoffrey L. (1985). *Single fathers*. Lexington, MA: Lexington Books.

Guidubaldi, John and Helen Cleminshaw (1985). Divorce, family health, and child adjustment. *Family Relations* 34: 35-41.

Guttman, Joseph (1993). *Divorce in psychological perspective*. Hillsdale, NJ: Lawrence Erlbaum Associates.

Guttman, Monika (1996). The split over divorce. *USA Weekend* (June 21-23): pp. 4-5.

Hanson, Shirley M. (1988). Divorced fathers with custody. In Phyllis Bronstein and Carolyn P. Cowan (Eds.), *Fatherhood today: Men's changing role in the family* (pp. 166-194). New York: Wiley.

Heaton, Tim B. (1984). Religious homogamy and marital satisfaction reconsidered. *Journal of Marriage and the Family* 46: 729-733.

Hobson, Charles J., Joseph Kamen, Jana Szostek, Carol M. Nethercut, James W. Tiedmann, and Susan Wojnarowicz (1998). Stressful life events: A revision and update of the social readjustment rating scale. *International Journal of Stress Management* 5: 1-23.

Hoffman, Saul D. and Greg J. Duncan (1988). What are the economic consequences of divorce? *Demography* 25: 485-497.

Holmes, Thomas and Richard Rahe (1967). The social readjustment rating scale. *Journal of Psychosomatic Research* 11: 213-218.

Inglehart, Ronald (1990). *Culture shift in advanced industrial society.* Princeton, NJ: Princeton University Press.

Jarvis, George K. and Herbert C. Northcott (1987). Religion and differences in morbidity and mortality. *Social Science and Medicine* 25(7): 813-824.

Jaynes, Gerald D. and Robin M. Williams (Eds.) (1989). *A common destiny: Blacks and American society.* Washington, DC: National Academy Press.

Jenks, Richard and Cynthia Woolever (1999). Integration and well- being among Catholics: Married, divorced, annulled. *Journal of Religion and Health* 38: 127-135.

Kain, Edward (1990). *The myth of family decline: Understanding families in a world of rapid social change.* Lexington, MA: Heath.

Kaprio, Jaakko, Markku Koskenvuo, and Heli Rita (1987). Mortality after bereavement: A prospective study of 95,647 widowed persons. *American Journal of Public Health* 77: 283-287.

Kauffman, J. Howard (1996). Mennonite: Family life as Christian community. In Airhart, Phyllis and Margaret Lambers Bendroth (Eds.), *Faith traditions and the family* (pp. 38-52). Louisville: Westminister John Knox Press.

KAYAMA (1997). <http://www.Kayama.org/bios.htm>.

Keith, Verna M. and Barbara Finlay (1988). The impact of parental divorce on children's educational attainment, marital timing, and likelihood of divorce. *Journal of Marriage and the Family* 50: 797-809.

Kelleher, Stephen J. (1973). *Divorce and Remarriage for Catholics?* Garden City, NY: Doubleday.

Kelleher, Stephen J. (1977). Catholic annulments: A dehumanizing process. *Commonweal* 104: 363-368.

Kelly, Kevin T. (1997). *Divorce and second marriage.* Kansas City: Sheed and Ward.

Kennedy, Sheila Rauch (1997). *Shattered faith.* New York: Pantheon Books.

Kennedy, Sheila Rauch (1999). *A respondent view.* Paper presented at the Annual Meetings of the Society for the Scientific Study of Religion, November 6, Boston, MA.

Kensky, Allan (1996). The family in Rabbinic Judaism. In Carr, Anne and Mary Stewart van Leeuwen (Eds.), *Religion, feminism and the family* (pp. 74-94). Louisville, KY: Westminister John Knox Press.

Kessler, Ronald C., Katherine A. McGonale, Shanyang Zhao, Christopher B. Nelson, Michael Hughes, Suzann Eshleman, Hans-Ulrich Wittchen, and Kenneth S.

Kendler (1994). Lifetime and 12-month prevalence of DSM-III-R psychiatric disorders in the United States. *Archives of General Psychiatry* 51: 8-19.

Knox, David and Caroline Schacht (1997). *Choices in relationships: An introduction to marriage and the family* (Fifth edition). Belmont, CA: Wadsworth Publishing Company.

Koenig, Harold G. and Linda K. George (1998). Depression and physical disability outcomes in depressed medically ill hospitalized patients. *American Journal of Geriatric Psychiatry* 6: 230-247.

Kosmin, Barry A. and Seymour P. Lachman (1993). *One nation under God: Religion in contemporary American society.* New York: Crown Trade Paperbacks.

Kposowa, Augustine J. (1998). The impact of race on divorce in the United States. *Journal of Comparative Family Issues* 29: 529-548.

Kurdek, Lawrence A. (1991). The relationship between reported well-being and divorce history, availability of proximate adult and gender. *Journal of Marriage and the Family* 53: 71-78.

Kurdek, Lawrence A. (1993). Predicting marital dissolution: A 5-year prospective longitudinal study of newlywed couples. *Journal of Personality and Social Psychology* 64(2): 221-242.

Lagges, Patrick R. (1991). Annulment: The process and its meaning. *Marriage and Family* April: 18-25.

Lasch, Christopher (1978). *The culture of narcissism.* New York: Norton.

Leary, Jan (1999). Is the annulment process a "pastoral" procedure? <http://www. saveoursacrament.org/fact.html>.

Lee, Gary, Karen Seccombe, and Constance Shehan (1991). Marital status and personal happiness: An analysis of trend data. *Journal of Marriage and the Family* 53: 839-844.

Lehrer, Evelyn L. and Carmel U. Chiswick (1993). Religion as a determinant of marital stability. *Demography* 30: 385-404.

Leonard, Bill J. (1996). Southern Baptist: Family as witness of grace in the community. In Airhart, Phyllis D. and Margaret Lamberts Bendroth (Eds.), *Faith traditions and the family* (pp. 8-21). Louisville, KY: Westminister John Knox Press.

Lester, David (1996). Trends in divorce and marriage around the world. *Journal of Divorce and Remarriage* 25, 169-171.

Levin, Jeffrey S. (1994). Religion and health: Is there an association, is it valid, and is it causal? *Social Science and Medicine* 38: 1475-1482.

Levin, Jeffrey S. and Harold Y. Vanderpool (1987). Is frequent religious attendance really conducive to better health? Toward an epidemiology of religion. *Social Science and Medicine* 24(7): 589-600.

Levinger, George and Oliver C. Mokes (Eds.) (1979). *Divorce and separation: Context, causes and consequences.* New York: Basic Books.

Linville, Patricia W. (1985). Self-complexity and affective extremity: Don't put all of your eggs in one cognitive basket. *Social Cognition* 3(1): 94-120.

Linville, Patricia W. (1987). Self-complexity as a cognitive buffer against stress-related illness and depression. *Journal of Personality and Social Psychology* 52(4): 663-676.

Litwack, Eugene and Peter Messeir (1989). Organizational theory, social supports, and mortality rates: A theoretical convergence. *American Sociological Review* 54: 49-66.

Loconte, Joe (1998). I'll stand bayou. *Policy Review* May/June: 30-35.

London, Kathryn A. (1991). Cohabitation, marriage, marital dissolution, and remarriage: United States, 1988. *Vital health statistics.* Hyattsville, MD: National Center for Health Statistics.

Macionis, John J. (1999). *Sociology* (Seventh edition). Upper Saddle River, NJ: Prentice-Hall.

Marks, Nadine F. (1996). Flying solo at midlife: Gender, marital status, and psychological well-being. *Journal of Marriage and the Family* 58: 917-932.

Martin, Teresa and Larry Bumpass (1989). Recent trends in marital disruption. *Demography* 26: 37-52.

Matusiak, Father John (2000). Interview by Richard Jenks. August 7.

Mauldin, Teresa A. (1990). Women who remain above the poverty level in divorce: Implications for family policy. *Family Relations* 39: 35-41.

McKenry, Patrick C. and Mack A. Fine (1993). Parenting following divorce: A comparison of black and white single mothers. *Journal of Comparative Family Studies* 24 (Spring): 99-111.

McMurray, Lucille (1970). Emotional stress and driving performance: The effect of divorce. *Behavioral Research in Highway Safety* 1: 100-114.

Minutes of the General Assembly (1992). Atlanta, GA: The Committee for Christian Education and Publications.

Myers, David (2000). *The American paradox: Spiritual hunger in an age of plenty.* New Haven: Yale University Press.

Nakonezny, Paul A., Robert D. Shull, and Joseph L. Rodgers (1995). The effect of no-fault divorce law on the divorce rate across the 50 states and its relation to income, education, and religiosity. *Journal of Marriage and the Family* 57: 477-488.

National Center for Health Statistics (1970). Mortality from selected causes by marital status. Series 20:8A and 8B. Washington, DC: U.S. Government Printing Office.

National Center for Health Statistics (1991). Annual summary of births, marriages, divorces, and deaths: United States, 1990. *Monthly Vital Statistics Report* 39: 13.

Neft, Naomi and Ann D. Levine (1997). *Where Women Stand: An International Report on the Status of Women in 140 Countries, 1997-1998.* New York: Random House.

Newport, Frank and Lydia Saad (1997). Religious faith is widespread but many skip church. *Gallup Poll Archives.* <http://198.715.140.8/poll/%5Farchives/1997/970329.htm>.

Norton, Arthur J. and Louisa F. Miller (1992). Marriage, divorce, and remarriage in the 1990s. *U.S. Bureau of the Census, Current Population Reports:* 23-180. Washington, DC: Government Printing Office.

Norton, Arthur J. and Jeanne E. Moorman (1987). Current trends in marriage and divorce among American women. *Journal of Marriage and the Family* 49: 3-14.

Orsy, Ladislas (1986). *Marriage in canon law.* Wilmington: Michael Glazer.

Orsy, Ladislas (1990). Questions concerning the matrimonial tribunals and the annulment process. In Roberts, William P. (Ed.), *Divorce and remarriage: Religious and psychological perspectives* (pp. 138-155). Kansas City, MO: Sheed and Ward.

Orsy, Ladislas (1994). Divorce and remarriage: A German initiative. *The Tablet* June 18: 787.

Ortega, Suzanne, Hugh Whitt, and J. Allen Williams Jr. (1988). Religious homogamy and marital happiness. *Journal of Family Issues* 9: 224-239.

Otto, Mary (1999). U.S. moves toward divorce reform. *Detroit Free Press,* March 5: 11A.

Paloutzian, Raymond F. (1996). *Invitation to the psychology of religion* (Second edition). Boston, MA: Allyn and Bacon.

Peterson, James L. and Nicholas Zill (1986). Marital disruption, parent-child relationships, and behavior problems in children. *Journal of Marriage and the Family* 48: 295-307.

Peterson, Larry R. (1986). Interfaith marriage and religious commitment among Catholics. *Journal of Marriage and the Family* 48(4): 725-735.

Peterson, Richard (1996). A re-evaluation of the economic consequences of divorce. *American Sociological Review* 61: 528-536.

Phillips, Roderick (1988). *Putting asunder: A history of divorce in western society.* Cambridge, MA: Cambridge University Press.

Pollner, Melvin (1989). Divine relations, social relations, and well-being. *Journal of Health and Social Behavior* 30: 92-104.

Poloma, Margaret M. and Brian F. Pendleton (1990). Religious domains and general well-being. *Social Indicators Research* 22: 255-276.

Queen, Stuart A., Robert W. Habenstein, and Jill S. Quadagno (1985). *The family in various cultures* (Fifth edition). New York: Harper and Row.

Ragen, Naomi (2000). The great "aguna" debacle. <http:www.irac.org/article_ e.asp?artid=263>.

Rasmussen, Paul and Kathleen J. Ferraro (1991). The Divorce Process. In John N. Edwards and David Demo (Eds.), *Marriage and family in transition* (pp. 376-388). Boston, MA: Allyn and Bacon.

Ratzinger, Cardinal Joseph (1997). Letter to *The Tablet.* In Kelly, Kevin T., *Divorce and second marriage* (pp. 183-185).

Respondents' Appeal to the Vatican Rota, The (2002). <rota.html.>.

Reyes, Fred (2002). Response from Lifeways Fall Festival of Marriage. Personal Communication.

Ripple, Paula (1990). Remarriage: Shaping the pastoral questions that facilitate life. In Roberts, William P. (Ed.), *Divorce and remarriage: Religious and psychological perspectives* (pp. 1-14). Kansas City, MO: Sheed and Ward.

Rogers, Richard G. (1995). Marriage, sex, and mortality. *Journal of Marriage and the Family* 57: 515-526.

Rogers, Stacey J. (1996). Mothers' work hours and marital quality: Variations by family structure and family size. *Journal of Marriage and the Family* 58: 606-617.

Ross, Catherine E., John Mirowsky, and Karen Goldsteen (1990). The impact of the family on health: The decade in review. *Journal of Marriage and the Family* 52: 1059-1078.

Rue, James J. and Louise Shanahan (1972). *The Divorced Catholic*. Paramus, NJ: Paulist Press.

Saluter, A. F. (1994). *Marital Status and Living Arrangements: March 1993*. U.S. Bureau of the Census, Current Population Reports, Series P20-478. Washington, DC: Government Printing Office.

Schwartz, Lita Linzer and Florence W. Kaslow (1997). *Painful partings*. New York: John Wiley and Sons, Inc.

Seiden, Anne M. (1976). Overview: Research in the psychology of women. II. Women in families, work and psychotherapy. *American Journal of Psychiatry* 133: 1111-1123.

Shehan, Constance L., E. Wilbur Bock, and Gary R. Lee (1990). Religious heterogamy, religiosity, and marital happiness: The case of Catholics. *Journal of Marriage and the Family* 52(1): 73-79.

Shehan, Constance L. and Kenneth C. W. Kammeyer (1997). *Marriages and families: Reflections of a gendered society*. Boston, MA: Allyn and Bacon.

Smith, Eliot R. and Diane M. Mackie (1995). *Social psychology*. New York: Worth Publishers.

SOS Goals (2002). <http://www.saveoursacrament.org/goals.html>.

Soule, W. Becket (1997). *The Catholic teaching on annulment*. New Haven, CT: Catholic Information Service.

Spilka, Bernard, Ralph W. Hood Jr., and Richard C. Gorsuch (1985). *The psychology of religion: An empirical approach*. Englewoods Cliffs, NJ: Prentice-Hall.

Spitze, Glenna (1988). Women's employment and family relations: A review. *Journal of Marriage and the Family* 50: 585-618.

Statement of Position on Divorce and Remarriage (1999). <http://www.anabaptists.org/tracts/divorce2.html>.

Stone, Lawrence (1990). *Road to divorce: England 1530-1987*. New York: Oxford University Press.

Tierney, Terence E. (1993). *Annulment: Do you have a case?* New York: Alba House.

Umberson, Debra (1987). Family status and health behaviors: Social control as a dimension of social integration. *Journal of Health and Social Behavior* 23: 306-319.

Varley, Irene (1999). Interview by Richard Jenks. October 31.

Vasoli, Ron (1998). *What God has joined together: The annulment crisis in American Catholicism*. New York: Oxford University Press.

Wallerstein, Judith S. and Sandra Blakeslee (1989). *Second chances: Men, women, and children a decade after divorce*. New York: Ticknor and Fields.

Wallerstein, Judith S. and Joan Kelly (1980). *Surviving the breakup: How children actually cope with divorce*. New York: Basic Books.

Weitzman, Lenore (1985). *The divorce revolution: The unexpected social and economic consequences for women and children in America*. New York: Free Press.

Weitzman, Lenore and R. Dixon (1986). The transformation of legal marriage through no-fault divorce. In Skolnick, Arlene S. and Jerome H. Skolnick (Eds.), *Family in Transition* (pp. 338-350). Boston, MA: Little, Brown.

White, Lynn K. (1991). Determinants of Divorce. In Booth, Alan (Ed.), *Contemporary families: Looking forward, looking back* (pp. 150-161). Minneapolis, MN: National Council on Family.

Wilde, Melissa (1999). *From excommunication to nullification.* Paper read at the Annual Meetings of the Society Study of Religion, November 6, Boston, MA.

Wineberg, Howard (1994). Marital reconciliation in the United States: Which couples are successful? *Journal of Marriage and the Family* 56: 80-88.

Wrenn, Lawrence G. (1973). *Divorce and remarriage in the Catholic Church.* New York: Newman Press.

Wrenn, Lawrence G. (1988). *Annulments* (Fifth edition). Washington, DC: Canon Law Society of America.

Wrenn, Lawrence G. (1995). Annulment. In Richard P. McBrien, *The Harper-Collins Encyclopedia of Catholicism* (pp. 53-56). San Francisco: Harper San Francisco.

Wu, Zheng (1994). Remarriage in Canada: A social exchange perspective. *Journal of Divorce and Remarriage* 21(3/4): 191-224.

Young, James J. (1979). Introduction: The divorced Catholics movement. In Young, James J. (Ed.), *Ministering to the divorced Catholic* (pp. 1-14). New York: Paulist Press.

Zinn, Maxine Baca and D. Stanley Eitzen (1999). *Diversity in families* (Fifth edition). New York: Longman.

Zunkel, C. Wayne (1976). Can a divorce be forgiven? *Brethren Life and Thought* 21: 155-160.

Index

Page numbers followed by the letter "t" indicate tables.

Order a copy of this book with this form or online at:
http://www.haworthpressinc.com/store/product.asp?sku=4621

DIVORCE, ANNULMENTS, AND THE CATHOLIC CHURCH
Healing or Hurtful?

_____in hardbound at $49.95 (ISBN: 0-7890-1563-3)
_____in softbound at $24.95 (ISBN: 0-7890-1564-1)

COST OF BOOKS_____

OUTSIDE USA/CANADA/
MEXICO: ADD 20%____

POSTAGE & HANDLING_____
*(US: $4.00 for first book & $1.50
for each additional book)
Outside US: $5.00 for first book
& $2.00 for each additional book)*

SUBTOTAL_____

in Canada: add 7% GST____

STATE TAX____
*(NY, OH & MIN residents, please
add appropriate local sales tax)*

FINAL TOTAL____
*(If paying in Canadian funds,
convert using the current
exchange rate, UNESCO
coupons welcome.)*

❏ **BILL ME LATER:** ($5 service charge will be added)
(Bill-me option is good on US/Canada/Mexico orders only;
not good to jobbers, wholesalers, or subscription agencies.)

❏ Check here if billing address is different from
shipping address and attach purchase order and
billing address information.

Signature_____

❏ **PAYMENT ENCLOSED: $**_____

❏ **PLEASE CHARGE TO MY CREDIT CARD.**

❏ Visa ❏ MasterCard ❏ AmEx ❏ Discover
❏ Diner's Club ❏ Eurocard ❏ JCB

Account # _____

Exp. Date_____

Signature_____

Prices in US dollars and subject to change without notice.

NAME_____

INSTITUTION_____

ADDRESS_____

CITY_____

STATE/ZIP_____

COUNTRY_____ COUNTY (NY residents only)_____

TEL_____ FAX_____

E-MAIL_____

May we use your e-mail address for confirmations and other types of information? ❏ Yes ❏ No
We appreciate receiving your e-mail address and fax number. Haworth would like to e-mail or fax special
discount offers to you, as a preferred customer. **We will never share, rent, or exchange your e-mail address
or fax number.** We regard such actions as an invasion of your privacy.

Order From Your Local Bookstore or Directly From
The Haworth Press, Inc.
10 Alice Street, Binghamton, New York 13904-1580 • USA
TELEPHONE: 1-800-HAWORTH (1-800-429-6784) / Outside US/Canada: (607) 722-5857
FAX: 1-800-895-0582 / Outside US/Canada: (607) 722-6362
E-mail: getinfo@haworthpressinc.com
PLEASE PHOTOCOPY THIS FORM FOR YOUR PERSONAL USE.
www.HaworthPress.com

BOF02